DISASTER RECOVERY PLANNING

DISASTER RECOVERY PLANNING

Managing
Risk and Catastrophe
in Information Systems

Jon William Toigo

YOURDON PRESS
Prentice Hall Building
Englewood Cliffs, New Jersey 07632

LIBRARY OF CONGRESS
Library of Congress Cataloging-in-Publication Data

Toigo, Jon William
   Disaster recovery planning : managing risk and catastrophe in
information systems / Jon William Toigo.
      p.   cm. -- (Yourdon Press computing series)
   Bibliography: p.
   Includes index.
   ISBN 0-13-214941-9 (Prentice Hall)
   1. Electronic data processing departments--Safety measures.
2. Data processing service centers--Safety measures. 3. Disasters.
I. Title. II. Series.
HF5548.2.T616 1989
658.4'78--dc19   88-20766
                                                           CIP

Editorial/production supervision
  and interior design: Elaine Lynch
Cover design: Ben Santora
Manufacturing buyer: Mary Ann Gloriande

 © 1989 by Prentice-Hall, Inc.
A Division of Simon & Schuster
Englewood Cliffs, New Jersey 07632

The publisher offers discounts on this book when ordered
in bulk quantities. For more information, write:
   Special Sales/College Marketing
   Prentice-Hall, Inc.
   College Technical and Reference Division
   Englewood Cliffs, NJ 07632

Printed in the United States of America
10 9 8 7 6 5 4 3 2 1

ISBN 0-13-214941-9

PRENTICE-HALL INTERNATIONAL (UK) LIMITED, London
PRENTICE-HALL OF AUSTRALIA PTY. LIMITED, Sydney
PRENTICE-HALL CANADA INC., Toronto
PRENTICE-HALL HISPANOAMERICANA, S.A., Mexico
PRENTICE-HALL OF INDIA PRIVATE LIMITED, New Delhi
PRENTICE-HALL OF JAPAN, INC., Tokyo
SIMON & SCHUSTER ASIA PTE. LTD., Singapore
EDITORA PRENTICE-HALL DO BRASIL, LTDA., Rio de Janeiro

CONTENTS

LIST OF ILLUSTRATIONS

CHAPTER 1

APPENDIX A

ACKNOWLEDGEMENTS

The author wishes to thank the following persons for their participation and support in the preparation of this book:

Mary Kern, her enlightenment born of experience, saw the need for disaster recovery planning and first placed me in the role of disaster recovery coordinator. She set the standards of performance by which I will judge myself for a very long time.

Judith Brugner, John Flint, Joan Kobernick, Tom Little, Ross Markley, Pat O'Connell, Judy Ryan, and the staff and membership of the Disaster Avoidance and Recovery Information Group provided observations and ideas that contributed much to the practical value of this book. The contributions of vendors and friends Steve Glantz, Kevin Hephner, and Mark Sher also deserve special note.

Edward Yourdon, Edward Moura and Patricia Henry are owed my deepest thanks for their steadfast belief in, and improvement of, both the author and the work.

Special thanks to Gary Eng, Mark Shulman, and Dennis Rapp of DataSouth, Inc., whose speedy and effective repairs to my PC averted the disaster of an unfinished manuscript and missed deadline.

Last but not least, my thanks and love to Jolanta, Alex, Max, and the entire Toigo and Suziedelis clans, who offered their support and encouragement. Without you, my dear family, this project would not have been completed.

MANAGEMENT OVERVIEW

The essence of good management is the rational, cost-effective use of resources. Next to personnel, a company's most important resource is information. Effective management of the information resource in a business enterprise is, therefore, a primary determinant of business success.

What does effective management of information mean? Today, the concept has become inexorably linked to the development, implementation, and refinement of technological tools for collecting, processing, and distributing information in a timely way. Effective information management has become synonymous with information systems management.

Information systems are now a basic component of nearly all business organizations. U.S. companies spent close to $30 billion on their information systems in 1987, and are reaping the fruits of their investments in the form of faster, more refined, more meaningful data—the kind of data that supports decisions and creates wealth.

However, there is a side to this symbiosis of business and machine that is rarely examined. It is business's dependency on the uninterrupted flow of information from its systems and the consequences to a company if the corporate oracle, the computer, were to be suddenly turned off.

xvi   Management Overview

These are the statistics:

1. The average company will lose 2-3 percent of its gross sales within 8 days of a sustained computer outage.
2. The average company that experiences a computer outage lasting longer than 10 days will never fully recover. 50 percent will be out of business within 5 years.
3. The chances of surviving a disaster affecting the corporate data processing center are less than 7 in 100. The chances of experiencing such a disaster are 1 in 100.

Despite these statistics and the numerous accounts of actual disasters that support them, many companies have ignored their vulnerability to a disastrous interruption of normal information system function. It was reported in 1986 that as many as 250 of Fortune 1000 companies had never planned for the possibility of an information system failure. The number of smaller companies without a disaster recovery plan is impossible to calculate.

In the financial industry, on the other hand, there has been a substantive trend toward disaster recovery planning. This trend has been spurred by federal and state legislation requiring the development and regular testing of disaster recovery plans. New laws have made bank managers and boards of directors personally liable for a failure to plan measures for reacting to, and recovering from, information system disasters.

Besides the frightening statistics and legal liabilities, there are other compelling and positive reasons to prepare contingency plans to protect corporate information resources. For one, disaster recovery planning can reduce corporate business interruption insurance premiums by 10 to 20 percent. This is because the planning process enables insurance requirements to be more accurately identified. In many cases, expensive blanket coverage can be replaced by more targeted policies.

In addition, many capabilities, such as uninterruptible power, that may be purchased for purposes of disaster prevention, may actually improve overall day-to-day system performance. Environmental maintenance can prevent costly equipment downtime as well as contamination-related equipment fires.

However, the ultimate impetus for disaster recovery planning is not financial. Disaster recovery planning is, after all, an overhead expense which demonstrates its worth in "non-events"—disasters that are prevented.

In the end, disaster recovery planning needs to be undertaken because of what it is: a fundamental component of effective resource management, the protection of vital corporate assets.

Chapter   1

Introduction

The history of business automation is fascinating and vast. For the purposes of this study, however, one aspect of the history is especially important. Driven by the incentives of cost-efficiency and competition, business has placed more and more of its critical information asset into automated systems and networks. This, in turn, has made business dependent upon the uninterrupted function of the machine, a dependency rarely perceived by those within the corporation who have no direct contact with the data processing service. The consequences of a loss of information systems to the business may never be considered until a disaster occurs. By then, it is often too late.

Recent business experience is replete with examples of companies that failed to recover from a disaster. Some were consumed by a flood or fire that demolished offices and data centers, leaving skeletons of twisted metal and smoking rubble. Others died gradually over several years, after being crippled by a catastrophe from which they could never fully recover.

However, in the same historical experience there are also examples of companies that suffered disasters of the same magnitude and survived. They emerged from the crisis, with critical operations intact, to regain their position in the marketplace and to continue their commercial pursuits.

One must ask the reason for the different outcomes. Why do some companies survive when others fail? Is it simply fate or chance that determines success or failure in disaster recovery?

Disaster connotes chance or risk. The word itself is derived from the Latin word for "evil star." However, mounting evidence supports the fact that companies can take measures that will improve the likelihood of full recovery following a disaster. Put simply, the difference between winners and losers in a disaster is often the presence or absence of an effective disaster recovery capability. Companies that plan for the possibility of a disaster, that formulate strategies for recovering critical business functions, and that train employees to implement those strategies, generally do survive disasters.

This book is about disaster recovery planning. It is designed to equip a company contingency planner with the knowledge and skills needed to develop an effective disaster recovery capability. It is also intended to serve information systems managers and business executives as a primer

3

in the critical and often-rarified discipline of disaster recovery planning, and as a guide for managing the activities of the planning project. Finally, it is a pragmatic reference describing the products, practices, and politics of the disaster recovery industry that has emerged over the past two decades.

Having read this book, the reader will understand the principles of contingency planning and be equipped with a model of the planning project that he or she may emulate to develop a workable disaster recovery plan. Along the way, the reader will be exposed to some of the current debates and emergent technologies of disaster recovery as well as first-hand experiences of numerous business planners in both the preparation and implementation of disaster recovery plans. All that will remain is for the reader to select and apply what has been learned to develop a workable plan.

The term disaster, as used in this book, means the interruption of business due to the loss or denial of the information assets required for normal operations. It refers to a loss or interruption of the company's data processing function, or to a loss of data itself. Loss of data can result from accidental or intentional erasure or destruction of the media on which data is recorded. This loss can be caused by a variety of man-made or natural phenomena.

Loss of data can also refer to a loss of integrity or reliability either in the dataset (or database) itself, or in the means by which data is transported, manipulated or presented for use. Corruption of programs and networks can interrupt the normal schedule for processing and reporting data, wreaking as much havoc within a company as would the loss of the data itself.

The above conception of disaster may suggest that only a major calamity—a terrorist bombing, an earthquake, or even a war—would qualify as a disaster. One envisions a smoking data center at Goliath, Inc., rather than an accidental hard disk erasure at the small business office down the block. In either case, if the result is an unacceptable interruption of normal business operations, the event can be classified as a disaster. Disasters are relative and contextual.

However, there are some constants about disasters. One is time. Because of business's growing dependency on customized data processing systems, alternatives to system-provided functions and information cannot be implemented readily. Yet, for a business to survive a disaster, the time factor for restoration of system functions is critical.

According to a 1978 study by the University of Minnesota, a data processing failure in a financial institution, one-half day in length, will degrade normal business activity by 13 percent for the two weeks following the failure.[1] A ten day outage will result in a 97 percent loss of business activity. Figure 1.1 depicts the impact of outages of varying lengths.[2]

The study also examined the relative vulnerability of specific industries and demonstrated the maximum downtime allowed by industry before recovery would be nearly impossible. As summarized in Figure 1.2, financial industries have the lowest tolerance to prolonged downtime, while insurance and manufacturing can tolerate slightly greater periods without business collapse.[3]

In manufacturing and distribution industries, however, even relatively brief outages entail substantial dollar losses. Figure 1.3 depicts the results of the 1978 analysis of dollar loss following a data center disaster in manufacturing or distribution industries with over $215 million annual gross sales.[4]

Although the Minnesota study is a decade old, experts still consider it to be an accurate portrayal of damage potentials confronting corporate data processing. However, the study did not account for the changes that have recently taken place in American business, including PC proliferation, the emergence of the private telecommunications switch, the growth of local area networks (LANs), and departmental computing. Thus, the study provides at best a conservative estimate of potential loss impact.

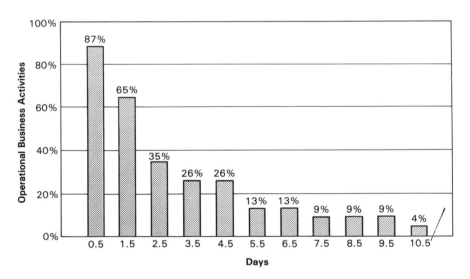

Figure 1.1 Decline in Operational Business Activities for the Finance Industry During the Two Weeks Following Complete Data Center Failure.

SOURCE: D.O. Aasgaard, et al., *An Evaluation of Data Processing "Machine Room" Loss and Selected Recovery Strategies* (Minneapolis; MISRC, University of Minnesota, 1979). Reprinted by permission.

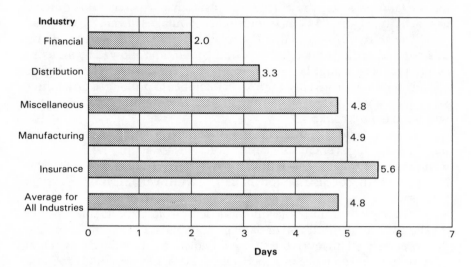

Figure 1.2   Maximum Downtime Allowed by Industry Type.
SOURCE: D.O. Aasgaard, et al., *An Evaluation of Data Processing "Machine Room" Loss and Selected Recovery Strategies* (Minneapolis; MISRC, University of Minnesota, 1979). Reprinted by permission.

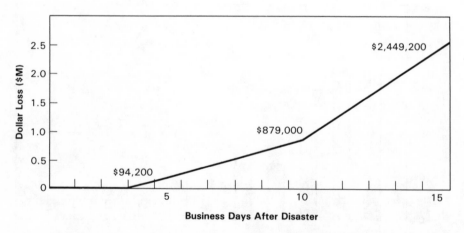

(Based on Manufacturing or Distribution Industry
with $215+ Million Annual Gross Sales)

Figure 1.3   Dollar Loss in Manufacturing or Distribution Industry Following a Data Center Disaster.
SOURCE: D.O. Aasgaard, et al., *An Evaluation of Data Processing "Machine Room" Loss and Selected Recovery Strategies* (Minneapolis; MISRC, University of Minnesota, 1979). Reprinted by permission.

In view of business's dependence upon centralized and decentralized computing and communications and its vulnerability to an interruption of normal information processing activity, it makes sense for a company to plan and prepare for this possibility. Recent events, including the 1982 Thanksgiving Day fire at Norwest Mortgage Corporation in Minneapolis and the 1986 fire at Steinberg's headquarters in Montreal, attest to the fact that those who plan for disaster fare better than those who do not. These companies both survived catastrophic losses because of effective disaster recovery planning. When a company does not have a tested set of procedures for reacting to and recovering from a catastrophe, it places all of its other plans and objectives in jeopardy.

The Need for Disaster Recovery Planning

The need for disaster recovery planning is usually self-evident to an information manager. Who, after all, has a more personal stake in the survival of a company's information processing systems than the manager whose position, prestige, and salary are directly dependent upon system performance? In addition to self-interest, information managers often manifest a protective, almost parental attitude toward "their" systems, especially systems developed in-house. Good data processing (DP) managers and management information systems (MIS) directors, like good parents, take an interest in the safety and health of their charges.

Beyond self-interest and psychological factors, the data processing professional has an ethical mandate to protect data integrity and ensure system survivability. Service level agreements between the data processing or MIS Department and company user departments are a manifestation of this commitment to quality and excellence in information processing. Contingency plans must exist if service level agreements are to be made in good faith.

Given all the compelling arguments for undertaking disaster recovery planning, it may seem redundant for auditors and federal law to require it. Unfortunately, a 1985 survey conducted by an independent consulting group revealed that less than 25 percent of the companies surveyed had written and tested disaster recovery plans.[5] (In a 1980 investigation of fifty government agencies conducted by the Office of Management and Budget (OMB), none had a plan that adequately covered its information systems![6]) Thus, auditors and legislators have assumed the responsibility for apprising corporate information managers of disaster recovery planning requirements and enforcing them as a matter of law.

Auditors tend to view disaster recovery planning as a facet of an organization's efforts to guarantee the security and integrity of its data processing capability. While some auditors are content with a regular schedule for off-site storage of backup tapes and a paper plan gathering dust in the DP manager's bookshelf, many auditors are becoming more concerned about their clients' disaster recovery capability.

Internal auditors are also taking a more active role in helping develop the company plan, often to ensure that corporate management (for whom they serve as the "eyes and ears") is not exposed to law suits or regulatory censure in the event of a disaster. Another reason for their interest is to ensure that security measures will remain in place even while processing is performed at a backup DP facility.

External auditors, especially "Big Eight" accounting/audit firms such as Price-Waterhouse, Coopers & Lybrand, and Deloitte, Haskins and Sells, are offering disaster recovery planning services to clients. The auditor-as-contingency planner opens some controversial issues that will be explored later in this chapter.

Information system audit handbooks now contain chapters devoted entirely to auditing the data processing department disaster recovery plan. Auditors will be paying increasing attention to the following areas as they examine a company's disaster recovery plan.

- **Plan revisions.** While EDP auditors may have no way to determine a plan's solvency or workability (unless they are invited to participate in an actual test), they may look to see when the plan was last revised. They are also interested in procedures providing for the regular review and revision of the document and for the regular reporting of system changes that must be accommodated within the plan. A list of revision dates should appear in the back matter of the plan document to answer these questions.

- **Plan test schedule and results assessments.** An untested disaster recovery plan cannot be presumed to provide an adequate measure of recoverability to corporate data assets. Tests provide the means for assessing the workability of strategies for evacuation and recovery that appear to work well on paper but may not perform well in real life. A schedule of regular testing and documentation of methods and results are important indicators to the auditor of management's attentiveness to the disaster recovery requirement. This is also typically added to the back matter of the plan.

- **Training and awareness.** It is often said at EDP Security and Disaster Recovery Planning seminars that disaster recovery plans are "living documents." A disaster recovery plan addresses two time frames: the future time frame, when the plan will be implemented to cope with some man-made or natural catastrophe; and the present time frame, when the plan is maintained and tested, plan participants are trained, and every corporate employee is made aware of the principles of disaster preparedness and prevention. These foci of disaster recovery planning presume an on-going training effort.

Thus, auditors may ask to see a schedule indicating the dates, topics, and attendance by key recovery personnel at training sessions covering the many aspects of the plan. They may also wish to see evidence of provisions made to increase safety awareness within the company as a whole. Awareness posters in dining areas and elevators, handouts for new employees, and even designated "disaster awareness days" may be some of the ways that this audit requirement can be satisfied.

In addition to these general items, there are many specific requirements of a disaster recovery plan that may be cursorily checked or verified by the auditor. These include:

- Documentation of relationships with other companies for mutual backup of data processing in the event of a facility disaster (service bureau agreements, see Chapter 5)
- Contracts with vendors of data processing backup facilities (hot sites)
- Contracts and schedules for regular off-site storage of paper files and magnetic media back-ups (off-site storage agreements, see Chapter 4)
- Provisions for on-demand rerouting or automatic switching of telecommunications lines to a designated alternative worksite (network recovery strategies, see Chapter 6)
- Network backup arrangements
- Specifications of fire protection systems, power continuation systems, water detection systems, and automated detection and alarm systems for other contingencies (disaster prevention capabilities, see Chapter 3)

In many industries, the dictates of commonsense and audit requirements are supplemented by legal mandates for disaster recovery planning. Many states are currently deliberating laws on this issue and some states, including Florida and Maryland, have already passed laws requiring contingency planning. Readers are urged to consult an EDP lawyer to determine the requirements in their respective states.

The federal government has also enacted legislation or passed regulations that require adequate disaster recovery planning within business and industry. The law that has had the greatest impact on companies across all industry categories is the Foreign Corrupt Practices Act of 1977.

The Foreign Corrupt Practices Act, although originally aimed at controlling the practices of companies conducting business outside the continental United States, contains provisions that apply to all companies regardless of industry, scope of marketing, or gross income. The law states that businesses must take measures to guarantee the security and integrity of assets—interpreted to include accounting and ledger information stored and processed on electronic data processing systems.

The act thus pertains to any company using computerized ledger, accounts receivable/accounts payable, or accounting systems. Furthermore, the act provides the means to prosecute individual managers and corporate executives for a failure to plan adequately for a disaster.[7] Individual fines of up to $10,000, five years in prison, and corporate penalties of more than $1 million have been established.

Another government regulation, Office of Management and Budget Circular A-71, requires government agencies that use data processing facilities to take adequate measures to safeguard those facilities. This rule has been interpreted to extend to government contractors and subcontractors, and is being rigidly enforced as a matter of national defense. Proponents of the circular argue that more and more of the design and production of military equipment and other contracted goods are being conducted or controlled using computers, and that the inadequate safeguarding of these systems represents an economic and military threat to the security of the United States.[8]

Financial institutions are subject to additional laws and regulations that are specifically designed for contingency planning within their industry. National banks must comply with the 1983 Banking Circular 177 (BC-177) which states that banks must "develop means to reduce the impact and/or risk of losing" data processing support. This circular makes bank management responsible for determining critical functions at the bank, assessing the risk and potential impact of a loss of EDP support for those functions, and developing plans to reduce the risk and/or impact of such a loss.[9]

BC-177 further requires that the board of directors annually review the plans of bank management, approve them, record their approval in the board minutes, and provide the minutes for review by the bank examiners. Thus, both the board and bank management are legally liable for a bank failure arising from inadequate preparation for an EDP outage.

A second banking circular, BC-187, was issued in 1985 to extend management accountability for disaster recovery planning to include the management of banks using service bureaus. Banks using service bureaus to process information are required to investigate the financial condition of their servicers annually and to develop alternate processing strategies if the servicer's financial condition is deteriorating or unsound. This circular is also interpreted to make bank management responsible for developing and implementing a contingency plan in the event of a service bureau outage.

The management and boards of both banks participating in the Federal Reserve System and of thrifts insured by the Federal Savings and Loan Insurance Corporation (FSLIC) are becoming increasingly targeted by the government for liability in the event of EDP-related interruptions and failures. Following a computer failure at the Bank of New York in 1985, senior officials of the bank were summoned to appear before a Congressional investigating committee which, at one point in its hearings, considered the possibility of removing senior managers from their positions for not adequately preparing for a disaster.[10]

Bank of New York, reputedly the state's largest broker of government securities, experienced an EDP outage which lasted approximately 27 hours. To continue operations, the bank was forced to borrow $22 billion from the discount window of the Federal Reserve Bank. It did so at an interest rate well below prime. The huge loan briefly destabilized the weighted rate of federal funds and cost the bank (or its insurer) $4 to $5 million in interest.[11] While Congress did not remove management in this case, the Federal Reserve did issue a circular that set the rate for borrowing in the face of an EDP failure at prime plus two.

The assignment of the ultimate responsibility—in legal terms—for the protection and preservation of corporate assets to corporate management is not without precedent. The Internal Revenue Service (IRS), for example, has articulated a number of strict rules pertaining to secure storage of business records. Management is often liable if IRS rules have not been observed and the records are lost.

For example, IRS Procedure 64-12 requires that recorded and reconstructible data be maintained in accordance with the Internal Revenue Code of 1954 and that program and source documentation be securely stored so that an audit trail from source documents to final accounting balances and totals may be demonstrated in the event of an IRS audit.[12] IRS Ruling 71-20 goes further to describe the requirements for retaining and safeguarding machine readable records (including punched cards, disks, and other machine-sensible data media) which may become material in the administration of any IRS law.[13] Corporate officers are subject to penalties if these rulings and regulations are not observed.

Besides making provisions for disaster recovery and secure storage of data, the U.S. government further requires all businesses to safeguard the health and safety of employees and to refrain from activities that could harm the community in which facilities are located. The Occupational Safety and Health Administration (OSHA) and the Environmental Protection Agency (EPA) have issued enforceable codes and regulations aimed at "disaster avoidance" which make company management prosecutable if avoidable disasters occur.[14] At the state level, numerous agencies and departments have followed the federal government's lead with fire, building, and emergency management codes that impact on disaster avoidance and recovery planning.[15]

This brief survey demonstrates that the disaster recovery planning project is propelled by a number of considerations, ranging from a common-sense business impetus to safeguard corporate assets from loss or damage to a natural desire to reduce legal exposure and personal loss. This is not to say, however, that corporate management is aware of all of the legal penalties, or even the risks, associated with not having an effective disaster recovery capability. Only in rare cases does a management consensus exist prior to its cultivation by an information manager or auditor. Even after a consensus is built to support the planning for business interruption and recovery, sustaining the consensus when it comes time to implement the paper plan—to install the recovery capability—can be difficult.

The reasons for the breakdown of the consensus are numerous. In some cases, management exhibits reluctance to spend money acquiring the services and products that are intrinsic to the plan. This often occurs when management does not fully understand the risks and exposures a company faces without a recovery capability.

Where legal requirements compel management to undertake planning, this must be communicated clearly. Where the law does not require a disaster recovery plan, other strategies have to be found to convince reluctant senior managers of plan benefits. Effective strategies are often difficult to find.

Strategies for Selling the Disaster Recovery Capability

Selling corporate management on shouldering the costs of the disaster recovery capability can often be a greater challenge than surmounting the technical problems involved in backing up critical systems and networks. In the final analysis, however, management will play the most critical role in the planning effort—the role of underwriter. Following are some typical problems reported by information managers who had to sell their plans to senior management, and the successful strategies they developed to overcome them.

 • *"You haven't cost-justified the plan."* This criticism usually reflects the disaster recovery planner's failure to document adequately the exposures and risks of not having a plan. The information manager can confront this problem even before any formal planning is authorized or risk analysis undertaken.

How does one cost-justify a capability that, in the best circumstances, will measure its success in nonevents? A good disaster recovery plan, after all, sets the stage for disaster avoidance by providing the means to detect and react to potential problems, in many cases, before they become disasters. Strategies for successfully addressing this problem generally fall into two categories.

The first strategy is to assign a dollar value to an hour of downtime. Calculate the average hourly earnings of an employee who uses the system for which a recovery capability is being sought. Multiply this average hourly wage by the number of users associated with the system who would not be performing productive work while the system is down. Assuming that the data could be entered at a later time without other adverse consequences, repeat the above calculation for one hour of average overtime salary (i.e., the amount of time all system users would need to work to make up lost time). Then, add the two dollar values as the total average labor cost for one hour of downtime. For users of larger systems, this number by itself could be sufficient to demonstrate the benefit of a disaster recovery capability that would avoid outages or minimize the duration of nonavoidable outages. By multiplying the number to reflect 10 hours, 24 hours, 48 hours, and so on, the statistic could be quite compelling.

Of course, other known values can be added to this estimated cost. Intangible costs—customer dissatisfaction, missed sales inquiries, blown deadlines, etc.—should be mentioned. This type of cost-justification has been successfully used in certain cases to obtain management support.

A second way to cost-justify the plan is to demonstrate the benefits of such a plan. An effective disaster recovery capability can actually reduce other business costs. Premiums for facility or business interruption insurance can be substantially reduced in many cases where disaster recovery planning identifies the specific coverages required and blanket insurance policies are replaced with targeted and less-expensive plans.[16]

Some disaster recovery capabilities, such as an uninterruptible power supply (UPS), can do double duty: sustain the business during a disastrous power outage as well as during the occasional surges, dips, and flickers of a typical business day. Furthermore, a backroom operations center—a facility designed to house users if the main business facility becomes uninhabitable for a period of time—can also be used as a training or conference facility. Similar benefits can often be discerned for most disaster recovery plan components given sufficient time and creative energy. When a particularly compelling benefit cannot be found to outweigh a cost, the impact of the cost may be softened if it is examined from the perspective of tax deductions, health and safety of personnel, or good corporate citizenship.

- *"Our insurance will cover an outage, so why do we need the plan?"* Even if a consensus exists for developing a plan on paper, management may resist spending money for implemention, especially if the disaster recovery capability is viewed as just so much more insurance. According to spokespersons for two DP insurers, the right DP insurance will cover operating costs that are above the normal costs of business operations, provided that the appropriate "extra" costs are spelled out in the policy. This business interruption insurance, however, should not be viewed as business resumption insurance.[17] An information manager may need to educate management in the following facts.

Insurers can readily cover the costs of facility damage (and, in some cases, replacement), and they can provide coverage for hardware and media. However, while insurers are willing to underwrite the *reconstruction* of data lost to a natural or man-made disaster, it would be cost-prohibitive to the client to underwrite the *value* of the data.

Without a disaster recovery plan, the client would be hard pressed to estimate the cost of reconstructing data or to buy adequate insurance for doing so. In all likelihood, without a disaster recovery capability, there would be nothing with which to reconstruct the data: no extant records, no systems, no location for personnel to work. Purchasing extra coverages under these circumstances would be pointless.

In a disaster situation, a company protected only by business interruption insurance is placed in the unenviable position of relying on the progress of the claims adjustment cycle to drive the recovery. While top flight insurers generally provide excellent turnaround on disaster claims and may even support the insured's recovery activities to reduce their own exposure, this is generally less desirable than controlling recovery within the business itself and capitalizing on the determination and commitment of trained recovery teams who are employees of the company.

- *"The purpose of the plan is to satisfy the auditors."* While it may seem blasphemous, information managers often express this sentiment in spoken or unspoken terms. One information manager of a national financial concern remarked, off the record, that the best disaster recovery plan he could get his company to fund was an up-to-date résumé. Sadly, in the absence of rigidly-enforced laws, auditors' comments are often the only incentive for management to undertake disaster recovery planning. Auditors seldom have the power to compel management to do anything it is not inclined to do.

One strategy for surmounting management indifference is to barrage corporate officers with news clippings about business disasters, although this may ultimately cost the sender some prestige or power. The object of this strategy is not to aggravate or frighten, but to create awareness in senior management that disasters do happen and that those who prepare for them generally recover normal operations far more readily than those who do not.

Another method for reducing senior management indifference is to demonstrate that the information manager understands and participates in management's priorities and objectives. This may be reflected in the methods used to create and articulate the plan. For example, every effort should be made to maximize the plan's protection while minimizing its cost. Despite his or her personal investment in systems, the information manager must strive to assess systems dispassionately for their criticality to the corporation. Certain applications are more vital than others. Target the largest share of plan expenditures for the most important applications and clearly communicate this rationale to senior management.

Furthermore, plans must ultimately encompass not only the recovery of data processing or MIS systems, but also the user departments. It makes little sense to restore systems if no provision is made to restore the user community. By involving the managers of user departments in the planning project, the information manager may be able to cultivate a corporate climate of support for disaster recovery planning. This, in turn, may reinforce senior management's perception of the value of the disaster recovery planning effort and result in a more comprehensive and effective recovery capability.

These are only a few of the common problems and strategies used by information managers to obtain senior management approval for disaster recovery planning costs. Other problems may develop that reflect the particular circumstances of a business, the distribution of information systems, or even the individual personalities of senior managers themselves. Whenever possible, disaster recovery planning should be depoliticized and depersonalized. Since the initial focus of the planning effort is on information systems, the information manager will play an important role in setting the stage for the entire corporate disaster recovery plan.

Who Should Write the Plan?

Once the decision has been made to undertake disaster recovery planning, the information manager must first determine the method to be used to develop the plan. One option is to hire a consultant to perform this task. Another is to develop the plan in-house. Valid arguments exist to support each option.

At first glance, hiring a consultant with X years of experience in developing this type of project may seem the best choice. Indeed, this approach has several distinct advantages.

First, the disaster recovery planning project is just as complicated as a major system development project and, in fact, parallels the systems' development life cycle (SDLC). (Figure 1.4 depicts the similarity.) Like a system development project, a disaster recovery planning project begins with an end user needs assessment called a risk analysis. Recovery strategies are then outlined and tasks are prioritized much in the way that an analyst would set forth a general system design. This general design is subjected to user review and, if it is approved, a detailed system description is articulated. At this point, development costs are specified and a project time-and-money budget is developed. In systems development, the project would be approved by management, and coding would begin.

Similarly, the disaster recovery planning budget is presented to senior management and, if approved, vendors are contacted, products and services purchased, and recovery procedures developed and documented. Plan testing and user training follow, just as comparable activities would follow the conclusion of coding. Finally, when the system is released or the plan is placed into effect, it is integrated into a change management system to provide for periodic review, revision, and maintenance.

An information manager, realizing the scope and complexity of the planning project, may decide that a consultant is needed to manage it. The information manager either cannot reassign an employee to manage the project, or feels that no employees are equal to the assignment.

There are other factors that may favor the consultant option:[18]

- Consultants bring specialized knowledge to the planning project that may facilitate the speedy development of an effective plan. An experienced consultant knows how a disaster recovery plan is constructed, knows the right questions to ask, and typically knows who's who in the disaster recovery products and services industry. Consultants who work within a specific industry may combine an understanding of the industry with a methodology for disaster recovery planning. This reduced learning curve, in turn, can help to speed plan development.

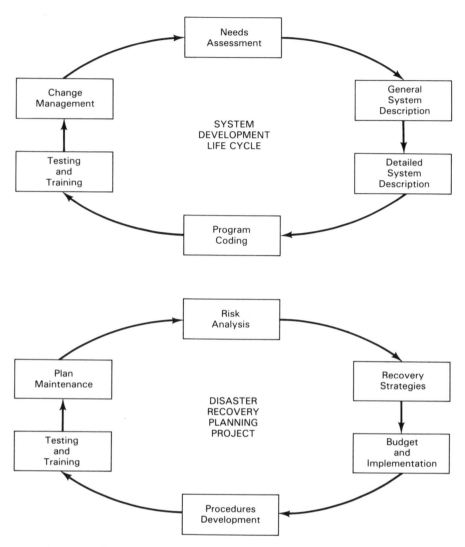

Figure 1.4 Comparison of System Development Life Cycle (SDLC) to Disaster Recovery Planning Project.

• Consultants can bring a "fresh eye" to the project, noticing recovery requirements that may be overlooked by someone who is too close to the data center he or she is seeking to protect. One consultant relayed a story about a client who had hired her to perform a risk analysis of a data center. In conferences, the client confidently reassured her that all vital processing equipment had been identified. Then, during a preliminary visit to the data center, the consultant nearly tripped over an ancient time card reader. She asked what it was and learned that no payroll checks could be generated without its use. A vital piece of equipment, yet it had not been mentioned anywhere in the lists which otherwise documented completely the state of the art hardware installed in the shop.

• Consultants are expensive. While this may be viewed as a drawback of the consultant option (and will be discussed later in this chapter), it may actually favor plan development in certain cases. Disaster recovery planning requires the interaction of users and information systems (DP and MIS) personnel. Within a large information systems shop, where rivalries frequently exist among applications support personnel, systems administrators, and operations, disaster recovery planning will also require the interaction of these groups. Often the only way to get all of the relevant parties to sit down as a group and discuss critical issues is to make it clear that a great deal of money is being spent for the consultant's time. Similarly, senior management, having invested a considerable sum of money for a consultant-developed plan, may be less inclined to withdraw support for the implementation of the plan.

Consultant-driven plans are similar to computer hardware acquisitions; they typically come with a maintenance agreement. For a fee, the consultant will return on a semi-annual basis to aid in the testing and updating of the original plan. Furthermore, since the plan usually reflects the favored methodology of the consultant, many consulting firms offer a training service to educate personnel in the client company who will maintain or use the plan.

Good consultants usually produce good plans and provide competent maintenance and training services. Unfortunately, not all consultants are good consultants. As of this writing, the disaster recovery planning consultancy is an unpoliced field. In the late 1960s, there were only a handful of disaster recovery consulting firms. Since that time, the number has increased exponentially. It is not uncommon for consulting firms to open and close their doors within the same year. This bodes ill for the industry as a whole.

During the last five years many "Big Eight" accounting firms entered the contingency planning business. In other words, the same firm that performs the company's annual audit will probably offer a disaster recovery planning service as well. The accounting firms argue that there is nothing incestuous about this, that their contingency planners are a separate entity from their auditing group. Yet, numerous information managers report that shortly after the absence or inadequacy of an EDP disaster plan was noted by the auditor, a marketing representative from the same firm contacted them to discuss their needs and offer their services. Concerned observers have asked how an auditor can objectively assess an EDP plan bearing the label of his or her own firm.

Undoubtedly there are good and bad consultants in the accounting firms just as there are in the "pure" disaster recovery consultancies. The information manager should use the same criteria when evaluating either type of consulting service. In particular, the information manager should observe the following guidelines when considering the use of consultants to develop the disaster recovery plan.

1. Check the qualifications of the consultant. It is important to know the name and background of the consultant who will be providing services. Find out how many and which companies the consultant has served and check directly with the clients for recommendations and criticisms. Be wary of using an inexperienced consultant even if he or she reputedly has access to more experienced hands. Ideally, the consultant will be able to demonstrate a knowledge of EDP, will understand the specific requirements within a prospective client's industry, and will have developed satisfactory disaster recovery plans for at least two other businesses.

2. Ask for a project roadmap. Ask for a proposal that shows the phases or tasks of the planning project. The consultant should not view this as an illegitimate request. Over the past few years, with the increasing commercial availability of excellent contingency planning project models and improved information on the techniques and methods of recovery planning, consultants have been hard pressed to portray what they do as secret, mysterious, or otherwise beyond the reach of non practitioners. Most consultants have generic plan methodologies that they adapt to accommodate specific client requirements. All the information manager needs is enough information about techniques and methods to evaluate the validity of the generic methodology. (For this reason, even if an information manager elects to use a consultant, this book will help the manager to evaluate the applicability of the consultant's planning methodology.)

3. Check and validate proposed time and cost estimates. Read consultant proposals carefully and note first whether time and dollar cost estimates have been assigned to parts of the project. Unless consulting services are packaged as fixed price contracts, there is no way that a consultant can develop meaningful time and cost estimates. The information manager should be especially wary if the consultant quotes exact prices or times before knowing anything about the particular requirements of the company.

Estimates provided by the consultant can be of value to the information manager in other ways. For example, valid time and cost estimates can provide a useful benchmark for comparing various consultant proposals, especially if each consultant states that he or she is basing estimates on similar projects performed for comparable businesses. This is about the only way comparison shopping can be performed for this type of service.

To ensure that the data being collected from each candidate is not skewed by anything other than unknown factors, ask whether all predictable costs, including the consultant's travel and lodging, are reflected in the estimated cost.

Information managers should be aware that consultants tend to push their premium service initially, and offer less-expensive shared-responsibility approaches only if they sense that they may be pricing themselves out of a contract. Faced with the prospect of losing a client, a consultant can often be very creative in finding cost-saving measures. One information manager reported that he cut the cost of consultant-aided plan development in half by arranging to place corporate word processing at the consultant's disposal for all written documentation, and by allocating one of his employees to work with the consultant on a full-time basis, thus replacing the assistant to be provided by the consulting firm. Other managers have discovered that they could purchase the consultant's PC-based disaster recovery planning tool and utilize the consultant's personal services only in the up-front analysis and data collection phases of the project. Substantial cost reductions resulted in each case.

One manager reported that the business ethics of the consultant could be discerned from the way in which he reacted to the manager's reluctance about costs. In one instance, a consultant offered to reduce costs by dropping the final two phases of the proposed project. These phases consisted of training personnel who would play key roles in the plan and maintenance of the plan document itself. Implied in this offer was the consultant's willingness to develop a paper plan that would sit on a shelf and satisfy a casual audit but provide no meaningful recovery capability!

4. Ask about the consultant's relationships with vendors of disaster recovery products and services. Information managers who are considering consultants also need to be aware that many consulting firms have formal or informal relationships with vendors of disaster recovery products and services. These relationships can profit the consultant's client in some cases. Using a particular consultant, for example, may qualify the client for discount rates on fire protection systems, off-site storage, or hot sites, data processing backup facilities.

There is, however, a potential for misuse of these relationships. An unethical consultant may be willing to sacrifice the objective analysis of client requirements in favor of recommending a product or service from which the consultant receives a kickback. It is valuable to know whether and with whom the consultant has marketing agreements, and how these agreements may result in price advantages for the client. Most vendors will openly admit to any special arrangements, particularly when they may profit the client and improve the marketability of their service. Some consultants argue that it is partly their extensive knowledge of the disaster recovery industry that qualifies them for the rates they command.

Should the information manager decide to use a consultant, whether or not the consultant admits having special marketing arrangements with vendors, he or she should pay particular attention to soliciting competitive bids for any product or service that the consultant recommends.

For many information managers, the cost of a consultant-driven disaster recovery plan is the major drawback. Plans can range from $20,000 to upwards of $120,000. This is generally perceived as a cost over and above the normal cost for plan development. Consultants respond that their price is reasonable from many perspectives.

A company electing to use in-house personnel to develop a plan must patiently wait for the novice disaster recovery coordinator to acquire knowledge that the consultant already possesses, and finance the coordinator's education and pay his or her salary while doing so. Plan development is a slower process when performed by a novice in the field. In the meantime, the company's vital information asset remains exposed. Consultants also point to the fact that most plans begun by in-house personnel are never completed.

Despite these arguments, many companies elect to use in-house personnel. Even consultant plans ultimately require that in-house skills and knowledge be developed. Someone must coordinate plan revisions and maintain the plan between visits by the consultant. In addition, much of the consultant's work must be overseen by in-house personnel since the consultant is essentially an outsider who does not participate in day-to-day business operations. Also, in-house personnel must perform all evaluations of products and services to be used in the plan, partly to ensure the honesty of the consultant.

Finally, in-house personnel now have access to information about disaster recovery planning techniques and methods through special training courses, published articles and books, and "sharing" groups so the learning curve for the in-house planner is drastically reduced.

Generic PC-based planning tools are also now available, and several consulting firms market their own software package containing their generic planning tool. These tools provide a structured approach to planning for common equipment configurations. They need to be modified by the purchaser to account for specific applications, networks, decentralized processors, and other characteristics peculiar to the customer site.

Although the PC-based planning tool does not provide comprehensive answers for the novice planner, it can offer valuable models that the planner can imitate when customizing the plan to meet his or her requirements. PC-based tools will be discussed in Chapter 9.

Another change that is supporting the development of disaster recovery plans by in-house personnel is the improvement of project management skills across all industries and business activities. The development of a disaster recovery capability is essentially a project with discrete tasks, milestones, resources and budget. Once the principles peculiar to disaster recovery planning are understood, any person skilled in the techniques of project management can develop a competent disaster recovery plan. (Many, including this author, have found that the only tools they require are old-fashioned research and communication skills, a user-friendly word processor, and a generic, off-the-shelf, PC-based project management software package.)

This is the book's approach. Each chapter provides cogent, practical information about the major tasks involved in developing a disaster recovery capability. Each chapter clearly defines the objectives of a development task, describes typical methods used to realize objectives, defines what resources are required, identifies sources and approximate pricing for specific products and services, and discusses methods for evaluating task fulfillment.

In some cases, the information manager serves as the disaster recovery coordinator for the company. In other cases, planning is undertaken by a group of users representing both information systems and the user community. If planning is undertaken by a group, however, it will need a person who will serve sometimes as researcher, sometimes as data collector, sometimes as honest broker, and ultimately as the person responsible for maintaining the plan in the face of almost daily shifts in recovery requirements. All these responsibilities are implied in the title coordinator.

Usually, the information manager will either hire a new employee to serve as disaster recovery coordinator, or transfer an employee to fill the position full time. The critical phrase is *full time*. In very small companies, the information manager is likely to serve as disaster recovery coordinator. In medium to large companies, developing and maintaining the disaster recovery plan is a full-time job.

Who is the ideal disaster recovery coordinator? There is no pat answer to this question. The coordinator does not need the highly technical skills set of a programmer, systems analyst, hardware specialist, or network administrator, but it is important that the candidate be able to communicate with technical staff and adequately interpret what they say in order to communicate it effectively to nontechnical users in reports, procedures, and other documentation.

It is important that the coordinator be organized, detail oriented, and a competent writer. The candidate should be able to work methodically through complex problems and issues and be experienced in managing vendors and evaluating product offerings. He or she should also be fluent in project management principles and techniques. In addition to these skills, the coordinator will need highly-developed qualities of patience, perseverance, and diplomacy.

There is a common theme in meetings of organizations for disaster recovery coordinators. Regardless of the initial level of enthusiasm and team spirit participants bring to the disaster recovery planning project, nearly everyone will ultimately develop resentment for the plan coordinator. DP operations will come to view the coordinator's insistence on routine backups as an unwarranted interruption of their already overcrowded processing schedules. Research and Development (R&D) programmers will find obnoxious the coordinator's requirement that they pause periodically to document changes made to programs and systems so that work can be reconstructed in the event of disaster. User departments may develop an intense dislike of the coordinator's constant testing and probing for possible gaps in their preventive and protective measures. Senior management may even come to disdain spending money on an enterprise without a tangible return on investment.

Thus, to supplement the skills that the coordinator brings to the job, the information manager will have to provide the coordinator with authority to quell dissent, visible (and budgetary) support and enthusiasm for the planning effort, and personal support for the coordinator's ego.

No statistics are available to demonstrate the stress level associated with the position of disaster recovery coordinator, but considering the nature of the job—the need to confront the dark side of business survival daily, and make the safety and security of fellow employees one's personal concern—the coordinator's stress level must rate somewhere between a dentist and a Chilean president's bodyguard. The information manager needs to recognize this and compensate for it, not only in salary, but by freeing the coordinator from other tasks and giving personal recognition and reinforcement for the valuable work that the coordinator is performing.

A Note on Methodology

A cursory examination of the literature will confirm that there are as many methodologies for developing disaster recovery plans as there are plan authors. This book seeks to find common ground by returning to the fundamental methodology of project management.

Fortunately, disaster recovery planning is too young an endeavor to have spawned argumentative schools of adherents to this or that guru's methodology. There are no gurus except, perhaps, those who have experienced and recovered from an actual disaster. Having talked with many of them in research for this book, they are wiser and somewhat modest about their accomplishment. Hardly the guru type.

This is not to say that there are not pretenders. In certain facets of disaster recovery plan development, one is almost certain to run up against a vendor representative, a plan author, or a risk manager who is convinced he or she has all the answers. The best policy is to listen. They may, after all, have a few worthwhile observations.

In the meantime, there are far more important and basic skills to master. One of the most important is one's ability to think systematically about the planning task. This is no mean feat: One must, after all, superimpose rationality on an event that is inherently chaotic—disaster. It cannot be overstressed that disaster recovery planning is not something that one can do perfectly the first time. Only by putting the plan on paper and testing it can its errors be realized and corrected. The only method is trial and error.

There are a few other points to make about the approach of this book to its subject. As previously observed, developing a disaster recovery plan is a project entailing the performance of many discrete tasks and the allocation of fixed resources. The end product of the effort is a plan document, that is, a roadmap for yet another project: recovery from an actual disaster.

To help the reader understand the objectives and alternative strategies that must be considered in the formulation of the plan, it is sometimes necessary to describe in detail how the plan will be implemented in a disaster *recovery* project. To help the reader, a simple diagrammatic distinction has been made between the plan project and the recovery project. When this book describes the plan development project, the accompanying illustrations use the techniques of data flow diagramming. When the recovery project is described, flow charts are used.

Data flow diagrams, or DFDs, seem appropriate to the description of the plan development project since the project generally consists of acquiring, processing, and presenting information.[19] Figure 1.5 provides the context for the disaster recovery planning project. It shows the plethora of organizations—including corporate departments, professional groups, and regulatory agencies—that shape the environment of the planning endeavor and form the reality against which plan adequacy is judged.

From this simple diagram, however, little can be discerned about the components of disaster recovery planning. Thus, in Appendix A, the reader will find another DFD that illustrates the major activities involved

Figure 1.5 The Context of Disaster Recovery Planning.

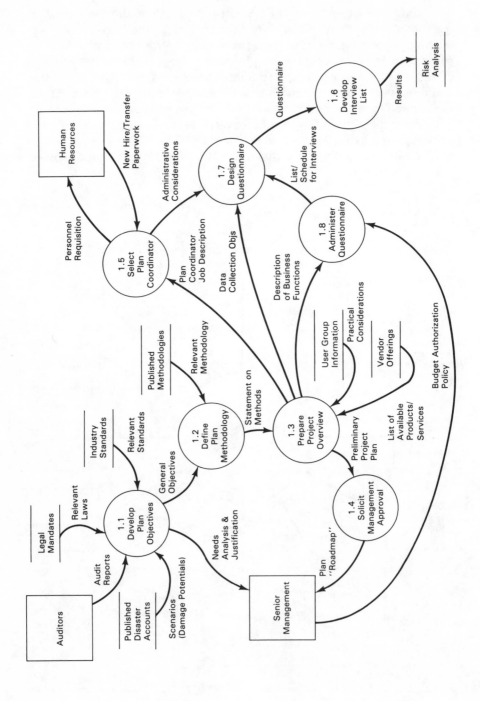

in the planning project. These major activities are then examined in more detailed DFDs appearing at the beginnings of most chapters in this book.

For example, Figure 1.6 is a DFD depicting data flows and activities described in chapter 1. Information resources, such as industry standards, published disaster accounts, and legal mandates, are used to develop a rationale for the plan development project for presentation to senior management. Data from these sources is used to define methods (consultant or in-house development) and to create project outlines. Other inputs and outputs are also presented to account for the numerous tasks involved in the initial start-up phase of disaster recovery planning.

DFDs do not necessarily show precedence or chronological order of tasks. They are flexible, spatial constructs that the reader, it is hoped, will find easy to apply to his or her planning requirements. As such, DFDs are preferable to the linear and rigid structure of a flow chart depicting tasks and milestones in the plan development project.

Elsewhere in this book, the reader will encounter flow charts that provide examples of master plans for various aspects of the recovery project. These flow charts attempt to superimpose order and sequence on recovery events. Flow charts are not intended as models to be rigorously followed, but as guides for creating and organizing one's own implementation plan. A concatenated flow chart appears on the reverse of the master DFD in Appendix A.

It is hoped that this distinction in illustrations will help to clarify any confusion that may arise between the planning project and the implementation project that is its product.

REFERENCES

1. D. Aasgaard, et al., "An Evaluation of Data Processing "Machine Room" Loss and Selected Recovery Strategies," *MISRC Working Papers* (Minneapolis, MN: University of Minnesota, 1978).

2. Ibid.

3. Ibid, adapted.

4. Ibid, adapted.

5. Jeffrey Gardner, "How to Assemble a Comprehensive Disaster Recovery Plan," *Computerworld*, Volume 19, Number 47, 25 November 1985.

6. CHI/COR Information Management, Inc., marketing literature, 1987.

7. "All About Disaster Recovery: A Special Datapro Report," Datapro Research Corporation, June 1985. Also, Jill Chamberlain, Vice President, CHI/COR Information Management, Inc., interview with author, 6 January 1987.

8. Chamberlain interview.

9. Datapro Special Report and Chamberlain interview.

10. Chamberlain interview.

11. Eddy Goldberg, "DP Nightmare Hits N.Y. Bank," *Computerworld*, Volume 19, Number 52, 2 December 1985.

12. William Perry, "The Auditor, EDP, and the Federal Government," in *Data Processing Management* (New York: Auerbach Publishers, 1979).

13. Ibid.

14. Ibid.

15. Inspector Roy Williams, St. Petersburg, FL Fire Department, interview with the author on 9 January 1987.

16. Maar Haack, EDP Underwriter, The St. Paul Insurance Companies, and Tom Cornwell, CHUBB Insurance Company, interviews with the author on December 5-6, 1987.

17. Ibid.

18. Jon Toigo, "Alternatives for Disaster Recovery Plan Development," *Data Security Management* (New York: Auerbach Publishers, 1988).

19. Data flow diagram (DFD) standards taken from Tom DeMarco, *Structured Analysis and System Specification* (New York: Yourdon, 1979).

Chapter   2

Analyzing The Risk

Just as a systems development project responds to user needs, a disaster recovery planning project responds to a corporation's needs for survival and business resumption in the wake of a disaster. In disaster recovery planning, defining corporate needs is synonomous with identifying risks and exposures. The proper methodological instrument for assessing these needs is a risk analysis.

Figure 2.1 is a DFD showing typical inputs and outputs of a risk analysis. As one can readily see, risk analysis is key to the development of objectives for many of the disaster recovery tasks that will follow. Its many activities involve interviewing company IS personnel and users, collating responses into a comprehensive view of the corporate information asset, and formulating criteria and objectives for the plans that will be created to safeguard this asset.

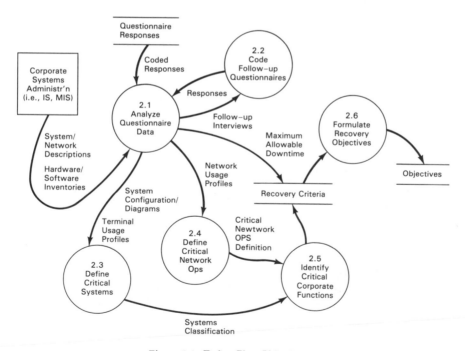

Figure 2.1 Define Plan Objectives.

The Purposes of Risk Analysis

Risk analysis is perhaps the single most misunderstood aspect of disaster recovery planning. To many, the term is vague and mysterious, connoting rarified techniques and unintelligible calculations known to only a very few privileged practitioners. To others, risk analysis is perceived as an irritating process of formalizing what is self-evident or obvious to anyone with a modicum of horse sense. As one information manager put it, "There is a generally accepted statistic that places the likelihood of a major disaster for any business at right around one percent. This is the risk. And when you have a disaster, you either have one or you don't. That's the exposure. That's all the risk analysis that you need. You just prepare for the worst."

This is an oversimplification, of course, but the meaning is clear. Risk analysis is a big term for what is essentially a straightforward application of good research and common sense. This is indicated by the three basic objectives of risk analysis:

1. Identifying company assets and functions that are necessary for business resumption following a disaster, and prioritizing them according to time sensitivity and criticality.
2. Identifying existing threats to assets and functions.
3. Setting objectives for developing strategies to eliminate avoidable risks and minimize the impact of risks that cannot be eliminated.

Identifying and Prioritizing Assets and Functions

Risk analysis consists of two basic operations: data collection and data analysis. The data collected in risk analysis should include a comprehensive list of computer and telecommunications hardware and a complete inventory of applications and systems software. From these data, system configuration diagrams are created and annotated to show the amount of activity, traffic, or use of each system in a typical business day, week, or month to provide critical business functions. To put this data in perspective, a single question should be asked: To what degree can the company tolerate the interruption of the functions that information and communications systems provide?

Typically, this data is collected from employees who use and manage systems on a daily basis. A questionnaire is sent to every user of a specific system or application (and to those responsible for maintaining the system or application) to identify its use in the performance of normal work. Technicians are asked more specific questions regarding file layouts, operational hardware configurations, etc. (A sample questionnaire is provided in Appendix D. The questionnaire developed for use at the reader's company may be more or less detailed than this one.)

The ultimate purpose of the questionnaire is to identify the criticality of each application or system. This is often accomplished by asking users how they would cope if the system were unavailable for a specified period of time.

The ability to cope with system interruption is called *tolerance*. In practical terms, tolerance may be expressed as a dollar value: It is the loss of revenues to the company from system outages of specific durations. If there is a very low tolerance within the company to the loss of a piece of equipment or to the interruption of the function it provides, this low tolerance is expressed as a high dollar value or cost. If, on the other hand, the company can tolerate to a significant extent the loss or interruption of a processing function, this high tolerance is expressed as a low dollar value or cost.

This concept cannot be overemphasized. The dollar value to the company of a given system may have little to do with the dollar cost of the hardware or software used in the system. A PC, using an off-the-shelf spreadsheet package and a few hundred kilobytes of corporate financial data, may provide a low tolerance business function whose loss would be far more expensive than the loss of any given application running on a mainframe.

Applications or equipment whose loss or outage would entail great costs for the company are termed *critical*. Conversely, high tolerance functions are referred to as *noncritical.*

For example, the loss of a telemarketing company's telecommunications switch would represent a low tolerance or high dollar loss. For each minute that the switch is down, the company is unable to do business and loses money. The telecommunications system, therefore, would be regarded as a critical system.

If, on the other hand, the same telemarketing firm were to lose the function of a computer application used to generate random telephone numbers, the financial impact of the outage would be very different. Since the company could readily change over to a manual system of random number generation, this application would not cost the company nearly as much as a telecommunications outage of the same duration. Thus, the application could be considered noncritical.

Of course, most companies use a variety of systems and applications whose loss or interruption can be tolerated to varying degrees. Thus, a spectrum of tolerances exists between those systems or applications that are critical and those which are noncritical. For this reason, the questionnaire provided to users might ask them to rate an application's criticality on some sort of a scale and to explain the reasons for their ranking.

For many users, the tolerance of an outage may be based upon the length of time that the system or application is unavailable for use. In an electrical power company, for example, users of the customer billing system may be able to revert to a manual method of billing for a brief period of time. However, because a large part of the customer base for a power company is transient (i.e., the customers associated with a given meter may change several times over the course of a month), the efficiency of manual billing may be degraded over time. It may become difficult to keep pace with the changes, driving up the costs of the manual system dramatically. Hence, over time, the utility's tolerance for the interruption of the application may decrease, and the criticality of the application may increase.

Variances in tolerance may also be linked to the time of the day or month an outage occurs. For many companies, a loss of their payroll system for a two-week period at month's end may be devastating. However, if the same outage occurred at midmonth, tolerance would be much higher. (Risk analysts, in general, assume that an outage will always occur at the worst possible time.)

It is not uncommon for users to identify mitigating factors, such as the timing of a disaster, when they assess the criticality of their systems. Time is a dynamic determinant of tolerance, for both economic and psychological reasons. When confronted with the news that a system is unavailable for use, the question that many users first ask is not why, but for how long. An outage of any length represents, in most cases, a need to make up time later—under stress—or in costly overtime.

It is also quite common for users to begin a criticality assessment by stating that all of their systems are critical precisely because they are *their* systems. Perhaps obtaining approval for system development was an uphill battle or the development project itself took a deep personal toll. Perhaps user ego influences their objectivity: Few users (or systems administrators) like to believe that the work they do, or the systems they use, are anything less than critical.

However, if the criteria used to classify systems are clearly explained, and the questionnaire asks not how critical a system is, but what steps a user group would take to perform the same function if the system were unavailable, then criticality typically becomes less problematic for the questionnaire respondent. More than one disaster recovery coordinator who has used the questionnaire method to gather information has discovered that users will provide a surprisingly fair assessment of their system's criticality.

One planner reported that three factors contributed to the success of a user poll at his company. First, each participant realized that other users were making similar concessions and complying with the classification scheme. Second, in group meetings held as a follow-up to the questionnaires, individuals who had displayed creativity or resourcefulness in developing coping strategies to deal with a hypothetical outage were given special praise or recognition by the coordinator. Third, everyone quickly realized that the classification of "their" system or application as less-than-critical applied only in the event of a disaster. The coordinator stressed that, under normal conditions, every system or application played a necessary, vital role in the achievement of company goals.[1]

Critical systems are often defined as such because, regardless of duration of the outage or the time of month in which an outage occurs, there are no substitute methods for providing the functions of the system. Typically, electrical power systems, telecommunications, or automated fluid control systems are classified as critical. Without backups or manual means of control, a loss of any of these systems *at any time* may represent a total cessation of normal business operations.

A well-designed user questionnaire asks the respondent to explain how he or she would deal with an outage that was one hour in duration, 24 hours, 48 hours, 72 hours, and so forth. If no coping strategies can be identified, the system is probably critical.

In the context of conventional data processing, applications may be defined on the following spectrum of tolerance:

- **Critical.** These functions cannot be performed unless identical capabilities are found to replace the company's damaged capabilities. Critical applications cannot be replaced by manual methods under any circumstances. Tolerance to interruption is very low and the cost of interruption is very high. Thus, for critical systems and applications, the company would need to arrange to have access to hardware comparable to its own, and, in an emergency, plan to transfer the application to the "backup" hardware in order to resume processing.

- **Vital.** These functions cannot be performed by manual means or can be performed manually for only a very brief period of time. There is somewhat higher tolerance to interruption and somewhat lower costs, provided that functions are restored within a certain timeframe (usually five days). In applications classified as vital, a brief suspension of processing can be tolerated, but a considerable amount of "catching up" will be needed to restore data to a current or useable form.

- **Sensitive.** These functions can be performed, with difficulty but at tolerable cost, by manual means for an extended period of time. Sensitive applications, however, require considerable "catching-up" once restored.
- **Noncritical.** These applications may be interrupted for an extended period of time, at little or no cost to the company, and require little or no "catching up" when restored.

Figure 2.2 illustrates this spectrum of tolerances. It should be noted that this classification scheme may also be applied to hardware, network operations, decentralized processing functions, and even to data.

Thus, one goal of risk analysis is to apply a classification scheme to each company function or asset that the disaster recovery plan will seek to protect. This same questionnaire-driven analysis, however, can go further to identify the costs of outages or interruptions as seen through the eyes of the users themselves.

In addition to asking users to classify their system's criticality and identify strategies for coping with outages, another question should be asked during initial data collection: How much would outages of the specified durations cost the company? User departments are often able to compile compelling cost analyses of the effects of downtime. They may collect dollar-cost data during normal operations for the purpose of demonstrating departmental performance. Many times this data can be

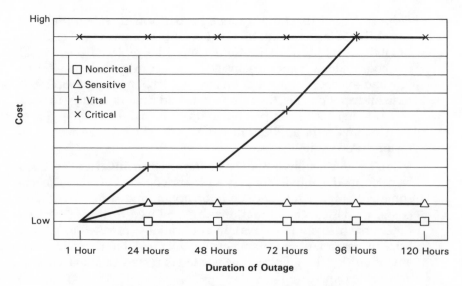

Figure 2.2 Relative Tolerances to System Failures.

adapted to show the dollar value of the work that would be lost if an interruption occurred.

For example, a marketing manager might keep data on the department's average daily sales of product in order to set sales goals for the next sales period. Using this statistic, the loss of on-line ordering systems for two days could be evaluated as a dollar loss. The permutations, as those who regularly perform risk analyses have observed, can be quite ingenious.

Identifying Threats to Assets and Functions

Once the criticality of systems has been assessed, the second objective of risk analysis is to identify what threats exist to normal information processing activity.

There are a variety of schemes for classifying threats. One scheme divides threats by causal origin, either man-made or natural. Another division is typically made between facility and regional disasters. These distinctions tend to blur more than they clarify. The dividing line, for example, between man-made and natural cause is often unclear until long after the disaster has passed (did a negligent employee or a bolt of lightning cause the fire?). The regional versus facility division also provides a poor analytical tool, since a regional disaster, such as a hurricane, may have a no less debilitating effect on business operations than would a facility disaster (and, in fact, a regional disaster will in many cases also damage the facility).

The best method for identifying threats is to look at the phenomena, regardless of origin, that typically cause a loss of normal system function. These may be summarized succinctly as:

- Water
- Fire
- Power failure
- Mechanical breakdown or software failure
- Accidental or deliberate destruction of hardware or software by hackers, disgruntled employees, industrial saboteurs, terrorists, or others.

Between 1967 and 1978, according to one study, fire and water damage accounted for 62 percent of all data processing disasters in the United States.[2] Because of improvements in fire detection and suppression systems and increased industry awareness to the threat of fire, flooding (water) is now considered the number one threat to data processing by major EDP insurers.[3]

Available statistics underscore the point. According to the Office of Insurance Support Services of the Federal Emergency Management Agency, claims paid to nonresidential Federal Flood Insurance policy holders reached $72 million in 1986.[4] Low-interest Small Business Administration loans, made to companies in disaster-stricken regions in the same year, amounted to $232 million.[5] Total damages due to torrential rains and six hurricanes that year exceeded $3.5 billion.

Water damage frequently results from firefighting techniques, but fires themselves claimed an annual average of 83 data centers and telephone switchrooms from 1980 to 1984. According to the National Fire Protection Association (NFPA), the average cost of a fire in a data center in 1984 was $2.6 million.[6] NFPA statistics do not cover noncomputer room fires. A fire at the U.S. Postal Service headquarters in October 1984, for example, claimed more than 500 PCs in user work areas and cost the U.S.P.S. approximately $20 million. At the time, disaster recovery planning did not extend to user work areas where PCs were in great use.[7]

Power failures, mechanical breakdowns, software malfunctions, and deliberate sabotage account for the balance of the average 300 data processing disasters that U.S. business suffered in a five-year period. These sources of disaster will probably continue to be a threat into the foreseeable future despite increased interest in machine and software fault tolerance, mean time between failure statistics, site uptime management, and general improvements in system and network security techniques.

The purpose of identifying the probabilities associated with various threats is not to create scare statistics. In risk analysis, it is valuable to know what the threats are in order to develop scenarios that will serve as the basis for planning prevention and recovery strategies. For example, it is valuable to know at what temperatures various media burn (see Table 1) in order to assess the protection afforded by fireproof cabinets of various ratings.

On the other hand, there is a hardcore group of risk managers and analysts who take this investigation to the extreme by quantifying the likelihood of each threat and expressing this percentage as a corporate financial exposure. However, the admonition of the information manager quoted earlier should be observed: "Either you have a disaster or you don't." Hence, the practical value of threat identification is twofold: (1) it serves to point out where disaster avoidance measures (such as halon systems, security access systems, and power protection systems) may be needed; and (2) it identifies specific vulnerabilities that plans and procedures must specifically address.

TABLE 1   Temperatures at Which Damage Starts to Occur

Computer equipment	175 °F
Magnetic tapes/diskettes	100–120 °F
Discs	150 °F
Paper/punched cards	350 °F
Microfilm/microfiche	225 °F
	(with steam)
	300 °F
	(no steam)

Another benefit of the threat identification process is less methodological than psychological. Focusing a group's attention on the threat potential can increase members' awareness and sensitivity. It can also facilitate group cohesion and unity in the disaster recovery planning effort as it helps the group recognize the importance of the work it will perform. This is extremely important, since there is much in the risk analysis process, including the classification of system criticality, to divide the group.

Threat identification may also serve to make participants more aware of the interdependencies that exist among them and build team unity by clarifying shared vulnerabilities. In this way, threat identification can set the stage for cost sharing in expensive threat avoidance systems and cooperation in other essential areas.

Developing Plan Objectives

Having classified system criticality, assigned costs to system outages of various durations, and identified threats to systems and data, it remains to analyze this data to formulate a set of specific objectives to guide the development of the recovery capability. The goal is to eliminate exposures that can be eliminated and to minimize the effects of those that cannot be eliminated.

This analysis does not lend itself readily to "group think," although follow-up interviews with users and system administrators may help the disaster recovery coordinator better understand requirements and set objectives. In fact, certain exposures do not fall under the aegis of the disaster recovery coordinator and, thus, require coordination with the security manager, auditor, or other authorized persons.

Threats related to the intentional abuse of systems by persons who are or are not corporate employees are typically viewed as security threats.

Obviously, if a hacker demolishes a network or erases critical data, these activities may have an impact equivalent to a disaster. Security planning is the twin of disaster recovery planning, and the two functions must work together to accomplish their respective goals.

To address effectively the other threats to normal operations, such as fire and flooding, the disaster recovery coordinator will need to work with individuals at practically every level within the company. This is because of the nature of the planning project.

As Figure 2.3 illustrates, the objectives of disaster recovery planning are to develop both a plan and a permanent, ongoing prevention and recovery capability. Installation of a fire protection system will require the cooperation of the data center manager or department manager for whom the system is being installed. Similarly, the coordination of a regular schedule of off-site storage for important records, storage media, and microfiche will require the full participation of those who create and use these items.

A clear set of stated objectives, identifying the conditions, tasks, and standards for each protection or recovery strategy, is often a prerequisite for justifying the strategy to those who will have to absorb the cost or modify existing procedures. Representatives of the department that will be affected and senior management will want to know what the coordinator is specifically seeking to do, and will want to see how all of the objectives fit together in a comprehensive recovery strategy.

The following is a generic, but by no means comprehensive, set of objectives that may result from a risk analysis. Each objective assumes that sufficient information has been collected to justify the need for the task. Objectives are organized under section titles that define the function or area that the objectives are designed to address. (If the objectives seem a bit like a job description for the disaster recovery coordinator, this is only

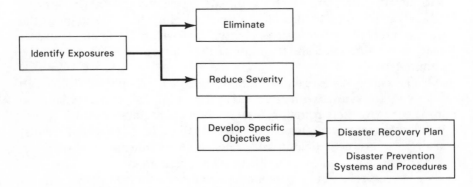

Figure 2.3 Objectives Development in Risk Control.

because they reflect the assumption made at the outset: Disaster recovery planning is a full-time task.)

Company Policy

1. The disaster recovery coordinator will develop and seek senior management approval for a company policy for the protection of people, property and assets (within a specified time frame) that meets current company standards and format for documentation.

This objective addresses itself to the need to undertake disaster recovery planning, to obtain management approval and support, and to generate a paper plan within a set time frame. It also assigns responsibility for the task to the disaster recovery coordinator.

Plan Maintenance

2. The disaster recovery coordinator will develop a schedule for periodic review and maintenance of the plan and advise all personnel of their roles and the deadline for receiving revisions and comments.
3. The disaster recovery coordinator will collate reviewer revisions and comments, and update the plan within 30 days of the review date.
4. The disaster recovery coordinator will arrange and coordinate scheduled and unscheduled tests of the disaster recovery plan to evaluate its adequacy.
5. The disaster recovery coordinator will participate in scheduled plan tests that will be performed four times per year on _____ (specific dates). For all scheduled and unscheduled tests, the coordinator will write evaluations of test results and integrate test results into the disaster recovery plan within 30 days.
6. The disaster recovery coordinator will develop a schedule for training recovery personnel in emergency and recovery procedures as set forth in the disaster recovery plan. Training dates should be scheduled within 30 days of each plan revision and scheduled plan test.
7. The disaster recovery coordinator will maintain records of disaster recovery plan maintenance activities (testing, training, and reviews) and submit these for examination by internal and external auditors.

This section sets forth the objectives for maintaining the plan and empowers the disaster recovery coordinator to initiate and supervise plan maintenance activities. It will be the information manager's job to ensure that the disaster recovery coordinator is provided with the authority to fulfill these responsibilities.

Physical Environment

8. The disaster recovery coordinator will collect information regarding company facilities and assess existing structures and facilities for their susceptibility to fire, water, and criminal intrusion, and will report the findings in memoranda to senior management, information systems management, and departmental management.

This objective specifically seeks to assess facility-related risk factors so that they may be addressed in the disaster recovery plan or through the development of loss prevention capabilities. (Facility-related risk factors are explored in greater detail in Chapter 3.) Obviously, the results of the departmental risk analyses are provided to those persons who will need to underwrite the costs of acquiring a specific avoidance or recovery capability. Risk factors and potential costs are typically communicated as a part of a cost-justification for the capabilities that are being proposed.

Organizational Control

9. The disaster recovery coordinator will work with departmental managers or systems supervisors to develop informational programs to advise all employees within the department of the assets and functions they are expected to safeguard, the irregularities they are to note and/or report, and the immediate actions they are to take.
10. The disaster recovery coordinator will work with departmental management to develop a formal "ownership" program in order to assign responsibility for each and every resource to individual employees within the department.

This section provides the means for employees and managers to aid the disaster recovery coordinator in the early detection and correction of potentially hazardous or debilitating conditions or practices. The disaster recovery coordinator may be called upon to draft these disaster avoidance procedures, or the task may be assigned to the department manager once the specific procedures and guidelines have been identified.

The second objective, to establish an "ownership" program, may be familiar to security planners with whom the concept originated.

However, system or application ownership has relevance in the context of disaster recovery planning as well.[8] The practice of assigning ownership of equipment or functions to employees is tantamount to giving the employee "owner" the right to say who may use the resource. At first glance, this may seem to invite friction and disputes among employees. However, the experience of many organizations that use ownership programs demonstrates that the opposite effect typically results.

Ownership programs often help employees become more attentive to the secure and qualified use of "their" resources. Abuse of systems, or misuse due to inadequate training, may be spotted sooner so that the detection and correction of errors can be undertaken before the problem creates an outage.

Human Resources

11. The disaster recovery coordinator will work with the human resources department to develop procedures for notifying information managers of pending terminations or separations within the user community.
12. The disaster recovery coordinator will work with the human resources department to develop procedures for maintaining a telephone directory to be used in contacting recovery team members in the event of a disaster.
13. The disaster recovery coordinator will work with the human resources department to develop a program designed to foster safety awareness among employees of the company.

The human resources connection is a vital one for a variety of security- and disaster recovery-related reasons. In some companies, human resources will be responsible for making employees aware of where to go to continue work in the event of a disaster. Human resources may also be called upon to set a policy providing for the immediate dismissal of employees who abuse systems, and to set into motion a procedure that will see a terminated employee's user permissions revoked and company property reclaimed.

Human resources may also be asked to assess the psychological strengths of employees who will be called upon to provide key recovery functions. Knowing how an employee is likely to behave under stress, and having access to the employee's personal data (marital status, home address, home and emergency contact telephone numbers), can be critical for evaluating his or her suitability to participate directly in recovery or salvage activities.

Operational And Access Controls

14. The disaster recovery coordinator will work together with systems administrators and data processing personnel to coordinate a daily schedule of routine backup of data and programs.
15. The disaster recovery coordinator will identify all documentation and forms required for continuation of normal operations following a disaster and ensure that adequate supplies are inventoried in a secure, access-controlled location.
16. The disaster recovery coordinator will document network and system integrity control measures.
17. The disaster recovery coordinator will ensure that master- and/or firmware-passwords and/or encryption/decryption standards are recorded and stored in a secure, access-controlled location.

Operational and access control measures are typical features of data processing or network operations; they are the backbone of security in normal, day-to-day operations. However, they can present a nightmare for disaster recovery. If systems administrators or operations personnel cannot be located at the time of a disaster, it is possible that the recovery of downed systems or networks will be delayed because master passwords or data encryption keys, known only to the administrator, are unavailable. A related concern: the lack of procedural or software documentation or preprinted forms used in normal operations, can also delay recovery.

Applications Development

18. The disaster recovery coordinator will develop and implement a schedule of routine backup and documentation for applications under development.

Applications development projects, which represent a substantial investment of company time and resources, should be backed up to prevent disastrous loss. If industry-accepted documentation standards are observed and enforced, this objective may have already been met. However, the disaster recovery coordinator should verify this.

Systems And Networks

19. The disaster recovery coordinator will quantify, to the extent possible, the dollar loss potential to the company of system failures of

fixed durations for every data site in the company, including mainframe, mini-, and micro-computer based systems and telecommunications systems and networks.

20. The disaster recovery coordinator will develop a disaster recovery capability that provides for recovery of critical applications within X hours.

21. The disaster recovery coordinator will document responsibilities of key recovery personnel in the event of a disaster.

22. The disaster recovery coordinator will develop minimum acceptable configurations for systems and networks that will provide emergency service levels for X hours, or until normal operations are restored.

23. The disaster recovery coordinator will develop strategies for the replacement of system functions by manual or automated means for a period of X hours in the event of a disaster.

24. The disaster recovery coordinator will develop sufficient alternative vendors or sources of supply for each resource required for system reconstruction in a minimum acceptable configuration in order to result in an acceptable level of risk.

These objectives begin to approach tasks that are generally recognized as the exclusive domain of disaster recovery planning. They set a timetable for recovery of downed systems in emergency mode. This number is expressed as a goal: Systems and networks will be up-and-running at emergency service levels within X hours.

Furthermore, the tentative recovery time frame is set forth: Systems and networks will need to be operated at emergency levels for X hours/days, which is the estimated time required to relocate to the original or to a new permanent processing site.

The term "minimum acceptable system configuration" in the above objectives is also significant. It refers to the fact that recovery systems and networks need not be mirror images of pre-disaster systems and networks. If only critical applications are being provided, user terminal requirements might be drastically reduced. Also, disk capacity requirements may not be as great if the size of the database required by partially-restored systems is reduced.

For voice and data communications, a smaller telecommunications switch might suffice to replace a full-sized private branch exchange (PBX). An analysis of capacity requirements might reveal that critical communications activity can be adequately sustained with fewer incoming direct inward dial (DID) trunks and fewer wide area service lines.

Whatever strategies are developed for system or network recovery, they must be cost-justified by demonstrating how much it would cost the company if it did not have the capabilities in the event of a disaster. The backup strategies and configurations that are formulated must be documented in advance, the documentation must be made available to those who will rebuild systems in an emergency, and provisions must be made for two or more sources to supply hardware and supplies that will be needed for reconstruction.

Backup/Off-Site Storage

26. The disaster recovery coordinator will assess and contract with a qualified vendor of off-site storage services according to the guidelines set forth by the Association of Commercial Records Centers (ACRC), or some comparable body.[9]
27. Having documented the criticality of data, applications, systems, and networks, the disaster recovery coordinator will identify the following resources for backup and/or removal to off-site storage:

    a. Hardcopies of system documentation, user manuals, operating procedures, vital paper records, disaster recovery plans, and other documentation that might be useful or essential to recovery.
    b. Critical, vital, and sensitive data stored on magnetic or photographic media.
    c. Stocks of forms and supplies that are necessary for recovery and subject to delays in resupply.

28. The disaster recovery coordinator or designate will inventory materials stored off-site at 60 day intervals and periodically audit materials for completeness and integrity in accordance with the latest update of the plan.
29. The disaster recovery coordinator will assess options and recommend strategies for system and network backup that meet plan requirements in the most cost-effective way.
30. The disaster recovery coordinator will make all advance arrangements that are necessary to facilitate the logistics of the transition from normal system operation to emergency system operation, including the transportation of resources, the acquisition and delivery of emergency supplies and materials, and the rerouting or activation of telecommunications networks.

These objectives go to the heart of the disaster recovery capability. When realized, they provide the means for recovery and the methods for implementing the recovery strategy.

Emergency Action

31. The disaster recovery coordinator will document all procedures and policies of civil or government organizations that might impact on the company's recovery strategy.
32. The disaster recovery coordinator will develop procedures that provide for the monitoring of all alarm sources, including fire alarms and weather and emergency radio.
33. The disaster recovery coordinator will develop clear decision "trees" (decision-making flowcharts) that assign specific personnel responsibility for invoking the disaster recovery plan. These procedures will fully identify the criteria for decisionmaking.
34. The disaster recovery coordinator will document the notification procedure that will be observed when the plan is invoked.
35. The disaster recovery coordinator will develop sound evacuation and immediate action procedures and train all personnel in their use. Periodic drills in evacuation will be conducted with the consent of department managers.

The orderly evacuation of facilities is prerequisite in disaster recovery planning, which seeks first and foremost to safeguard human life. In addition to the need (and legal requirement) to assign evacuation routes and drill employees in their use, it is also necessary to identify how and by whom the disaster recovery plan will be invoked to initiate recovery strategies.

Some disasters occur suddenly and without warning. Others, such as hurricanes, may develop over a period of time, allowing for a last minute backup and an orderly shutdown of systems. These differences would be reflected in the logic of a decision "tree," a decision-making flowchart included in the plan.

Furthermore, the procedures for warning and evacuating populations used by civil government authorities can have a direct impact on the implementation of the disaster recovery plan. In hurricane-prone areas, for example, it is not unusual for businesses in vulnerable areas to be evacuated while a storm is still quite distant and has a very small chance of striking anywhere in the vicinity of the business. Evacuation orders employ the logic of mass population movements, not of business resumption. Thus, the timetable with which government emergency managers work may be very different from the timetable of the disaster recovery plan.[10]

Articulating Objectives

These 35 objectives are general and generic. Those developed for a particular company will reflect the company's specialized needs in the area of disaster recovery. Once developed, plan objectives should be articulated to those who will provide spending authorization and those who will actually develop strategies and procedures based on the objectives.

Procedures development can be a lengthy process involving hours of research, consulting, writing, reviewing, and rewriting. During this process, the coordinator should take some immediate steps to provide basic protections for the data centers and user departments. These protective measures are the subject of Chapter 3.

R E F E R E N C E S

1. Kenneth N. Myers, "Avoiding a Crisis," Datamation, (1 February 1986).
2. Statistics taken from a presentation by Marsh & McLennen Protection Consultants, Inc., circa 1985.
3. Maar Haack, EDP underwriter for St. Paul Fire and Marine, taped interview with author, 9 January 1987.
4. Claudia Murphy, planning specialist, Office of Insurance Support Services, FEMA, statistics provided in a letter to author, 16 September 1987.
5. Jerry Pico, Small Business Adminstration, interview with author, 3 August 1987.
6. Carolyn Daily, public relations officer, NFPA, interview with author, 3 August 1987.
7. Steve Skolochencko, data security branch, USPS, interviews with author, 4 August and 6 October 1987.
8. Security Assessment Questionnaire, IBM Data Security Support Programs, May 1985.
9. See "Commercial Records Center Evaluation Form," Association of Commercial Records Centers, 1985.
10. Jon Toigo, "Storm Alarms Sound," Databus, (August 1986).

Chapter 3

Facility Protection

Formulating the strategies and documenting the procedures for disaster recovery are complicated and time-consuming processes. However, there are usually a number of action items, identified during risk analysis, that may be implemented at the same time as procedures are being developed. These include the purchase and installation of systems to safeguard against avoidable disasters such as fire and flooding.

Figure 3.1 is a DFD showing many of the generic activities that aim at securing disaster avoidance capabilities for a company's user departments and information processing facilities. As the chart suggests, the evaluation, selection, cost-justification and installation of these capabilities may be undertaken concurrently with the development of the paper plan.

The acquisition of disaster avoidance systems is rarely a simple matter of cutting a purchase order. Vendors must be identified, products evaluated, bids solicited, costs justified, and expenditures approved. Furthermore, depending on the type of system, there may be an additional set of tasks to coordinate system installation (with the data center or user department), schedule work, prepare the installation site, or provide for the interruption of normal operations for training or installation work.

Preparatory steps differ depending on a number of factors, ranging from the type of disaster avoidance system being installed to the work schedule of the affected department. Under ideal circumstances, systems are installed during the preparation of new company quarters. However, more often than not, disaster avoidance capabilities are add-ons to existing facilities and must, to the extent possible, be implemented around normal business activities.

The following sections discuss several common disaster prevention and protection strategies that can be implemented to provide a disaster avoidance capability.

Water Detection

As noted previously, flooding is the main threat to data processing and records management facilities. Annual costs to companies resulting from water damage are in the millions of dollars.

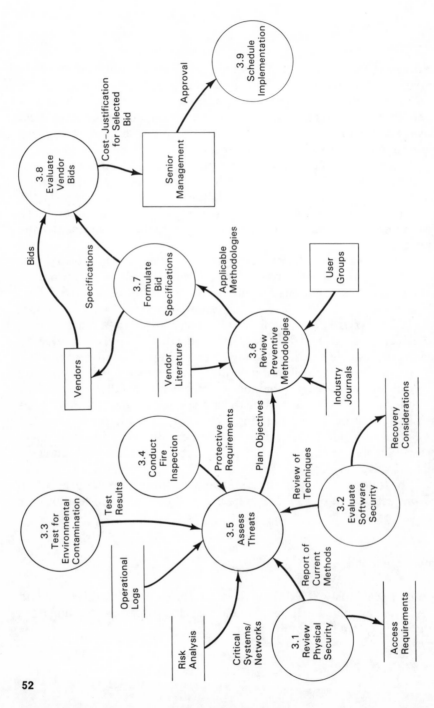

Figure 3.1 Disaster Prevention Systems Selection and Implementation.

Water can intrude into sensitive information processing and storage facilities in a variety of ways and from a variety of sources. Some common sources of flooding are:

- **Facility plumbing leaks.** Although the well-designed data processing or storage facility should be located away from building plumbing, they often are not. Water and sewer pipe leakage, particularly in multistory buildings, can travel along pipes and duct work and drain into the data or records storage center.
- **Air conditioning.** Spot coolers and subfloor air conditioning plants can produce water, either through leakage or condensation.
- **Water cooling systems.** Some larger mainframes are cooled, not by air, but by water. Leaks in the cooling system can show up as underfloor puddles.
- **Sprinkler systems.** Faulty, dripping sprinkler heads or sprinkler piping can deposit water in the center.

Many hardware vendors suggest that their equipment is impervious to water damage and it is not uncommon to hear a sales representative state assuredly that water poses no threat to deenergized equipment. If the computer is deenergized and becomes wet, says the rep (or service technician or field service agent), just disassemble it, dry it out, put it back together, and it will work properly. This presumes that the information manager or computer operator will have the prescience to know when water will enter the facility and come into contact with energized equipment, and that he or she will enjoy the luxury of spare time in the processing schedule to shut down until a leak can be traced to its origin and repaired.

With the exception of the times when facilities are intentionally evacuated in response to natural threats, such as hurricanes, storm surges, or rising water, there is rarely a clear indication of imminent water intrusion. Thus, it is likely that water will contact energized equipment causing short circuits and damage.

Even if it were true that electronic components are waterproof if deenergized (and according to a U.S. Air Force study, this is certainly not the case [1]), the period required to dry and test components before reenergizing them is protracted. Thus, the claims of many vendors about the tolerance of their hardware to water intrusion is a moot point: Disasters are disasters because they stop normal processing operations for an unacceptable or intolerable period of time.

What is needed, therefore, is a means of anticipating water intrusion, or detecting it before equipment shutdown is required. Systems—ranging from simple battery-operated alarms to sophisticated sensing cables—are available to detect the presence of underfloor water before it becomes hazardous to equipment and personnel. Cables, placed in a grid-like pattern on the subfloor, can pinpoint the exact location of water intrusion, and when strategically positioned around subfloor air ducts, pipes and fixtures, they can provide information about the probable source of the leak. In addition to signaling leakage with an alarm, systems can also provide the means for automatically deenergizing equipment when water intrusion is detected.

Figure 3.2 portrays sources of water in the data center. In Figure 3.3, a typical sensing cable installation, the numbers indicated along the cable correspond to sensing points in the cable itself and activate sensor readings on a digital monitor in combination with the alarm signal.

Sources of Water

Data Center Application

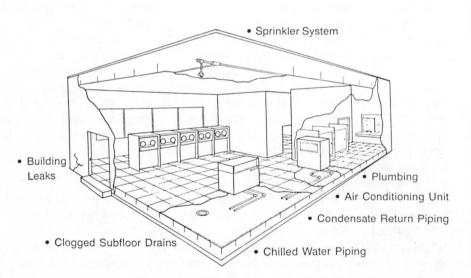

Source: TraceTek™, Raychem Corporation Reprinted by permission.

Figure 3.2 Sources of Water: Data Center Application.

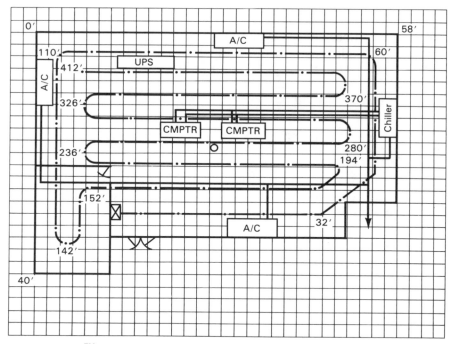

Source: TraceTek™, Raychem Corp. Reprinted by permission.

Figure 3.3 Typical Water Detection Layout.

Fire Protection

Although water is statistically the cause of the greatest number of facility disasters, it is fire, not water, that is generally perceived as the chief threat. Fire prevention begins with facility design and construction. Fire-resistant construction materials, fire wall placement, and facility compartmentalization can play major roles in limiting the scope, duration, and destructiveness of a fire. Also, when building codes and associated fire codes are observed, many building-related fire hazards can be minimized or eliminated.

However, despite the existence of some very thorough building and fire codes (Disneyworld's EPCOT code being one of the most advanced), state laws differ in enforcing contractor adherence to the codes. Some states have adopted National Fire Protection Association standards *in toto*, while others have adopted the codes only in part. Nearly every state lacks sufficient enforcement personnel to inspect all new and existing construction for code adherence, and violations often become evident only after a fire occurs.

A good starting point for the disaster recovery coordinator or information manager interested in installing fire detection or fire suppression systems is to contact the local fire department. Fire inspectors are generally willing to visit a site and provide practical (and legal) insights into the adequacy or inadequacy of existing capabilities.

The inspector may find code violations in the building structure that will need to be rectified regardless of the type of fire suppression system being considered for installation. (However, few inspectors will penalize facility owners or tenants for less-than-life-threatening code violations discovered in an investigation prompted by an invitation, provided that they are remedied within a reasonable period of time.)

If inadequate detection or suppression capabilities are noted by the fire inspector, this finding can often be used to support the case for spending money on an effective capability. The inspector's comments should be requested in writing.

Another way in which fire departments may assist during disaster recovery planning is by identifying the techniques that will likely be used if a fire occurs. More than one company has learned, to its chagrin, that the expensive Halon fire suppression system it purchased proved useless in the case of a major fire originating in another part or on another floor of the building.

A halogenated agent, to be effective, must reach a certain concentration within the atmosphere of the environment. Thus, the environment must be sealed. Firefighting techniques, however, may require that the integrity of the Halon-protected environment be violated by breaking windows or opening sealed doors.

In fact, fire inspectors can often advise, based on facility design and probable firefighting techniques, whether or not Halon is even appropriate for a given facility. In the case of one facility, an inspector observed that the data processing department's Halon would be useless: "We'd just open the doors at one end of the building and hose everything through the doors at the other end, and on into the parking lot. Computers, cubicles, chairs, the works."

This is not meant to imply that Halon systems are inappropriate in every case. It is important, however, to keep in mind facility design and fire-fighting principles when considering their installation. Fire inspectors are usually competent in analyzing building diagrams and can use their experience and knowledge to offer valuable advice. In the case of the facility described above, Halon was installed despite the inspector's graphic description of how the fire department would handle a fire. The information manager's objective was to suppress any fire that broke out in his center *before* it became a conflagration requiring fire department assistance.

In addition to advice on the selection of systems and the determination of facility structure hazards, fire inspectors can often identify fire hazards within company offices and recommend corrective measures. The coordinator should accompany the inspector through the facility and note any comments he or she may make. Some common observations and concerns may include:

- **The presence of combustibles located near potential igniters.** In a DP environment, for example, this may include cartons of paper located in close proximity to heat-generating hardware.
- **The UL rating of extension cords and electrical devices.** The Underwriting Laboratory rates a wide range of products for, among other things, their potential for causing fires. Many products do not bear the UL label and this may be a factor in determining fire risks.
- **Company smoking policy.** Lighted tobacco is an obvious hazard. However, in addition to the immediate danger of a fire, cigarette smoke can also invade and damage sensitive storage media and drives.
- **Fire-related health hazards posed by certain types of fabrics and materials.** Some fabrics and materials, when burned, can release poisonous particles and gases into the atmosphere. Phosgene, hydrogen chloride, and hydrogen cyanide may be released by the burning of common plastics, while PCBs may be released from fires involving transformers and other electronic equipment. These toxic by-products can not only result in the loss of human life, but they can also delay reentry into the facility following a fire.

Besides hazards within the facility, a fire inspector is often in a position to warn the disaster recovery coordinator about neighbors with high potential for disaster. In multi- story buildings, it may be valuable to know the lines of business of other occupants. If a neighbor engages in an activity that poses a substantial fire risk, this might affect the selection of fire avoidance systems. Also, if a facility is located in close proximity to one engaged in the refinement of chemicals, the manufacturing of volatile products, and so forth, the fire inspector typically knows this and can notify the disaster recovery coordinator.

Knowledge is power. However, knowing the risks does not necessarily mean that all threats can be eliminated. Just as the disaster recovery coordinator may have no control over the initial construction of the facility, he or she may have no control over where the facility is located in relation to high potential risks. The best one can do is to eliminate potential risks that can be eliminated, and minimize exposure to those that cannot. This strategy involves both preventive and prophylactic measures. Protecting against fires means identifying possible causes and controlling or eliminating them.

An important and often overlooked cause of fire in DP facilities is environmental contamination. Contamination, the entry of airborne contaminant particles into electronic equipment, can cause short circuits and even flash fires in data processing equipment. Moreover, contamination has been the indirect cause of more data processing downtime than all the fires, floods, hurricanes, earthquakes, and disgruntled employees combined.

Contaminants are microscopic particulates bearing such grandiose names as crystallines, carbonaceous particles, organic and synthetic fibrous particulates, and metallics. Without a degree in chemistry, an information manager can be unimpressed by the reports and analyses conducted by research labs that explain how contaminants effect sensitive disk media, circuitry, and microswitches. Also, due to the minute size of many contaminants, industry specialists report that they are often hard pressed to convince an information manager that a contamination problem exists.

Concern with the destructive potential of contamination has long been an issue for agencies of the U.S. Government. In the late 1960s, the General Services Administration issued federal air standards for cleanroom and workstations in federal agencies. These were revised in 1973 and issued by the GSA under the unassuming title, Federal Air Standard 209B.

209B set forth three scientific classifications of environmental contamination and mandated that federal agencies and contractors comply with them. Class 100 facilities included certified clean rooms, such as those employed by NASA and the Department of Defense for the development of sensitive electronic devices. Class 10,000 facilities included government hospital operating theatres. Class 100,000 facilities included all federal data processing centers. The classification nomenclature—100, 10,000, and 100,000—referred to particulate concentrations. It was determined that environments having less than 100,000 particulates (no larger than 0.5 microns in size) per cubic foot of air were optimal for data processing hardware.

While this standard has not been enforced in the private sector (except in the case of certain defense contractors and within certain facilities regulated directly by the federal government), it indicates the correlation the government has drawn between environment and system integrity.

Various methods have been developed to demonstrate the presence and concentration of contaminant particles in the data center. Some of the more popular methods are:

- **"White glove" method.** As the name suggests, this method assesses the level of contamination by wiping the exposed surface of a piece of equipment with a white glove. The particulates in the glove are analyzed to determine the type of contaminant in the center environment.

- **Petri-dish method.** With this method of checking contamination, a petri dish is used to collect particulates that fall out of the air.[2] After a period of time, the contents of the dish are analyzed to determine the amount and type of fallout.

- **Aspirating pump.** This method involves the installation of a pump in an area where air quality is to be measured. Air samples are collected through an air intake, and the contents are analyzed following several hours of operation.

- **Electronic particulate counter.** The electronic counter, until recently the most advanced method of contaminant data collection, literally counts the number of particulates that come into contact with its sensing tip over a period of time. To analyze the contaminants themselves, counter probes are wiped with a swab and the swab is then microscopically examined.

- **VICON^{TM} Detector System.** By far the most advanced contaminant measurement apparatus available, VICON^{TM} detectors provide a more comprehensive picture of facility contamination than do fallout and static detection methods. Many of the most damaging particulates (propelled by air conditioning within the sub-floor environment at an average velocity of 50 linear feet per minute, and through perforated floor tiles at approximately 500 linear feet per minute) do not readily settle out of the air stream. The VICON^{TM} monitor is designed to measure contamination in circulating air and to trap airborne contaminants. The monitor is active 24 hours per day, avoiding the false readings of other methods involving momentary collection or counting. This monitoring system uses a filter card on which filtering media of various types are assembled. Analyses of these filtering media can provide an accurate picture of contamination levels in the data center *by type of contaminant.*[3]

Once the presence of contamination in the data center has been demonstrated and its threat in terms of equipment failure, overheating, and combustion are understood, next it is necessary to develop strategies for eliminating or reducing contamination levels. A good way to begin is to answer the question: "How are contaminants introduced into the clean environment of the data processing facility?"

While certain contaminants are carried in by operators (including clothing fibers, hair and skin particles, and even cigarette smoke and ash), most particulates are airborne and are transported into sensitive equipment through the computer room subfloor air supply. Examples of the more common contaminants follow.

- Cement dust, sand, plaster and brick dust may be produced by the gradual erosion of the subfloor surface beneath a data center's raised floor. Even if the subfloor has been properly sealed with poly-acrylic sealants, the dust that was generated during raised floor installation may settle on the subfloor. This cement dust, propelled by air conditioning, can enter bottom-cooled equipment at high velocity and damage board components.
- Urban pollution, including carbon/coal dust, can enter the subfloor air supply by way of the air conditioning system. The wearing of drive belts or printer components and the release of laser printer toner can also introduce these contaminants to the DP area. These particulates are a special problem since they can conduct electricity and cause short circuits and cross-tracking.
- The electrically-conductive particulate metallic can be traced to equipment wear, wear of the air-conditioning plant, floor and ceiling suspension systems, and even to good old-fashioned rust (iron oxide). Metallic contaminants are even more dangerous than carbon residue because they tend to "plate out" on components where they will cause the most damage.

Nearly any contaminant can conduct electricity—even paper dust. If the contaminant can absorb moisture, it can wreak the same sort of damage as the "bug" of computer legend which, when it straddled two poles of an open switch with its legs, made a circuit and short-circuited the first computer. As in the case of the first bug, it is almost impossible to determine the cause of the short circuit since fiber or paper particles disintegrate in the heat generated by the short.

Fortunately, there are several steps that the information manager can take to eliminate certain types of contamination and to minimize the impact of contaminants that cannot be completely eliminated. The good news is that most of these steps do not require that the equivalent of a NASA clean room be established in the DP facility.

1. Forbid cigarette smoking inside the data center. If smoking is now permitted, smoke particles and tar are already harming the health of computer equipment.
2. Remove wastepaper baskets and bulk paper containers from the computer room. These are prime sources of fiber and paper dust—highly water-absorbent, therefore conductive, particulates.

3. Invest in a hand-held vacuum that is fitted with brushless rotors and microstatic filters for use in general cleanup of paper handlers and printers in the center. Most portable vacuum cleaners add more contamination than they remove. Especially dangerous are the metallic particles from the motor brushes that are expelled in the vacuum exhaust and collected by sensitive equipment in the center.

4. If space permits, move printers—especially laser printers—out of the room where CPUs, tape drives, telecommunications switches, and disk drives are stored.

5. Observe proper computer floor tile maintenance practices, as recommended by the manufacturer. For example, perform all tile alterations outside the raised-floor environment. Cutting a tile inside the center will flood the environment with fiber and aluminum contaminants. In addition, always replace a tile in the same direction as it was removed. Replacing tiles incorrectly can cause them to wobble and wear, depositing contaminants into the plenary air supply below the raised floor.

6. Ensure that all equipment is fitted with the best filters that the equipment vendor can provide. This will not eliminate contamination altogether, but it will keep some of the larger particulates out of drives and switches.

For example, most of the so-called "absolute" filters available from mainframe vendors for hardware and drives provide protection only from particles of 1 to 2 microns in size or larger. One micron is equal to 39.36 microinches. The headfly height—the distance between the reading head and the disk media—of many disk drives is 50 microinches. Thus, particles that are small enough to pass through absolute filters are still large enough to seriously impair the operation of the equipment on which the filters are installed. Figure 3.4 illustrates the comparative sizes of contaminant particles and Figure 3.5 depicts the development of a disk drive head crash due to contamination.[4] A head crash of this type has been aptly compared to a 747 flying three feet above the runway at 750 miles an hour that encounters a 3'1" rock. The effects can be disastrous.

So-called sealed drives are also at risk from contamination. Despite vendor claims that the drives are impervious to environmental factors, these drives are equipped with breather filters that contaminants can and do penetrate. When the smallest contaminant penetrates this shield, it has enormous destructive potential. The read/write head on a thin-film type drive flies only 10 to 15 microinches above the platter.

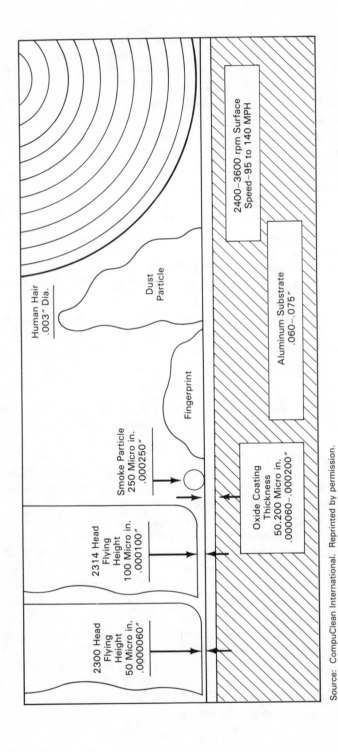

Human Hair
.003" Dia.

Dust
Particle

Fingerprint

Smoke Particle
250 Micro in.
.000250"

2314 Head
Flying
Height
100 Micro in.
.000100"

2300 Head
Flying
Height
50 Micro in.
.0000060"

Oxide Coating
Thickness
50.200 Micro in.
.000060–.000200"

Aluminum Substrate
.060–.075"

2400–3600 rpm Surface
Speed–95 to 140 MPH

Figure 3.4 Relative Sizes of Contamination Particulates.

Source: CompuClean International. Reprinted by permission.

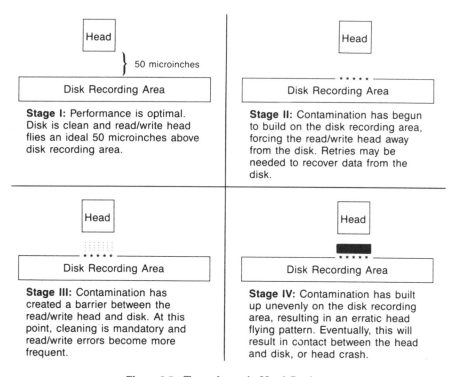

Figure 3.5 Chronology of a Head Crash.

SOURCE: Jon William Toigo, "Environmental Contamination: Averting a Microscopic Threat to Data Center Operations," *Data Center Operations Management* (New York: Auerbach Publishers, 1987).

In addition, the clogging of filter media by trapped particulate matter over a period of time may increase temperatures within sealed drives beyond narrow ranges of tolerance. The result of the temperature change on the disk media is termed *platter warble*. Platter warble (or warping) occurs when heat inside the drive exceeds the upper limits for the disk media and the media undergoes a molecular change that warps its surface. As with contamination buildup, an irregular surface caused by warping can lead to head crashes.

7. Consult an engineer to determine how (and at what cost) a positive pressure air system can be established in the data center. In a positive pressure air system, air blows outward when the integrity of the raised-floor room is violated. If air blows outward, airborne contaminants are less likely to find ready access to the facility.

8. Remove all ion-generating air purifiers from the center environment. Also, de-install any humidifiers or "toaster-element" space heaters and set up a schedule for thorough maintenance and inspection of air conditioners. All of these are major contributors to the contamination of environments where they are present. Ion-generating purifiers, nicron wire heating elements (like those in a kitchen toaster), and the electrostatic precipitators found in some older model air-conditioning units produce electrostatic particulate that seeks out electronic components.

Perhaps the most important step to take to control contamination is to contract with a reputable computer room maintenance company to perform routine cleaning. Unfortunately, a number of firms claim to be competent in the field of computer room cleaning, and selecting one requires some savvy about the causes of environmental contamination and proper cleaning techniques.

For example, many janitorial companies are more than willing to clean a company's computer facility using the same techniques that they use to keep other office areas neat and clean. The fact is that contracting with one of these services could well add to the problem of contamination.

Stories abound of janitorial services that wax and buff tile floors, creating a wax barrier that impairs the static grounding ability that was part of the floor's design. Another DP shop found piles of sawdust under the computer room floor, deposited there by janitors to absorb water. More than one DP shop has experienced costly damage because janitors took up 20 or 30 raised-floor tiles at one time to clean the subfloor beneath them "more efficiently."

According to industry specialists, most janitorial services do not know enough about the data processing environment to provide a service that will effectively reduce contamination. They use improper techniques and equipment that do more harm than good and possibly cause even more contamination-related downtime.

What should an information manager look for in a cleaning vendor? First, the best cleaning companies use only shielded, brushless-rotor equipment to avoid releasing ferro-magnetic pollutants into the atmosphere and to prevent electro-magnetic interference from affecting data processing equipment.

Furthermore, the cleaning company should clean tiles using OSHA-approved, non-ionic solutions and lint-free towels, and should clean equipment exteriors with silicon-treated cloths that leave a silicon film that repels dust.

Reputable firms recommend that information managers look for vendor endorsements of the cleaners they are considering, and check the credentials of the vendor with other DP shops.

In the final analysis, the solution to the problem of contamination-related equipment failure and downtime will never be a comprehensive one. At best, an informed DP manager, aided by a competent high-technology environmental maintenance service, will be able to reduce the amount of costly downtime and greatly offset the possibility of fire from this cause.

In addition to fire prevention through facility design and maintenance, it is necessary to take other measures to detect and suppress non-preventable fires. Detection systems are required by most states to counter the threat to human life posed by fire. Legal requirements for installing suppression capabilities vary, however, from state to state.

The tell-tale signs of fire are, of course, heat and smoke. These byproducts of fire can do substantial damage in an area, such as a computer facility or records storage area, that is never touched by flame itself. Heat can destroy data centers by destroying CPUs and storage media. Furthermore, heat in the presence of water generates steam that can destroy microfilm and fiche at a substantially lower temperature than heat in the absence of steam. Finally, smoke can render equipment unusable, and corrosive gases can make the facility uninhabitable.

Heat and smoke detectors are available in a variety of types, shapes, and sizes to alert personnel to hazardous conditions. Some types are:

- Photoelectric detectors, which detect the smoke produced by smoldering fires and fires that involve PVC insulation.
- Ionization detectors, which detect fires involving more flame than smoke.
- Temperature detectors, which detect heat in excess of a preset value.

It is advisable to select, purchase, and position these devices on the advice of a fire protection official or a knowledgeable fire protection contractor since DP environmental conditions (air conditioning, air streams, etc.) can impede the effective detection of hazardous conditions.

Once a hazardous condition is detected, the purpose of the detector is to alert on- and/or off-site personnel to the situation. Alarms may be connected to signaling systems that also automatically shut down equipment, notify personnel in an area that is constantly staffed (a security desk or operator station), auto-dial the DP center manager at home, or arm automatic fire suppression systems. Thus, the purpose of the signaling system is to facilitate both evacuation and reaction.

Responses to fire alarms may include notifying the fire department or suppressing the fire using whatever means are available. Typical fire suppression capabilities include:

- Portable fire extinguishers. These should be used only in emergencies and only with small fires. For electronic equipment, Halon-1211 extinguishers are the currently-recommended choice. For paper storage areas, stored-pressure, water-based extinguishers are preferred. Again, recommendations about appropriate ratings and sizes are best obtained from a fire protection professional.
- Sprinkler systems.
- Halon-1301 systems.

An ongoing debate between the advocates of Halon and water should be mentioned. The potential water damage to energized equipment suggests that alternatives to sprinkling data processing centers need to be found. Advocates of water state that if detectors are used to shut down equipment prior to sprinkler activation, the point is moot.

Other detractors point to the unreliability of sprinkler systems due to leaks from system piping not only of water, but also of the pressurized-gas charge designed to ready the sprinkler to activate (so-called preactivation systems). Water enthusiasts recommend that nitrogen rather than compressed air be used for preactivation. Nitrogen leaks, they argue, could be detected as readily as Halon leaks.

Both water and Halon advocates agree on one point: The use of water in the data processing facility will delay facility reentry with cleanup and dry-out activities. However, water advocates suggest that delays would be inevitable in any case, especially where poisonous gases have been released in the fire or fire department personnel have employed standard fire-fighting methods.

Halon advocates present several other points. In a Halon-suppressed fire, there is generally no postdisaster cleanup—simply vent the room. Also, Halon is more effective than water against fires involving polystyrene (a common substance used in magnetic tape spools) and plastics. In some cases, in fact, the use of water to suppress fire can result in the production of dangerous chemicals, including gaseous hydrochloric acid.

Halon advocates also point to the declining price and new modular designs of their systems. Installing Halon-1301 systems no longer requires major modifications to piping and ductwork. Halon containers, or "spheres," may be installed in the ceiling and moved when the data center changes or moves.

Finally, while water has been found to be particularly debilitating to removable disk packs and drives, Halon harms neither personnel nor media.

Again, the specific features and requirements of a facility will determine whether Halon or water is more appropriate. Consulting with a knowledgeable fire protection professional is the best way to decide which option best meets fire suppression needs.

Power Failure

Another cause of data center downtime is electrical power failure. Providing alternatives or backups for the facility power supply is one method to insulate the company against external conditions that are beyond its ability to control. Interruptions in electrical power can result from a variety of factors, such as:

- Transformer failure or line damage.
- Lightning damage.
- Utility company failure.
- Inadequate power-handling capacity in multitenant or single tenant buildings.
- Sabotage and terrorism.

In addition to prolonged power outages are a host of day-to-day problems including line dips and surges, transverse and common-mode interference or "noise," and in some areas of the country, brownouts. All can bode ill for computer equipment.

As its name implies, only an uninterruptible power supply (UPS) can provide protection against both momentary and prolonged power outages. (Because a UPS can reduce the amount of daily downtime as well as provide a hedge for disaster avoidance and recovery, it may also be easier to sell to senior management.)

What is a UPS? Basically, it is an interface between critical electrical devices in a company (collectively termed the critical load) and the local power company. The five typical components of a UPS are:

- **Rectifier/battery charger.** The rectifier converts utility company power into DC power both to charge the UPS storage batteries and to supply the UPS inverter.
- **Inverter.** The inverter converts DC power from the rectifier or storage batteries into a clean, continuous AC power supply for use

in driving connected equipment (the critical load—computers, air conditioners, telecommunications switches, elevators, emergency lights, etc.)

- **Storage batteries.** Typically, these are lead-acid or nickel-cadmium cells that remain constantly charged and in reserve unless a power outage occurs and they are called upon to supply power to the load.
- **Bypass switch.** Essentially a protective device should the UPS itself fail, the bypass switch will effectively remove the UPS from the circuit and feed power directly from an alternative AC source (often a second utility power line) directly to the load.
- **Control logic.** The hard-wired or programmable logic that provides the basis for UPS operation.

The UPS described above is an on-line UPS. That is, the UPS remains in the line between the critical load and the power company at all times. Other UPS models are available for off-line operation. Generally speaking, it takes longer for an off-line UPS to activate and replace failed commercial power than an on-line model. Thus, it may not prevent equipment failures resulting from split-second line voltage drops (such as those experienced during a lightning storm).

At root, the UPS is a battery backup to commercial power. Depending on the load that it supports and its battery capacity, the typical UPS may provide sufficient power to sustain its load through outages that are no more than 15 to 30 minutes in duration. To protect against outages of substantially longer duration, many companies elect to install a private power generator in conjunction with the UPS. At some point, before UPS power is exhausted, the generator is activated, supplies AC to the UPS, and the UPS batteries—returned to standby mode—are recharged.

Selecting the right UPS for a facility requires technical expertise. The assistance of engineers, power company representatives and vendor specialists may be needed. Some of the factors to be considered are the following:

1. **Power requirements.** Once the critical load has been determined, the power requirements in kw and kva need to be assessed. Device power requirements are provided on most equipment, although these should be double-checked by an electrician or engineer. Base the size of the UPS both on current requirements and future anticipated needs.

2. **Reserve power.** Determine how much battery backup (in terms of minutes of battery power) is required. If a generator is to be used in conjunction with the UPS, this figure may be however long it takes

to start the generator. If only enough power is required for safely shutting down equipment, ensure that the time required for shutdown is known and used in sizing the UPS. Ensure also that the *efficiency* of the UPS (input kw/output kw) is adequate to support the reserve power requirement.

3. **Reliability.** Determine what demands may, in an average 24 hour period, be made of the UPS. An analysis of facility power characteristics will determine whether the UPS will be called upon to support the critical load once, or 30 times, in a given day. This analysis is used to determine the required mean time between failure (MTBF) and mean time to repair (MTTR), characteristics that must be accommodated by the selected system.

Other factors, including overload capacity, environmental and safety requirements, and compatibility with load equipment, must also be considered in the selection of the right UPS.

The acquisition and installation of a UPS are complicated planning tasks. Once the appropriate UPS has been selected and approved by senior management, facility preparation may be extensive. Most vendors are extremely helpful with advice and information, and some even provide an installation planning team. Ensure that warranties and maintenance agreements are clearly understood and that thorough documentation and training are provided to those who will manage the system.

According to Kenneth Brill, the dean of what has been termed "uptime management science," the UPS is only one of 11 power-related subsystems that must be installed and maintained in an information processing facility to prevent disaster. Others subsystems include: lightning protection; building switch gear (and utility-service entry); critical power buses; UPS air conditioning (without it, a UPS won't stay up); frequency conversion equipment; UPS batteries (considered a component of the on-line UPS described above); emergency generators; off-line testing; and computer room power distribution and grounding. Overall reliability of power backup systems, according to Brill, is determined by the "weakest element" in this 11-subsystem chain.[5] It is important, therefore, that power protection systems, like other disaster prevention systems, be inspected and tested regularly and maintained in top operating condition.

Physical Access Control

Although commonly regarded as a security concern, facility access is another area with which the disaster recovery coordinator may need to become involved. An increasing number of disasters are the result of intentional or accidental damage to equipment and facilities by employees and others who have access to the data center. Disgruntled employees, corporate saboteurs, negligent users or vendors, and a host of others, may cause fires, damage media, disrupt processes, or otherwise impair normal operations.

This has led to the installation of physical access control systems ranging from locked doors and security guards to closed-circuit cameras and electronic card key systems to laser scanning of the retina. It is essential for the disaster recovery coordinator to fully understand systems that are already in place and to spearhead the physical security issue if no access control methods have been provided.

The reasons for involving the disaster recovery coordinator in security are twofold. Effective access security can greatly reduce the risk of man-made disasters. The second reason reflects the twin-edged sword that is security. It is important to know how to *circumvent* security measures in the event of a disaster in order to evacuate personnel, to perform last-minute backups, and to access and remove secure information that is at risk of loss or damage.

The latter concept is sometimes difficult for security administrators to accept. Implicit is the threat that security-breaking methods will become common knowledge, and that expensive and time-consuming systems will be rendered impotent. Considerable diplomacy and common sense may be required to arrive at a mutually-agreeable solution to the issue of security versus survivability in a disaster.

There are several steps that the disaster recovery coordinator should take when considering the physical security aspects of disaster avoidance and recovery which are discussed in the following paragraphs.

- **Consult with experts.** If the data center is currently without an access security capability, consult with one of the many vendors of security products and services to provide a preliminary analysis of data center security requirements. Do not be surprised if the representative seems a bit paranoiac or seems to have mistaken your data center and its security requirements for those of the CIA. Security vendors are bombarded daily by stories of terrorism, computer embezzlement, and other darker aspects of the industry. They tend as a group to take their work very seriously and to perceive any data or function worth securing as an asset that any number of nefarious persons would like to destroy or disrupt. They communicate this view coldly, suspiciously, and often without humor.

In addition to vendors, auditors can help identify facility security requirements. There are also a number of competent books on the principles and techniques of security. Reading the literature and terminology can be of great assistance in selecting and implementing an appropriate security capability.[6]

• **Develop an understanding of security systems that are already in place.** If security consists of a locked door, cabinet, or drawer, find out who has the keys. Similarly, if a master card key, or special code number, or other device exists that will open all doors, find out who possesses the information or device. It may be that the security administrator will need to be made a member of the recovery team. However, even where this is the case, it will be necessary to provide the means to other team members to circumvent security if a disaster occurs and the security administrator is unavailable.

• **Learn what is being safeguarded by security measures and determine if it is needed in day-to-day work at the facility or if it would be better stored off-site.** In this way, the disaster recovery coordinator can ascertain whether the security issue is also a disaster recovery issue.

In a financial environment, for example, checks and other executable financial documents, printed on a daily basis, are often stored on-site in locked cabinets. Also, registers and logs, which are used to track the use of checks, may be stored in the cabinets where they can be accessed to record check processing runs. Assuming that a supply of checks is readily available from off-site storage or from vendors in the case of a disaster, the disaster recovery coordinator may see no reason to change the current security arrangement. However, the registers are also important and, in many cases, nonreplaceable. Thus, the coordinator may need to make provisions for accessing registers in order to remove them to a safe location in the event of an emergency.

• **Verify that external conditions cannot create a nonrecoverable situation.** This guideline is admittedly vague, but only because it reflects a host of facility-specific considerations. Basically, it means: Make sure that the security systems do not create more problems than they prevent. The following examples may help to illustrate this principle.

If secure doors respond to computer-recognized I.D. badges, ensure that manual means also exist in case power is lost or the computer fails. Ensure that exit is not impeded by the same system that restricts unauthorized entrance. In an emergency, not everyone will be able to maintain the rationality required to punch a lengthy series of memorized numbers into a keypad doorlock. Similarly, entrance to restricted areas should never be so mindless as to prevent prompt response to an emergency. If a center manager sees an operator being sucked into a paper shredder through the window of the shredder room, the manager should not have to recall an encrypted code to enter the room and aid the operator.

• **Make provisions for the restoration of physical security at the recovery site.** It is important to ensure that security controls are reestablished at the same time as systems and networks are restored. Controls should also be established to safeguard data during evacuation and transport to the backup site.

The point is that physical security, while vital to safeguarding normal center operations, is less important than business survivability in an emergency. Only by providing the means for replacing standard security procedures with emergency security procedures will the objectives of both security planning and disaster recovery planning be met.

In addition to physical security considerations, a host of application and network security measures may also need to be accounted for in the disaster recovery plan. These will be discussed in greater detail later in this book.[7]

REFERENCES

1. *Report of Test Results: Halon 1301 vs. Water Sprinkler Fire Protection for Essential Electronic Equipment*, Document ESL-TR-B2-28, Air Force Engineering and Services Laboratory (Tyndall AFB, FL: AFESL, 1982), pp. 75-76. Conclusions about water damage to computer equipment included: "water . . . produced many deleterious side effects, primarily through corrosion and staining of sensitive electronic components" and that "considerable downtime [was required] to dry out the electronic equipment and repair water damaged components."

2. According to studies published by the American Society of Heating, Refrigeration and Air Conditioning Engineers (ASHRAE), *Handbook of Fundamentals*, (Atlanta, 1986), particles have a calculable settling velocity. A particle one micron in size that is suspended in the air of a room eight feet tall, under ideal conditions of still air, will take nearly 19 hours to settle out. A .1 micron particle, under the same conditions, would take 72 days. In a typical data center—with doors opening and closing frequently, air conditioners blowing, and machines moving and generating electrostatic, thermal and frictional influences—the settling rate would be very much prolonged. For this reason, contamination detection methods that rely on settled particulate are inherently flawed in their findings.

3. Portions of this discussion were drawn from Jon Toigo, "Environmental Contamination: Averting a Microscopic Threat to Data Center Operations," *Data Center Operations Management* (New York: Auerbach Publishers, 1987).

4. Ibid.

5. Kenneth G. Brill, "Keeping Up Your UPS," *Datamation*, Volume 33, Number 15 (15 July 1987).

6. Two good references on security are *Security: Checklist for Computer Center Self-Audits* (Reston, VA: AFIPS Press, 1979), and Richard Mansfield, ed., *Data Security Management* (New York: Auerbach Publishers, 1987). See Endnote 7 for other references.

7. If the reader's company is without an Information Security Officer, or if more information is desired regarding the methods and techniques of information systems security, readers are encouraged to contact American Society for Industrial Security, an association for computer security professionals located at 1655 North Fort Meyer Drive, Arlington, Virginia, (703)522-5800.

   For further reading on IS security, consult *Data Security Management* (New York: Auerbach Publishers, 1987), a compilation of some of the best literature on data security available, or write to the National Bureau of Standards, U.S. Department of Commerce, Gaithersburg, MD 20899, and ask for NBS Publications List 91, "Computer Security Publications."

   One final suggestion for readers having access to a modem. Telephone the Computer Security Bulletin Board at (301)921-5718. The board is also a National Bureau of Standards' Institute for Computer Sciences and Technology activity. The baud rate is 300 or 1200, 8 data bits with no parity, or 7 data bits with even parity, and 1 stop bit.

Chapter 4

Off-Site Storage

Many experts believe that effective off-site storage of critical data is the single most important determinant of successful business recovery following a disaster. They argue that alternate processors can usually be found "on the fly," that network backup strategies can be developed *ad hoc,* and that temporary user quarters can be set up just about anywhere. Without a backup of programs and data, however, all the other logistics and strategies of disaster recovery plans are meaningless.

While one cannot discount the value of advance planning for other aspects of recovery, off-site storage is certainly one of the most important components of an effective disaster recovery capability. To understand the importance of effective off-site storage, the information manager needs only recall some of the issues discussed earlier in this text.

As previously indicated, business interruption insurance can provide only for the restoration—not the replacement—of data. Restoration frequently requires that source documents or recent tape or disk backups be available.

To guarantee that backups and source documents are not consumed in the same disaster that renders production systems unusable, these items should be stored at a safe location, preferably at a facility other than the one that houses the production systems. In response to this common sense dictate, many companies elect to use commercial off-site storage facilities that specialize in the storage of backup media, paper records, and fiche. In the event of a disaster, information stored off-site may be accessed and used to restore business functions. (In the case of computer data, this assumes that other ancillary procedures exist for regular backup and removal of daily transaction records to safe storage, and for the replacement of systems, programs, and hardware with comparable configurations at an alternate site.)

In addition to this practical rationale for backup and storage of vital data, a number of legal requirements pertain to records retention and off-site storage. The IRS has adopted several procedures, policies, and rulings requiring that businesses retain (and safeguard) data that may be called for in audits and other activities. Other government agencies have also mandated that certain types of records be retained for specified periods of time.

Be it in response to common sense or to legal mandates, the development of a data backup plan and storage strategy is one task for which the disaster recovery coordinator is typically made responsible. Off-site storage planning includes the analysis and classification of data, the review of existing backup procedures, the evaluation and selection of a storage vendor, and the formalization of schedules for regular or routinized removal of data to storage. It is often undertaken concurrently with development of other backup strategies and procedures in the disaster recovery planning project. The data flow diagram in Figure 4.1 provides an overview of the complex network of activites involved in creating and maintaining an effective off-site storage plan.

Identify the Information Asset

Providing the means for restoring business activities and system functions using information stored off-site requires that the "right" information—information that will be used to reduce downtime and speed recovery—be identified:

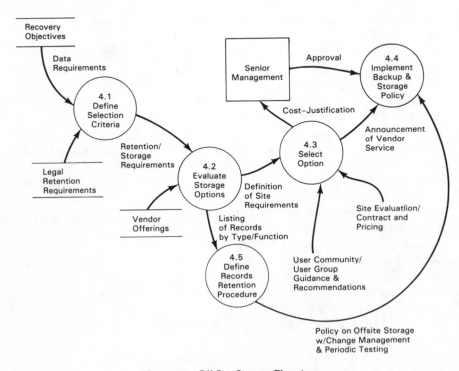

Figure 4.1 Off-Site Storage Planning.

- Identify data and source documents required for production database restoration. This information should be available from the results of the risk analysis undertaken at the outset of disaster recovery planning. First, critical and vital systems should be identified. Next, inputs and outputs of those systems should be defined. Inputs may comprise source documents that are coded or otherwise rendered machine-readable by system users. These source documents (or copies of them) should be identified for removal to off-site storage on a regular, suitable basis.

Output documents, such as reports or summaries, may also be critical because they are auditable records, they are used in important historical analyses, or they are used by others in their performance of vital work (e.g., in their work with interdependent systems). These documents and/or the photographic or magnetic media on which they are recorded should be listed for regular removal off-site.

Of course, programs, systems software, and electronic backups of the current production database, system software, and applications software should also be earmarked for off-site storage.

- Identify documentation required for restoring systems and data. In addition to data and source documents, a number of other items must be stored off-site to facilitate the recovery. These may include written inventories of hardware serial numbers and other documentation required for efficient processing of insurance claims, operations and user manuals, preprinted forms, and—of course—a copy of the disaster recovery plan.

- Identify data that must be preserved to satisfy legal requirements and to reduce business loss. Auditors can assist in identifying records and documents that must be preserved to satisfy legal requirements. In addition, there may be a host of documents, including drafts of contracts and designs for prototype systems, that would not be needed to restore vital business operations or to satisfy legal mandates, but which do represent substantial investments of company resources. These may be difficult, costly, or impossible to replace and would be a substantial business loss if destroyed. These documents, too, probably belong in secure off-site storage.

The identification of items for off-site storage can be a laborious and time-consuming task. It is exacerbated by the proliferation of records and their wide dispersal (due to PCs, LANs, etc.) in most corporations.

Statistics underscore the problem. One recent study showed the average growth of production records across all industries at 8 percent annually. Other studies have suggested that up to 50 percent of a company's records are duplicates, that 25 percent of the remaining volume are worthless, and that as many as 85 percent of filed documents are never referred to again.

If a company has no established policy on records retention, sifting through corporate records to identify those which belong in secure storage may be a herculean task. For this reason, the disaster recovery coordinator may want to consider the following strategies for identifying records for storage.

1. For existing records—establish departmental "owners" of information. With the assistance of auditors and other knowledgeable persons within the business, establish criteria for identifying the relative importance of records. The following generic method of classifying importance may be adapted to the needs of a specific company. As will become apparent, the same categories that are applied to systems or applications in risk analysis may also be extended to data required to restore the systems or applications.

   Critical—Data or documentation that must be retained for legal reasons, for use in normal business activities, or for restoration minimum acceptable work levels in the event of a disaster.

   Vital—Data or documentation that must be retained for use in normal business activities, which may not be required in a disaster recovery situation but which represents a substantial investment of company resources that may be difficult or impossible to recoup. Information that requires special secrecy or discretion may also fall under this category.

   Sensitive—Data or documentation that is needed in normal operations but for which alternative supplies are available in the event of loss. Data that can be reconstructed fairly readily but at some cost could also be classified as sensitive.

   Noncritical—Data or documentation that can be reconstructed readily at minimal cost, or duplicates of *critical*, *vital*, or *sensitive* data that have no prerequisite security requirements.

     With the help of auditors and in-house experts, it may be possible to correlate certain types of data (i.e., forms with specific form numbers and reports) with the generic categories above. Once this is done, representatives of the departments that produce or store the data may be called upon to sort through their files and collect the data classified as *critical* or *vital* and to indicate what is currently being done to safeguard it. Based on the results of this analysis, measures may be taken to store data off-site.

2. For future records. The disaster recovery coordinator may find it helpful to seek management approval for applying the data clas-

sification scheme as a matter of company policy. If information can be classified on an ongoing basis, it will be easier to identify new off-site storage requirements when plan revisions are undertaken.

Of course, classifying data entails many of the same problems as classifying applications and systems that were discussed earlier. No one likes to believe that the data he or she "owns" is anything less than critical. However, most owners will concede that third-generation copies of original documents are less critical than the originals, and many will comply with a definition of criticality that does not imply that their data is useless in day-to-day operations.

Options for Records Storage

Once data has been identified and classified, special attention must be paid to identifying any current methods that are being used to safeguard data from loss. Disaster recovery coordinators may find that the fear of potential data loss has motivated "owners" to develop their own strategies for safe storage. A host of capabilities may already be present within the company that provide varying degrees of records protection. In certain areas of the company, auditors may have left their mark. Their comments about the security and recoverability of vital records may have led to the purchase of fireproof cabinets or to informal storage arrangements with the vendor who prepares microform versions of paper or magnetic records, or to any number of other strategies to safeguard data.

Ferreting out these existing strategies can be an obstacle to consolidated off-site storage planning, not only because they are often extremely informal and poorly documented, but also because they may be a source of pride for those persons who formulated them. The disaster recovery coordinator needs to be cognizant of the personal stake that people sometimes have in the most innocuous things. Applaud the ingenuity of the owner who has perceived the need for security and survivability and stored his or her backups in the safe deposit box at the local savings and loan. Be diplomatic when telling the owner that a new strategy is being developed that will consolidate his or her off-site storage arrangements with those of less conscientious departments. Perhaps the owner can be recruited to assist in identifying and classifying other information assets in the company.

Once these steps have been completed, it is time for the disaster recovery coordinator to begin working toward a corporate solution to safe storage. The word off-site has been used frequently in this chapter and is part of the chapter title. In fact, off-site storage is a common part of an overall strategy for data protection and survivability. However, off-site storage may be neither required nor appropriate for every data asset. The following options for data storage provide varying degrees of protection. A typical data protection strategy may integrate one or more of these approaches.

- Fire rated safes and cabinets. A variety of fire- resistant cabinets and safes are available to safeguard data at the location where it is produced. Vendors typically reference the ratings that are accorded their products by the Underwriting Laboratories, and often state the appropriateness of safes and cabinets to media storage in terms of the National Fire Protection Association (NFPA) Standard 75, "Protection of Electronic Computer/Data Processing Equipment." Table 1 summarizes the NFPA records classification scheme and the minimum amount of protection NFPA recommends for each type of record.

NFPA standards state clearly the need to store duplicates of key, expensive-to-replace records in a location where they will not be affected by a disaster affecting the originals. This implies that storing records in and

TABLE 1   NFPA Records Classification Scheme and Fire Protection Requirements

Type	Description	Fire Protection Requirements
Class I: VITAL	Essential, irreplaceable, or necessary to recovery.	Duplicate and store in an area not subject to the fire or associated effects that may involve the originals. Store in approved Class 150 one-hour or better record protection equipment.
Class II: IMPORTANT	Essential or important but reproducible with difficulty or at extra expense; not vital to recovery.	Same as VITAL.
Class III: USEFUL	Records whose loss would be inconvenient, but which are readily replaceable; not essential to recovery.	Paper- or plastic-based: Store in closed metal files or cabinets; metal-based records require no special protection.
Class IV: NONESSENTIAL	Records, which upon examination, are found to be no longer necessary.	No protection required.

Source: *National Fire Protection Association (NFPA) Standards*, "Protection of Electronic Computer/Data Processing Equipment 1976," (Boston: NFPA, 1976).

around the data center (or operations area of the business) in which they are produced or used is ill-advised. Other options to strictly on-site storage, therefore, need to be considered.

• Shell game. Perhaps the least expensive storage option is to place data in a different (though local) facility. If company quarters are dispersed over several buildings in an office park development, for example, copies of the records from one building may be stored in another building. This strategy has the advantage of ready access by those who would need records in an emergency. However, local storage may be vulnerable to the effects of the same disaster that damages the originating facility.

It may also be prohibitively expensive to outfit a second building with the physical protection capabilities that have been installed in the originating facility. Storage rooms used for magnetic media have many of the same requirements as the production environment, including temperature control, humidity control, static grounding, fire protection, water detection, environmental maintenance, and physical security. Table 2 summarizes NFPA recommendations on room-size limitations based on the type of fire suppression system that is installed.

Another variation on the local storage option, which might reduce some of the expenses, is to share a storage room with another business. This, of course, is replete with issues of security and access control.

• Commercial records storage facilities. One of the most utilized options for secure, off-site storage is the commercial storage facility subscrip-

TABLE 2 NFPA Storage Room Fire Protection Requirements

Type of Records	Type of Fire Suppression	Maximum Room Size
Plastic-based records in combustible containers	Fire extinquisher	10,000 cubic feet
Plastic-based records in combusitible containers	Automatic water sprinkler or Halon system	20,000 cubic feet
Plastic-based records in non-combustible containers	Fire extinquishers	20,000 cubic feet
Plastic-based records in non-combustible containers	Automatic water sprinkler or Halon system	40,000 cubic feet
Paper records	Fire extinquishers	50,000 cubic feet
Paper records	Automatic water sprinkler or Halon system	100,000 cubic feet

Source: *National Fire Protection Association (NFPA) Standards*, "Protection of Electronic Computer/Data Processing Equimpent 1976," (Boston: NFPA, 1976).

tion. Commercial storage facilities are of two basic types: those offered by banks and moving-and- storage companies, and those offered by companies that specialize in off-site data and records storage.

Banks and moving-and-storage companies often make space available for records storage without knowing the types of records that are to be stored. Thus, their facilities do not generally meet the security and environmental requirements of data processing media or microform storage. Other drawbacks of using these facilities are that records are not available at all hours of the day, facilities are shared, access controls are insufficient, and physical storage sizes are limited.

Commercial off-site storage facilities cost about the same as bank or moving-and-storage company services. However, in these facilities, ideal environment, security, accessibility, and services are possible. Off-site storage centers are designed with magnetic and microform media storage requirements in mind. A well-designed facility is similar in all respects to one that an information manager might wish to construct at his or her own facility, although costs are generally much lower because several customers make use of the same facility. What makes the commercial facility preferable to the shared business records storage area, however, is the use of commercial facility personnel to control access to stored data. Rarely are client personnel allowed to access their storage directly; they must rely instead on storage center staff to pull tapes and storage boxes.

For most medium to large companies, a combination of the preceding options are used to provide safe storage of critical and vital information. For example, companies may set up an in-house records center to facilitate day-to-day information requirements, may utilize a local, but off- premises, storage area for tape backup storage, and they may contract with a commercial off-site storage vendor for longer-term media and records storage.

Other companies have seen wisdom in the idea of redundant backup and redundant off-site storage. To wit, the case for redundant backup holds that if original data is lost, and damage occurs to backed-up media while in transit to the backup site or during the effort to restore a system, a second backup would be needed to complete the system recovery process. Other proponents of redundant backups point to the possibility of disasters that are regional in scope (i.e., hurricanes in coastline states, earthquakes in western North America), which might affect both the subscriber company and its off-site storage facility.

Redundant backups would ideally be stored at separate locations: on-site, off-site locally, and off-site remotely. For many data processing centers, a three-cycle retention program is observed as a matter of standard operating procedure. "Grandparent" and "parent" backups are removed to remote and local off-site storage, respectively, while "child" backups are retained in-house for use in conjunction with day-to-day mishaps.

The point is that most businesses with a backup storage plan utilize a combination of redundant data backup procedures and complementary storage options to lessen their exposure to critical data loss. Most use, as part of their backup storage strategy, a commercial off-site storage vendor.

Selecting an Off-site Storage Vendor

One of the most controversial issues in disaster recovery planning revolves around criteria for selecting a vendor of off-site storage services. This, in part, reflects the nature of the data processing industry and the explosion of new companies that have formed to fill this niche over the past five to ten years.

The first commercial off-site storage facilities for magnetic media (and records generally) were designed for archival storage over decades or even centuries. Some were specifically constructed to withstand the anticipated force of an atomic explosion. (See Figure 4.2 for an example of a so-called bombproof facility.) Records were rotated in and out of these centers at the relaxed rate of once per month. Today, with an increased awareness of the need for off-site storage in the face of other threats somewhat less devastating than nuclear war, numerous above-ground centers have been built for local and regional users.

In fact, one reason that commercial off-site storage facilities have become less expensive is that there are more and more facilities. In most metropolitan areas of the country, information managers now have a choice among several vendors. Added to this number are the dozens of vault-equipped banks, thrifts, and moving-and-storage companies who market their own facilities for media backup. This explosion of facilities has led to increased competition and relatively low prices; it has also had the positive effect of promoting a drive to establish "THE RULES" for identifying what makes one off-site storage facility superior to another.

In the search for distinction, vendors advertise that their facilities comply with a any number of authoritative guidelines, including those articulated by the Association of Commercial Records Centers (ACRC), the Association of Records Managers and Administrators (ARMA), the National Fire Protection Association (NFPA), American National Standards Institute (ANSI), the U.S. Government's National Bureau of Standards (NBS), the Underwriters Laboratory (UL), and various state and local

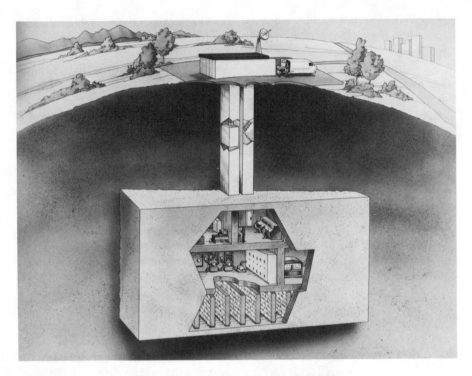

Figure 4.2 Underground Data Storage Vault.
Source: AT&T. Reprinted by permission.

agencies. Compliances often follow the facility logo in advertising literature like alphabet soup.

Despite all these guidelines, there is not a single set of rules that
defines the "best" off-site backup facility. None of the above organizations,
in fact, claim to have defined rules for *selecting* anything. Rather, each organization cites environmental or operational characteristics of a well-
designed facility. Adherence by vendor facilities to these standards is a
plus, but facility design alone is not a sound basis for selecting a vendor.

For example, the fact that a vendor complies with ANSI standard on
temperature, humidity, and air purity requirements says little about the
safety of the data of the business who uses the vendor. Similarly, vendor
adherence to NFPA standards for vault construction or fire protection offers little consolation if the vendor has internal management problems,
cannot effectively manage its stored inventory, or fails to answer emergency calls from clients over holidays.

There is some truth in the arguments of some vendors who do not comply with certain standards in their facilities when they claim that technological advance has outpaced guideline revisions. Today's media may be more resilient to heat, water, or dust than yesterday's media. Storage facility management may decide that complying with outdated standards is less cost-effective than providing appropriate security as well as other quality services. For this reason, the selection of the right backup storage facility is less a function of counting compliances than evaluating vendor performance and capability.

At a minimum, the following evaluative criteria should be considered:

- **Reputation.** How long a facility has been in existence, its association with a larger corporate entity, its financial statement, its record with the Better Business Bureau, and even its reputation within the community of information management professionals are all important factors in selecting an off-site storage vendor.
- **Site security.** Security at the storage site should be no less (and possibly a good deal more) stringent than at one's own facility. Some questions to consider:
  - What are the access controls in the facility?
  - Is visitor access restricted?
  - Are client names concealed, even from one another?
  - What security measures are observed during the transportation of media? (Unmarked vehicles, security in vehicles, employee monitoring, etc.)
  - How are employees screened?
  - Are cameras, videotape, or other devices used to monitor facility traffic?
  - How are emergency calls handled in terms of authorizations, etc.?

- **Media management.** A very important factor, how the facility manages client records, may present the following questions:
  - How is media of several clients segregated?
  - Is magnetic media stored separately from microform and paper? Are there certain types of media that will not be stored in the facility?
  - Is media transported in plastic containers or cardboard boxes?
  - Are employees trained in proper media handling?

- Are media maintenance activities, including periodic tape rotation, performed as standard operating procedure?
- What kind of inventory management system is used? Is it backed up?
- How often is a physical inventory of media performed?
- What controls exist to monitor the flow of media in and out of the facility?

- **Environmental factors.** Although much abused, there are a number of environmental standards that are important in off-site vendor selection. Vendors should recognize the standards, and if they do not comply with them, have a good case for not doing so. Of course, to determine whether a vendor complies, one must first understand the standards involved. Table 3 lists several references with which the disaster recovery coordinator should become familiar prior to meeting with vendors.

  Having become familiar with the standards, the disaster recovery coordinator should seek answers and documentation from the vendor on the following points:
  - What capabilities are installed to detect and signal smoke, heat, flame, water, and intrusion?
  - What extinguishing capabilities are available?
  - Is the alarm system tied directly to fire, police, and security services?
  - How are temperature, heat, humidity, and contamination controlled?
  - What are the facility's backup power requirements and how are they provided?
  - How frequently are environmental protection and backup capabilities checked or tested?
  - What is the company smoking policy?

- **Transportation.** There are statistics that purport to demonstrate that data is most vulnerable while in transit between the client facility and off-site storage house, and between the off-site storage facility and a data processing backup facility. In short, tapes and records are at higher risk of loss or damage while riding in the back of a van on a well-traveled street or highway, or in the luggage compartment of an airplane than when they are sitting in a climate-controlled, fire-protected, contamination-reduced storage room. This underscores the fact that the transportation capabilities of the off-site storage ven-

TABLE 3   References for Storage Facility Standards

Source	Title	Abstract
ANSI 1430 Broadway New York, NY 10018	*American National Standard for Photography (Film)– Storage of Processed Safety Film* (ANSI PH1: 43)	Humidity, temperature, and air purity conditions for the medium- to long-term storage of microforms.
ARMA Standards Board 4200 Sommerset Drive Suite 205 Prairie Village, KS 66208	*Records Center Operations: Guidelines*	General guidelines covering facility design and operational functions.
Kodak Company Department 412-L 343 State Street Rochester, NY 14650	*Storage and Preservation of Microfilms* (Eastman Kodak Pamphlet D–31)	Environmental considerations for microfilm storage, plus assessments of the hazards of micropscopic blemishes, chemical contamination, fungi.
National Bureau of Standards Superintendent of Documents U.S. Govt. Printing Office Washington DC, 20402	*Care and Handling of Computer Magnetic Storage Media* (NBS Special Publication 500–101)	Covers tape management systems, tape maintenance schedules, and environmental conditions for archival storage of computer media.
NFPA Batterymarch Park Quincy, MA 02269	*Protection of Records (232) Archives and LRecords Centers* (232 AM) *Central Station Signalling Systems* (71) *Automatic Fire Detectors* (72 E)	Standards covering the topics provided; NFPA standards are adoped with and without amendment by numerous state and local government agencies.

dor must be examined as part of the evaluation and selection task. The following questions can yield valuable insights:

- Is media transported by vendor employees or by an independent courier service?
- Is media subjected to ambient climatic conditions during transport or are vehicles climate-controlled?
- Under what conditions may drivers make stops, route changes, etc.?
- Are vehicles equipped with anti-theft devices, two-way radios, etc.?
- How is media stored in the vehicle?
- What is the longest estimated time to make a regular delivery? An emergency delivery?

- Are different vehicles used to make emergency deliveries?
- Does the vendor provide an airport delivery service?
- Does the vendor provide preparatory services (i.e., special services for readying media for long distance travel, including selection, crating, air or freight carrier contact, scheduling, delivery, destination transportation arrangements, etc.)?

The answers to all of the above questions should be verified, insofar as possible, with an on-site visit. Also, ask the vendor for the names of customers who would be willing to speak about the vendor's performance. Despite the security requirements of many companies, the vendor usually has the permission of several clients to disseminate their telephone numbers to prospective customers for validation and endorsement. Be aware, however, that the vendor will nearly always provide only the names of satisfied customers.

Once all evaluative criteria have been met and validated to the satisfaction of the disaster recovery coordinator, the next task is negotiating the contract and the schedule for regular pickups and deliveries. Contracting for off-site storage is essentially a task of assigning a cost to each of the services that the vendor will provide. Contracts may be as straightforward as an initial invoice and a handshake, or they may be multipaged, fine-print documents that need to be reviewed by a lawyer and/or auditor. Costs vary widely, and some storage facility managers have more latitude to negotiate than others.

Before examining the elements of an off-site storage contract, however, it is important to know what information the vendor will require about the prospective client prior to contract negotiation. Initially, the client will be expected to provide two items of information. The vendor will need to know approximately how much storage (and of what media type) the client will require. If the number of tapes or cartons can be estimated before the negotiation of a contract begins, this will help speed the process of setting a price for the service.

The second item of information concerns the frequency of pickups and deliveries. Are all records and media to be rotated to the facility daily? Are some to be rotated back to the client daily, some monthly, and some stored permanently by the vendor?

Until the disaster recovery plan is fully written, tested, and approved, the exact quantity of off-site storage and frequency of rotation may be difficult to determine. However, it may be possible to develop an interim off-site storage plan (for example, covering the storage of weekly system backups and daily transaction backups, plus the archival storage of critical and vital records) that will serve as the basis for negotiating the contract.

Some of the fees in an acceptable contract are the following:

• **Regular pickup and delivery fee.** This fee covers only the cost to the client of the courier's trip to the client facility on a regular or routinized basis. It should state how often, and at approximately what time of day, the courier will arrive to drop off and/or pick up materials. The fee may be written as a per visit charge, or as a monthly aggregate.

• **Emergency delivery fee.** The contract should identify what "emergency delivery" means, whether all nonroutine visits are considered emergencies or only those visits in which an emergency time frame for delivery is invoked. Some facilities will make nonscheduled deliveries on a nonemergency basis by allowing the courier to deviate from his or her route during daily deliveries. If this is the case, it should be included in the contract and the fee stated.

If an emergency delivery is defined as a visit made to the client site at a time other than normal vendor operating hours, be sure to have the vendor's working hours and holiday schedule spelled out in the contract.

• **Tape (or container) handling fee.** Delivery fees often cover only courier visits and media transportation. They do not necessarily cover the handling of media in and out of the storage facility. A per-tape or per-container fee for handling is often assessed, especially by vendors who must hire special staff to place, track, log, and maintain stored goods. For archival storage, particularly of tape, there may be a fee in addition to a handling fee, to pay for the rotation of archived tapes.

• **Storage fee.** In addition to delivery and handling fees, many facilities charge an additional fee for the actual amount of space occupied by client data. This rent is typically assessed on a monthly basis. If the amount of stored information changes during the month, the charge is usually assessed on the basis of the maximum amount of space occupied by client data at any time in the month.

• **Preparatory service fees.** Some vendors offer disaster recovery services in the form of preparing stored records and media for transportation to a recovery facility in the event of a disaster. These services may include boxing records and media for long distance travel by plane or freight, coordinating transport through freight routing services, moving media to an airport or train station, and arranging for the transportation (at the point of destination) of the records and media to the recovery facility.

These services may be charged as a regular monthly fee, or charged to the customer after the fact. If a regular fee is assessed, ensure that the vendor will provide one thorough-going test of the capability per year.

• **Other fees.** There are a host of other fees that are becoming increasingly prevalent in the industry. These range from special insurance fees to cover media replacement (if the vendor is not insured or bonded for this eventuality, find out why!); schedule revision fees (charged to customers who revise their regular pickup and delivery schedules); plan maintenance fees (for customers who use the vendor to write the section of the plan pertaining to preparatory services); and special fees for upgrades to facilities (sometimes employed instead of price increases). Some facilities offer media maintenance and cleaning services that are also charged on a fee basis. All fees should be clearly spelled out in the contract.

Besides fees, there are other items of information that the disaster recovery coordinator should secure in writing from the off-site storage vendor. The vendor should indicate the exact steps that will be taken if records or media are misplaced in the vault or warehouse. The vendor should also identify the procedure for requesting and receiving a delivery, including emergency contact numbers, authentication of requests, and emergency delivery time frames. The contract should also supply a complete definition of the vendor's liability for media in its charge, and identify the details of the vendor's insurance or bonding.

Cost-Justify Off-Site Storage

Once the disaster recovery coordinator is satisfied that a vendor will provide competent, cost-effective service for the foreseeable future, the next step of the procedure may be to cost-justify the service to senior management. Pointing out a number of factors may help simplify this effort.

1. Off-site storage is not only a data processing-related expense. Every department, even administration, may have records and documents that need to be stored off-site. Most senior managers recognize the value of safe, secure storage when it comes to documents such as contracts, agreements, and accounting data.
2. As off-site storage is a solution to a business's overall vulnerability, it may be possible to divide the cost among all corporate departments. Better yet, off-site storage may be handled as a strictly administrative expense item, and may, in many cases, be tax deductible.

3. Off-site storage is rarely a politically-charged issue. If the disaster recovery coordinator couches his or her rationale for storage in terms of protecting corporate assets, few detractors can persuasively argue against it.

4. Because of increased competition among vendors of off-site storage, the expense of the service is rarely prohibitive.

Of course, cost-justifications must reference benefits that accrue to the company from the acquisition of a subject product or service. In the case of off-site storage, cost-justifications devolve from the same risk analysis that was generated to identify corporate exposures. While it is difficult to assign a dollar value to the data that is being stored, it is a relatively common practice to demonstrate the cost to the company of prolonged downtime. Therefore, the coordinator can provide a scenario in which the cost of downtime to the company is attributable to the lack of backup data needed to restore the system.

The disaster recovery coordinator can further demonstrate the cost-effectiveness of the off-site option by developing a prospectus showing the costs of developing a comparable capability within company-owned facilities. In addition to the cost of environmental control, fire protection, water detection, furniture, shelving, and security, a "home-grown" shell for storage would also require the hiring of additional personnel.

Controlling the Storage Schedule

Once approval has been granted, the disaster recovery coordinator must finalize a schedule for removal of records to permanent off-site storage. The coordinator may need to coordinate with the IS executive to establish a routine for the preparation and rotation of computer media and other records requiring periodic update.

Special attention should be given to the requirement that users of PCs and user-administrated departmental computers become participants in an off-site storage plan. For the first several weeks, their cooperation may need to be closely monitored. According to one recent study, there were nearly 8.5 million mini- and microcomputer hard drives sold in 1987 with an average of 20Mb each. This is expected to increase to more than 13 million drives by 1990, averaging 40Mb capacity per unit.[1] This represents a truly staggering potential for data storage and data loss.

Obtaining the cooperation of users and administrators of decentralized systems may be a major hurdle, but it must be overcome if a company's disaster recovery capability is to be fully developed. There may be a need to involve senior management in forging corporate policy regarding data backup and participation in an off-site storage plan. Even then, it may be necessary to monitor the compliance of PC and mini-based systems users for a period of time until their participation becomes automatic. The coordinator may also find it helpful to disseminate information about the program throughout the company so that new storage requirements or requirements that were not originally considered may come to light.[2]

To establish controls, a formal log should be kept to record movement of media and records from of the tape library and record center to the vendor site. This log documents when couriers were on site and what they took or delivered. The log may also be useful in billing issues or in assessing vendor compliance with established delivery schedules. The log further provides a backup that may be used to track down media or records that are misplaced at the off-site storage facility. The more detailed the log, the better its use in resolving probelms.

Once schedules and controls are in place, the disaster recovery coordinator needs to arrange periodic reviews of the off-sight storage program. Depending on how rapidly company procedures and systems change, this review may have to be conducted quarterly or semiannually in order to identify changes in off-site storage requirements. This review should include an investigation of the following:

- **Vendor performance.** Periodically, the record of the vendor should be checked to ensure that billing is correct, media is being properly handled and stored, promised emergency delivery time frames are being met, and media is being rotated on schedule and without apparent damage. This check should include an inspection of the vendor facility, a review of vendor financial statements, and a sampling of opinions of the information management community regarding vendor performance generally.
- **Adherence to classification criteria.** Determine whether company information is being properly classified according to the scheme set forth in the development of the off-site storage plan. This may be done by sampling some of the records and documents as they are prepared for off-site storage. Trace the origins of the documents identified in the spot check, and ask the individual who classified the data to explain his or her rationale for the classification applied.
- **Changes in disaster recovery requirements.** An inventory of data and forms stored off-site should be discussed at a meeting of data "owners" to assess whether it is obsolete or otherwise irrelevant to company requirements. In some companies, this is done as part of departmental review of their sections of the company disaster

recovery plan. If some materials stored off-site are no longer necessary or relevant to business recovery, have them removed. Be sure to have the vendor revise the storage fees if there is a substantial reduction in the volume of data being stored.

- **"Awareness" programs.** Verify that awareness programs established at the outset of the off-site storage program are continuing. This may include revising a handout on key characteristics of the storage program and disseminating it to department managers, system users, and new employees within the company.

    It is especially important, with the proliferation of PCs within companies over the past several years, that new PC users be indoctrinated in procedures for backup and off-site storage of critical data. Having users read, initial, and return a memo covering their responsibility to participate in off-site storage may facilitate this requirement.

Off-site storage is not the most glamorous aspect of disaster recovery planning, and it may not pose as many interesting technical problems as the formulation system or network backup strategies, but it is essential to successful recovery from a disaster. Without backups of critical data, most companies will never recover from a major disaster, regardless of other preparations they have made.

REFERENCES

1. Dataquest projection cited in "Trends," *Personal Computing,* Vol. 11, no. 10 (October 1987).
2. This underscores another advantage of the local area network (LAN) that utilizes a file server. File backup may be accomplished from a single server location far more readily than through the cooperative efforts of individual users scattered throughout the company.

Chapter 5

Strategies
for System Backup

To many people, disaster recovery planning means planning for the restoration of mainframe operations following a catastrophe. This should come as no surprise considering that the traditional focus of disaster recovery planning was the corporate computer, almost without exception a mainframe. Disaster recovery plans dealt primarily with replacing a damaged or inaccessible mainframe with compatible hardware. Often disaster recovery planning was an activity confined to the data processing department of the company.

Today, more and more, disaster recovery planning encompasses a wider set of objectives. It aims at the recovery of critical business functions rather than the restoration of data processing operations alone. This, in large part, is a response to changes in the environment in which disaster recovery plans are developed. Decentralization of data processing functions, the rise of personal computing, and the emergence of local area networks are just some of the environmental changes that have forced contextual alterations in the field of disaster recovery planning.

Departmental Computing

With the development of powerful minicomputers—billed as "departmental processors"—traditional data processing functions have become increasingly decentralized. "Ownership" of these systems and their data often resides with nontechnical departmental managers, supported by service technicians from the equipment manufacturer and software support services from application vendors. In some companies, an IS or MIS department may also support departmental computing; in others, MIS exerts no control whatsoever over the selection, acquisition, installation, or on-going maintenance of departmental systems.

This trend toward decentralized control and management of data processing mitigates the value of disaster recovery planning techniques that narrowly focus on mainframe systems replacement. Additionally, decentralization may pose practical problems for effective disaster recovery planning. Issues may include the following:

- The "Tower of Babel" phenomenon. When departmental processors are selected and installed without reference to a consolidated strategic technological plan within the company, a host of proprietary languages and disparate operating systems may be in use throughout the company. This, in turn, can complicate efforts to develop cost-effective ways and means to backup critical systems in the event of a facility disaster.

• **The "Beckett" effect.** Departmental managers and their systems experts may stray from IS conventions or standards for application development, producing software that is difficult (or impossible) to port to (or run on) replacement hardware even if compatible hardware is forthcoming.

Unfortunately, the incentives for developing applications without the assistance of IS personnel are often great: Most IS departments have large application development backlogs, or have a strategic plan that favors development of new applications using more costly or time-consuming techniques (the argument being that this will simplify system integration downstream). Thus, given some competence in his or her own staff, a department manager may see some tangible, immediate benefits from developing his or her applications with nonIS personnel.

In many cases, "home-grown" software, developed within the department, may be poorly documented, if at all. This factor, combined with staff turnover, may result in a situation in which only one user has sufficient knowledge about the design of the software to aid in its recovery. This, in turn, makes for a potential disaster recovery nightmare: If the expert cannot be reached following a disaster, the recovery of a critical system may be delayed beyond an acceptable time frame.

Cooperation of departmental management, of course, is the key to resolving these difficulties. Managers, however, may perceive any efforts to change their systems—even if the intention is to facilitate disaster recoverability—as an intrusion. When departmental independence is given precedence over business recovery planning, the planning project cannot succeed.

• **The "Compartmentalization" factor.** Strong feelings of ownership that sometimes go hand in hand with departmental processing may lead to the development of some very esoteric security measures in departmental systems. Convincing departmental managers to reveal their secret master passwords or to divulge how their access security works can be difficult. Often this is less the result of paranoia about possible abuse than the manager's heartfelt belief that the data in his or her system is "cleaner" (i.e., less in error, having a high degree of integrity or accuracy) than the data in someone else's system. Since one common disaster recovery strategy for multiple homogeneous departmental processors is to *combine* applications and data for use on a single (albeit, more capable) processor, there is often the fear that recovery would corrupt the "good" data.

There may also be a fear that system combination would reveal that separate processors are not needed by each department, overturning senior management consensus that a department manager fought long and hard to build.

Micros and LANs

Another challenge to traditional disaster recovery planning methods comes from personal (micro-) computers, or PCs. PCs are an increasingly familiar part of the basic equipment for company employees at every level of the business. Some PCs may be used to run "fire and forget" applications that produce one-time output rather than stored databases. These applications are often relatively easy to safeguard by simply removing a copy of the software to off- site storage and providing for the availability of a PC in the disaster recovery plan.

On the other hand, an increasingly voluminous amount of vital business data is being stored on PC hard drives and floppies. For example, more and more departmental managers use decision support software in conjunction with original or extracted databases to map trends and plan for company growth and expansion. These plans, representing substantial investments of resources, may be impossible to reproduce should the PC data be lost.

The critical nature of some PC applications and data has led many major corporations to designate PCs as "data sites," which corporate disaster recovery coordinators must plan to recover with the same zeal as they have always devoted to the data center (mainframe). The disaster recovery coordinator for one of the largest U.S. corporations has publicly observed that, besides his company's 21 data centers, his plan needed to account for the recovery of more than 20,000 data sites, representing PCs used by corporate employees nationwide.[1]

Mainframes are still important, to be sure, and one day the pendulum may swing back to centralized DP. (There are a number of indicators that suggest this reversal may already be happening.) However, just as minis and micros did not replace mainframes, it may be safely assumed that the ascendancy of mainframes will not displace departmental and personal processing.

Moreover, an entire industry is evolving whose sole objective is integrating "data processing sites" (all processors great and small) through the use of local area networks, interface software packages, and data communications links. These LANs and links are also an increasingly important concern for disaster recovery planners as they may reflect an incremental or "assembly line" approach to providing a critical corporate function.

The bottom line is that the disaster recovery coordinator must think in terms of protecting and restoring "systems" rather than CPUs. Systems include not only hardware, applications, and databases, but also business functions and the users who provide them. Planning only for the replacement of a computer is no longer sufficient, if it ever was.

Developing System Backup Strategies

As indicated above, system backup means more than hardware replacement and entails more than software or data backup (i.e., copies for off-site storage). System backup strategies are interdependent with off-site storage schedules and plans and other disaster recovery procedures. For this reason, system backup strategies are best developed *concurrently* with off-site storage plans and *before* procedures for using the strategy are finalized. Figure 5.1 shows some of the relationships among these activities.

Developing strategies for system backup is central to the disaster recovery planning project. While primarily a technical problem, system backup also requires the coordinator's complete understanding of the business function that the system provides. Thus, data acquired during risk analysis is very important.

The risk analysis provides the following information that will impact directly on the strategies developed for system backup:

• **What applications are critical or vital?** One task of risk analysis was to rank the relative criticality of applications to business recovery following a disaster. Critical and vital applications were defined as those that facilitated key business functions and for which alternatives were unavailable. In short, these applications would need to be restored within a short time following a disaster if business recovery were to be accomplished.

Having identified critical and vital applications, the disaster recovery coordinator can begin defining the systems of which the applications are components. Systems include users, input data and forms, output data and forms, processing hardware and necessary peripheral devices, and documentation. (The identification of these other system elements is not a matter of conjecture or deduction. Many of the system elements are also defined in the process of risk analysis.)

• **What is the minimum acceptable hardware configuration?** Once application criticality is defined, the risk analysis goes further to identify the hardware (both CPUs and storage devices) that is used by the applica-

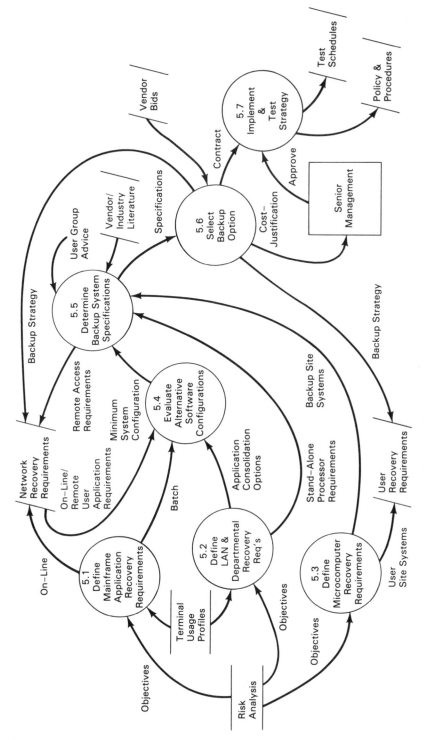

Figure 5.1 System Backup Plan Development.

tion in performance of the critical or vital business function. From the perspective of disaster recovery planning, it may be possible to view hardware capabilities utilized by all noncritical and nonvital applications as "spare capacity." Hence, during its emergency operations, the business may be able to settle for far less CPU/storage capacity than it normally utilizes. The ramifications of this view are twofold.

If less capacity is needed to run critical and vital applications, recovery hardware need not match production hardware on a one-to-one basis. A high-end model CPU may be adequately backed-up with a lower-end processor of adequate capacity.

It also follows that, if critical and vital applications run on several homogeneous (or compatible) processors in normal business operations, it may be possible to replace several low-end processors with a single high-end processor. Through the use of the right operating system software, even applications that reside on heterogeneous processors may be able to run successfully on a single processor. Again, the total capacity requirement of the backup processor and related storage devices may be substantially less than those of production equipment.

The net result of this analysis is what may be called a "minimum acceptable hardware configuration." This configuration, which must be implemented quickly in the event of a disaster, may require substantial technical assistance to design, and still more assistance to develop and test, but a workable minimum configuration can drastically reduce the costs of the disaster recovery capability.

• **How many users?** The risk analysis also identified the number of users who would need access to applications to continue business functions at emergency levels. The number of personnel needed may be far fewer than the number employed in normal business operations. (Presumably, other staff would be utilized to provide other business functions by manual means, or to aid in other aspects of the recovery.)

From the size of the "skeleton crew" using restored applications to provide critical and vital business functions, certain other facts may be discerned. For example, the number of users will define how many terminals, controllers, data lines, etc., will be required in recovery operations. This information, too, must be taken into account by the system backup strategy that is developed. The strategy must account for peripheral devices as well as CPUs and mass storage devices. It must also provide for a location where users will work in addition to providing an environment where processors, tape drives, and disk drives will be operated.

• **What are the business function requirements?** Besides application and user requirements, risk analysis also identifies, for each critical (and vital) job or business function, what inputs are required and what outputs are produced. Through the analysis of this data, much can be learned that will aid in the identification of an appropriate system backup strategy.

For example, the analysis of inputs and outputs may be used to identify how critical functions are related to one another. If an output of function *A* is used as an input for function *B*, the restoration of applications used in function *A* must take precedence over those used in *B*. This would be reflected in the procedures governing system restoration.

Going further, the relationship between function *A* and *B* may reveal that function *A* requires on-line terminals, while function *B* is essentially the product of batch processing and could be performed using an intelligent workstation and a downloaded data set. A study of the relationship may reveal that users of function *A* applications need access from 9 A.M. to 5 P.M., while system access for function B users may be limited to the time required to upload work files from their workstations once a day and download the data set for the next day's work.

Of course, besides showing the relationships between functions, the analysis of inputs and outputs also provides information about the system requirements of the functions themselves. For example, if reports are a necessary output of a given function, a printer may need to be added to the minimum configuration of the recovery system. Also, if some input data needs to be received, via data communications, from remote sites— as in the case of "lock box" transmissions used to update customer payment records—the system configuration would need to provide for the transmission lines, modems, and related communications software.

The business function analysis will also identify any special preprinted forms required for work as well as any voice communications, photocopying, facsimile transmission, and U.S. mail resources needed to complete the job.

From this brief overview, it should be evident that most components needed to develop an effective system backup strategy are available from the risk analysis. Given this information, it is up to the coordinator, in conjunction with technical staff, to select the best strategy for the restoration of critical and vital business functions.

Mainframe Backup Strategies

As pointed out earlier, system recovery strategies were once limited to strategies for replacing mainframe computers. While this is not an adequate context for business recovery, the focus on mainframe backup has yielded some time-tested techniques that can provide useful information for more sophisticated system recovery plans.

The following are typical strategies for backing up the corporate mainframe. The explanation of each strategy identifies the merits and demerits that have come to be associated with it.

• **"Next box off the line."** One strategy used by many companies in the past to backup their data processing mainframe was to absorb the impact of the disaster until a comparable mainframe could be installed to replace the lost CPU. In the interim—until a new mainframe became available—the company would "make do" with manual procedures, locate and prepare a new facility or refurbish the existing facility, and retrieve a current backup of system and application software and data from storage. When the new mainframe was installed, IS personnel would load the software and data backup and users would frantically input interim data until files and records were up-to-date.[2]

The drawbacks of this strategy are numerous. First, the plan could work only in an environment where there were no critical systems. That is, if viable, manual alternatives existed to all computer-provided business functions, no computer application would be considered critical to business survival. Only in such an environment could the open-ended time frames involved in replacing computer equipment with new hardware be tolerated. Certainly, very few companies today would find their automated systems so easily replaced with manual means.

Second, this option does not provide, in advance, for a facility in which the new mainframe can be installed. Locating a suitable facility may not be a very difficult task, but the preparation of such a facility, including the installation of a raised floor, air conditioning, UPS, electrical wiring, security systems, fire protection, etc., would be a major undertaking. In short, even if the "next box of the line" were available in a timely way, the facility might not be.

• **Cold site.** The cold site (or shell site) strategy is similar to the "next box off the line" option in that the actual restoration of mainframe operations is on hold until replacement hardware can be obtained. By using the cold site strategy, however, the business has already prepared a facility with the requisite physical capabilities to serve as an alternate data processing site.

Company-owned cold sites have the drawback of being expensive to outfit with security and protective systems. However, the facility may be used for other purposes, including off-site storage or new employee training, when not in use for disaster recovery.

• **Commercial cold site.** This option is identical to the cold site strategy above except that a commercial cold site is a leased facility. The facility may be located in the subscriber's vicinity or distant from it. Or, a cold site may be able to be moved to the customer's location. (Mobile cold sites, while prevalent in Europe, are just beginning to be offered in the United States See Figure 5.2.) The fact that a number of businesses share the cost of the facility reduces the cost to the individual company of having this capability.

Like the first two backup strategies, however, this approach to mainframe backup assumes that the company can absorb the impact of being without a mainframe until one can be obtained from a lessor or vendor. For many companies this option is unacceptable.

As with any cold site option, there is no way to test the effectiveness of this recovery option until a disaster actually happens. For example, a

Figure 5.2 Mobile Cold Site Offering.
Hotsite®, Division of RMI Company, Niles, Ohio. Reprinted by Permission.

company cannot verify its estimates for system restoration without testing restoration procedures on actual hardware.[3]

• **Reciprocal backup agreement.** To address the problem of facilities and hardware backup in companies unable to manage for extended periods of time without their mainframe, one option, popular several years ago, was the reciprocal backup agreement. Two similarly-configured companies—each having spare processing time and hardware capabilities—would formally or informally agree to backup each other's critical applications. If Company *A* experienced a disaster, Company *B* would allow Company *A* to restore its critical applications on Company *B*'s hardware. The reverse would be the case if Company *B* had a failure.

The problems with this strategy, even at the time that it was popular, were twofold. First, it was extremely difficult for a company to find a partner who had the right hardware, spare capacity, and the inclination to participate in such an agreement. Location was also a factor: The potential partner could not be colocated to the company seeking the arrangement, since the same disaster that affected Company *A* might, at the same time, affect Company *B*.

Second, if a suitable partner were found, it was difficult to find a mutually-agreeable time to test the arrangement. An untested strategy is nearly as bad as having no strategy at all. It was also difficult to maintain the relationship on mutually acceptable terms. Managers chafed at having to notify their partners of changing configurations or new processing requirements. One could not cost-justify to one's own management the need to acquire a new item of hardware on the grounds that it would facilitate the disaster recovery capability of another company.

These arrangements also carried the risk of domino-type disasters. The relocation of Company *A*'s processing capability to Company *B* might also disrupt Company *B*'s operations. Company *B* would need to activate its emergency service levels, requiring that its business operate in disaster recovery mode until Company *A* was recovered. Needless to say, this was unacceptable to Company *B*'s user community.

Today, these arrangements are rarely seen, except perhaps in large companies with numerous subsidiaries. Even in these cases, it is rare that enough spare processing time or equipment capability exists to support a mutual backup arrangement.[4]

• **Service bureaus.** Some companies elect to back up systems against failure by contracting with a service bureau for emergency processing services. For example, the vendor of a loan administration application used by mortgage banking companies may offer a "service bureau" capability for the application.

Software vendors providing service bureaus typically market the service to customers who prefer not to invest in their own computer systems and software. User terminals are installed in the client offices, and jobs are submitted to CPUs located at the vendor service bureau via data communications. In some cases, printers are also installed at the client office so that reports and other output can be printed locally.

For customers that purchase vendor software but operate independently of the vendor's service bureau, the service bureau offering may still be available in a disaster recovery situation. Service bureau backup may be part of a software sales contract, or may be a separately negotiated arrangement.

What are some of the potential drawbacks of this approach? Vendor service bureaus are typically application-specific. They process customer data all together, then distribute output to individual customers. This may create some difficulties for a company that has several critical applications, including some for which recourse to a software vendor's service bureau is not available. Also, the prospect of dividing numerous applications among several vendor-provided service bureaus is unsettling.

For a service bureau arrangement to be effective, several conditions must be met. First, the disaster-stricken company must have an extant facility where user terminals and printers can be set up. Second, the customer's data backups must have been saved from the disaster that consumed the originals, and these data backups must be in the proper format for speedy integration with the service bureau database. If vendor-recommended maintenance procedures have not been observed, or if applications have not been updated to the most current software release, or if file formats have been "customized" to better suit the business's needs, there may be incompatibilities with the service bureau application that will be difficult and time-consuming to correct.

• **Hot sites.** Hot sites are rather like generic service bureaus. Typically, they are free-standing, fully-equipped data processing facilities to which a number of companies having compatible hardware subscribe. Machine time is made available to subscribers for the purpose of testing their recovery procedures, and this testing schedule can be quickly interrupted so facilities can be made available to any customer who declares a disaster.

Once a disaster is declared (and this is usually done in conjunction with the payment of a disaster declaration fee to prevent frivolous use of the facility), the customer sends its backup media and a team of operations personnel to the hot site. Critical applications are mounted and tested, users are provided with terminals and modems at their location, and data processing service is restored.

Unlike a service bureau, a hot site is usually equipped to run any application that is compatible with its hardware and operating system. Hot sites are often equipped with technical support personnel to assist the company operations team in their efforts to get the system up and running. In addition to the fixed complement of hardware at the hot site, specialized equipment can be added to satisfy the customer's backup requirement. This, however, is often done at the customer's expense if the required equipment is not integral to the requirements of other facility subscribers.

Some hot site vendors also offer cold sites that a customer can lease if disaster conditions persist for an extended period of time. Hot site vendors may also provide assistance in obtaining replacement hardware for use in the cold site or for delivery to the customer's own new or refurbished facility.

Hot sites are increasingly becoming the mainframe backup option preferred by medium to large companies. Their reliability and recent notable successes in recovering companies in the throes of a disaster have greatly offset initial concerns about their price. (Some considerations and cautions in selecting a hot site are provided later in this chapter.)

• **Redundant systems.** Of course, the single most reliable system backup strategy is redundant systems. While most companies cannot afford to build and equip two identical data centers, those that can enjoy the comfort of full confidence in their ability to recover from almost any disaster.

In the event of a disaster, redundant systems at a separate facility—which must be far enough distant so as not to have been affected by the same disaster—are brought on-line. Users are either transported to an operations center that is colocated to the backup site or are provided remote access terminals and printers and connected to the backup CPU via data communications.

Besides being the most reliable method of systems backup, redundancy is also the most expensive. A commercial hot site, for this reason, is often a more acceptable alternative.

This spectrum of alternative mainframe backup strategies are graphed in Figure 5.3 to show the relative measure of confidence afforded to the company whose survival is dependent upon each strategy. The highest measure of confidence is afforded by the redundant systems strategy in which hardware availability is immediate, facilities mirror those that were lost, and backup systems duplicate production systems

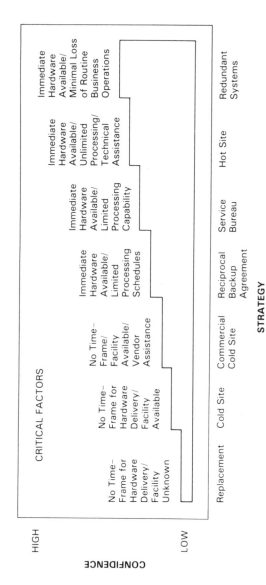

Figure 5.3 Mainframe Backup Strategies and Confidence Levels.

111

so closely that only minimal adjustments to normal business functions are required. The least confidence is placed in the "next box off the line," or replacement strategy: It has no timetable for system replacement or restoration of business functions as hardware delivery dates, facility location, and preparation dates, and other factors are unknown.

Figure 5.3 assumes that a company has several critical or vital mainframe-based applications, some developed internally, and that other departmental applications may be consolidated for installation and utilization on a mainframe. This is not atypical for the data processing center of a medium-size financial company.

As noted throughout this book, the financial industry is among the most vulnerable to total disruption by a disaster and is the most heavily regulated of all industries from the standpoint of disaster recovery planning requirements. In view of these characteristics, the results of a survey of banks by CHI/COR Information Management, Inc., provides an interesting picture of the system backup options preferred by the financial industry as a whole.[5]

According to the 1986 CHI/COR study, cooperative arrangements (mutual service arrangements) were at the top of the list, commanding 56 percent of the 110 survey respondents. The preponderance of this group were "medium and small banks" with total assets of $1 billion or less. Most of these respondents indicated, however, that they felt their hardware backup arrangements and testing programs needed improvement. The vast majority also conceded that they had never performed a risk or impact analysis pursuant to the development of their disaster recovery plan.

On the other hand, as Figure 5.4 illustrates, the hot site option was selected by the majority (57.1 percent) of "large banks" (assets: $1 to $4 billion) and the majority (77.8 percent) of "very large banks" with assets in excess of $4 billion. This could reflect of a number of factors, a prime one being that the number and sheer processing requirements for the critical applications of larger banks mandate a more reliable backup strategy than the mutual service arrangements preferred by smaller banks.

In fact, the predeliction of small to medium banks for mutual assistance arrangements may be a reflection of financial considerations rather than of actual preference. As Figure 5.5 suggests, many disaster recovery coordinators in medium-sized banks feel that their plans need improvement in the hardware backup area. They also sense the need for better testing (testing is difficult to perform in a mutual assistance arrangement), and for coordination with other business recovery plans.

Currently, the hot site industry, which has catered primarily to large systems backup, is undergoing several changes. Many of the smaller vendors are consolidating into full-service shops for the small- and medium-sized client. Several vendors of departmental mini- and

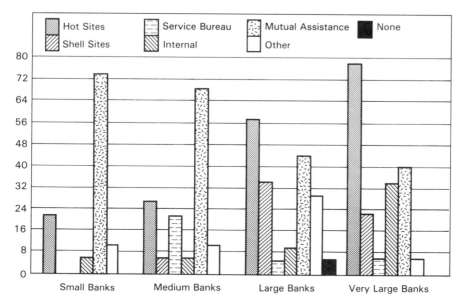

Figure 5.4 Hardware Backup Strategies.
Source: "1986 Computers in Banking Survey," CHI-COR Information Management, Inc.
Reprinted by permission.

superminicomputers are also beginning to offer a hot site capability for their users. Wang, for example, offers customers a backup Wang system and consulting assistance in disaster recovery plan development.

Driven by stiffer penalties for failure to safeguard systems and the increasing likelihood of lawsuits by customers against bank management and boards of directors, internal bank auditors will likely develop a more stringent attitude in the next decade toward untested and nonviable hardware backup strategies and an increased interest in hot sites as the strategy of choice. Larger companies have simply been driven by technical and legal requirements to adopt the hot site strategy first; many smaller companies are certain to follow as other options are exhausted.

Selecting a Hot Site

Of course, not every company will become a hot site user, although financial companies—given their great exposure to loss from business inter-

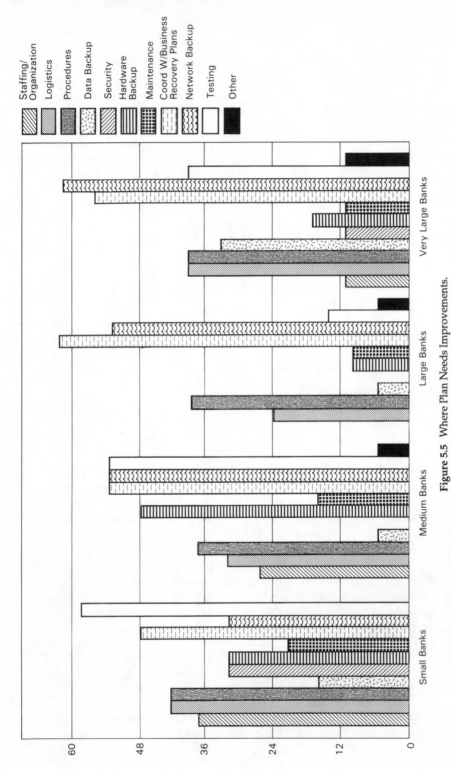

Figure 5.5 Where Plan Needs Improvements.

Source: "1986 Computers in Banking Survey," CHI-COR Information Management, Inc. Reprinted by permission.

ruptions—may find this the only viable option. However, the trend over the past five years has been toward the use of hot sites as the primary mainframe backup strategy. Hot sites remove many of the unknowns inherent in strategies that involve the acquisition of replacement hardware in a disaster situation (i.e., replacement, cold site, and commercial cold site). Increasing diversity of installed software products and a concurrent increase in the utilization of hardware capacities have rendered service bureaus and mutual backup agreements anachronistic as competent mainframe backup strategies. And, today, as in the past, few companies can afford to build and outfit duplicate data centers.

Thus, hot sites, such as the facility pictured in Figure 5.6, are now available for nearly all brands and sizes of mainframes. Even some of the more prominent minicomputer vendors sponsor hot sites to accommodate their users.

Figure 5.6   Mainframe Hot Site in Niles, Ohio.
Source: Hotsite®,Division of RMI Company, Niles, Ohio. Reprinted by Permission.

Selecting a hot site is a straightforward process, but one that requires the disaster recovery coordinator to have (1) a detailed understanding of the company's minimum acceptable hardware configuration (and operating system software), and (2) some savvy about the hot site industry and its practices. Armed with this information, the coordinator will be better able to identify the vendor offering that best fulfills a company's mainframe backup requirements.

Since minimum acceptable hardware configurations are company-specific, they cannot be treated here in any detail. Suffice it to say that considerable technical assistance may be required to determine whether all critical and vital applications—both those that are mainframe-resident and those which are installed on departmental processors—can be mounted on a single mainframe processor. Once this analysis has been completed, it is a good idea to have a list of hardware and system software before going hot site "shopping."

Data communications requirements of critical and vital applications should also be identified. Data communications telephone lines or specialized networks will probably be the methods employed to connect local users to remote hot site systems. Thus, the number of user terminals and other local peripherals (printers, primarily) comprise one set of data communications requirements that the hot site must be able to fulfill.

Also, if critical or vital applications require the exchange of data—via telecommunications, satellite or other means—between locations other than the user location and the hot site, these communications requirements must be specified in as much detail as possible. Information about the location and type of communicator, the communication methods, the access methods, protocols, encryption standards, and even the timing of scheduled communications should be at the coordinator's fingertips when he or she sits down to define backup requirements with a vendor marketing representative.

Technical suitability is a primary criterion for selecting a hot site vendor. However, there are several other factors that the coordinator would be well-advised to consider. Many of these factors can be derived from the experience of other information managers who have developed effective mainframe backup strategies in conjunction with hot site facilities.

There are other considerations reflecting the problems that information managers and disaster recovery planners have had in dealing with an industry plagued by fly-by-night companies who misrepresent facilities and capabilities. Unfortunately for the legitimate vendors, it takes only one unethical vendor—collecting large monthly fees for non-existent, or phantom, hot sites on the gamble that a customer will never have to declare a disaster—to soil the image of the industry generally.[6] For this reason, the legitimate vendors invite close inspection and careful evaluation of their operations along the lines described in the following paragraphs.[7]

1. Meet with the marketing representative. One of the first steps in selecting a hot site is to meet with a regional marketing representative of the vendor. During this meeting, the representative will seek information about company backup requirements, minimum configurations, communications requirements, and even the current status of the company disaster recovery plan.

Obviously, the representative will strive to inform the prospective customer about the merits of his facility, identify some of its more prestigious subscribers, and even recount instances (if there are any) in which the facility rescued a subscriber in distress. Be sure to ask for the names of contacts in several subscriber companies for later use in vendor evaluation.

Do not accept the representative's word for the fact that his facility can meet recovery needs. Only in rare cases can a marketing rep make such a determination without input from the hot site technical staff. (Even if a technical support person has accompanied the marketing representative, verbal assurances are not enough.)

Ask the marketing representative to develop, within a specified time, a written proposal summarizing the backup requirements of the prospective customer as they have been explained to him; it should clearly define how the hot site will fulfill each requirement. As hot site vendors are highly competitive, legitimate vendors will go out of their way to ensure that the prospective customer has all the information needed to make the right choice (presumably, a choice that favors their service).

The proposal should detail costs associated with both subscription to and actual use of the facility. It should also provide details of other vendor offerings. Many hot site vendors also maintain cold sites that are available to customers in the event that the recovery period becomes protracted. Some will help the customer locate and install new hardware in the vendor cold site or at some other specified location. Some vendors are subsidiaries of larger concerns involved with disaster recovery consulting, equipment leasing, or other data processing services. A list of the vendor's other services and interests may be a factor in coordinator's decision.

2. Inspect the facility. Once two or more potentially suitable hot site vendors have been identified and their proposals and credentials have been evaluated, the coordinator should go no further until a physical inspection has been made of each candidate's facilities. It is often a good idea to have a systems expert and an auditor accompany the coordinator during the inspection, as their observations and criticisms may go beyond the scope of a purely disaster recovery-oriented focus to identify important vendor inadequacies.

Some hot site vendors will even buy the plane tickets for serious prospects. The coordinator should strive to avoid being influenced by these or other perks that the vendor provides. Weighed against the monthly fee that the vendor will charge once the prospect signs a subscriber contract, these perks amount to very little indeed.

One of the purposes of the facility visit, besides ensuring that the hot site facility actually exists, is to evaluate the vendor's nonemergency operations and staff. The coordinator should find out how processors are used during nondisaster periods: Are they idle, are they in constant use for customer tests, or are they used to provide other services?

If vendor applications reside on processors during nonemergency operations, or if the processors are utilized to provide service bureau functions, the coordinator should ask for an explanation of how the disposition of these processing functions will be handled in the event of a customer emergency.

It is also important for the coordinator to ascertain how many subscribers are assigned to the facility. This factor has positive and negative dimensions. A large subscriber base may indicate that the hot site has some tenure in this new industry and that it is reputable in the information processing community. However, an excessive number of users assigned to a fixed set of processing capabilities can also be a warning sign. The coordinator should tread cautiously around vendor promises that a new site will be built to take the overload within X months.

Whether or not the number seems high, the coordinator should follow up by asking how multiple, simultaneous disaster declarations would be accommodated. The coordinator should also ask for a list—or at least a count— of hot site customers located in the same geographic region as his or her company. This is extremely important if the region is especially vulnerable to regional hurricanes or earthquakes.

3. **Contract for service.** Based upon information collected from the marketing representative, research, the vendor proposal, and the on-site visit, a final decision must be reached. In the best of circumstances, the ultimate decision will come down to price differences among two or three qualified candidates. There is, however, another method that will help identify the best-suited vendor in the group. The coordinator should clearly explain the situation to each vendor involved in anticipation that the vendors will probably react in one of three ways:

- The vendors will criticize their competition. Some vendors will respond by criticizing their competitors. They may relay "off the record" information about competitor incompetence or competitor failures in supporting customers in actual disaster situations. While this practice is ethically questionable, it may provide a basis for further investigation of the subject vendor. It may also say something about the vendor who is doing the criticizing: If criticisms are found to be patently false, how much trust can one vest in the critic?

- The vendors will negotiate their rates. Like auto salesmen, some vendors representatives have a certain amount of latitude in the pricing of their services. If they perceive that they are losing a prospective customer because of price, they may seek to lower the originally quoted price. Since the proposal solicited at the outset of the selection process was intended to show the vendor's best offer, some valid questions about negotiations and good faith may be raised by this practice of price cutting.

   This issue is also brought to the fore by vendors who will not provide pricing until competitive bids are known to them. Once the best offers of the competition are known, these vendors will proceed to undercut their price.

   Costs are as important in disaster recovery planning as in any other business activity. However, the coordinator must weigh pricing against the value of good faith negotiations, realizing that the latter, more than the former, may indicate how conscientiously the vendor will execute its responsibilities under the hot site agreement.

- The vendors will offer pre-subscription testing. Faced with the impasse of several qualified candidates, some hot site vendors will seek to reinforce their bid by inviting the prospective customer to conduct a live test at their facility to demonstrate that they can deliver what has been promised before a contract is signed. The coordinator would be well-advised to accept the vendor's offer. The test can provide important information not only about vendor capabilities but also about the solvency of the backup strategy itself. (Be sure to read Chapter 9 on plan testing in this book before conducting a precontract test.)

   The willingness of the vendor to provide precontractual testing may demonstrate sincerity and a willingness to go beyond the stipulations of the contract to aid subscribers that are experiencing disasters. The value of this business ethic cannot be understated.

Any of the above factors can provide the intangible, yet compelling, basis for selecting one vendor over several technically qualified candidates.

When the selection has been made, focus shifts to the contract itself. Hot site agreements, like off-site storage agreements, typically contain a number of provisions that the coordinator should understand and examine thoroughly.

- **Subscription fee.** This is the fee (typically expressed as a dollar amount payable to the vendor on a monthly basis) for the base equipment configuration that will be made available to the subscriber. Equipment covered will generally include all CPUs, storage devices, input devices (other than user terminals), output devices, and communications equipment that is held in common with other subscribers. A schedule of the exact equipment covered by the fee should appear in the contract. There is often a discount on the monthly fee for subscribers who contract for service over a period of many years.
- **Extra equipment fee.** This fee (also payable monthly for most facilities) covers special hardware that is not used by a preponderance of subscribers but which is made available at the hot site for emergency use by companies that subscribe for it. The fee may also cover additional storage devices, tape drives, etc., that are not a part of the base configuration. Extra equipment should be listed on a schedule that appears in the contract.
- **Annual test time allocation and additional test time fee.** The hot site contract should spell out how many hours per year the subscriber will have to test its plan without charge, and indicate the hourly fee for test time over and above this amount.
- **Disaster notification fee.** This fee is typically assessed to discourage frivolous use of hot site facilities. Fees may be nominal or quite expensive, depending on the vendor. In addition to stating the fee, the contract should indicate how the customer declares a disaster and when the fee will be collected.
- **Daily usage fee.** This fee is included in the contract to show daily (or hourly) rates for use of the hot site in a disaster situation. Other associated fees may be assessed for technical support, maintenance services, administrative office space rental, and cold site use. The hot site may also provide facilities for local and off-site storage of data and supplies. These charges should be spelled out in the contract.
- **Plan fees.** The hot site vendor may also contribute to the development of a disaster recovery plan and testing strategies, and the documentation of tests. These services may be provided on a fee basis or at no charge to the customer.

- **Multiple simultaneous disasters.** The methodology that the hot site will observe in allocating resources among customers that experience concurrent disasters should be spelled out in the contract. In some cases, resources are allocated on a "first come, first served" basis, while vendors with multiple facilities may offer primary and secondary recovery sites.

- **Subscriber limitations.** The hot site contract should also indicate the maximum number of subscriptions that will be taken on any extant facility.

- **Prior notice of price increases.** The contract should stipulate how much notice the subscriber will be given of fee increases. Ninety-days advance notice seems to be standard.

- **Equipment modifications and additions.** The contract should clearly describe how equipment changes and resultant changes in configuration fees will be handled. Contracts typically provide 60-day prior notice of hardware changes that significantly affect the configurations for which the subscriber has contracted.

- **Hot site liability.** The hot site contract should indicate the extent to which the hot site assumes responsibility for providing services at contracted levels. Typical components include a "reasonable care" clause and a *force majeure clause*. The former is the vendor's guarantee that it will exercise reasonable care in the handling and processing of subscriber media and data. The vendor should also provide client confidentiality. *Force majeure* releases the vendor from liability for outages resulting from Acts of God, nuclear wars, etc. These caveats are fairly common to service contracts of any type.

Hot Sites and System Users

In the preceding discussion, some critical assumptions have been made that merit additional discussion. The first assumption is that the disaster recovery coordinator has selected a facility that is not located near the company data center.

The rationale for selecting a distant hot site is fairly straightforward. Considering the company's exposure to regional disasters (hurricanes, earthquakes, telephone company CO failures, power company failures, etc.), it makes little sense to select a backup facility that might be affected by the same adverse conditions as the company data center.

Hot sites are available in numerous locations throughout North America. Thus, the hot site selected will probably be as near the company data center as possible (to save on travel expenses) without being so close as to be consumed by the same disaster that damages or interrupts normal operations at the company data center.

This assumption leads to another. Since the hot site is located at a distance, chances are that relocating the entire management and staff of the company to the vicinity of the hot site would be cost-prohibitive for most businesses. Hence, the assumption is made that users will need to be restored independently of systems, then connected to remote systems via data communications.

The nature and scope of the disaster confronting the company will ultimately determine the requirements for restoring users. If the disaster affects only the data center, but leaves company offices and work areas intact, then user relocation will be unnecessary. Recovering user functions will consist mainly of reestablishing contact with operations at the remote processing site via data communications. Of course, if only critical and vital systems are restored, user function recovery may also entail the implementation of manual systems for nonvital applications as well.

If, on the other hand, user facilities and the data center are destroyed or rendered unusable by the same disaster, user relocation may be required. Users will need to be directed to a work site outside the disaster perimeter, in new quarters equipped with all that is necessary to continue work at emergency levels—telephones, office supplies, terminals, preprinted forms, typewriters, and a myriad of other essentials.

This scenario presumes planning. Without advanced planning, not only will employees not know where to go, but they will also have no means for performing work when they get there.

Advanced planning is required in six discrete areas. These are: location of a backup facility, employee notification procedures, employee transportation arrangements, redirection of telecommunications traffic, supply logistics, and employee accomodations.

• **Location of a backup facility.** This component of a system backup strategy is often given little consideration in disaster recovery planning. Noting the lack of attention that traditional disaster recovery plans paid to nondata center issues generally, it is understandable why these plans failed to account for user work areas. However, plans that aim for recovery of all business functions, and not only computer operations, must consider this issue.

There are basically four approaches to planning for user recovery facilities. The first approach is the least expensive to the planning project, but quite possibly the most expensive for the company hit by a disaster. This approach involves locating a facility only after a disaster occurs.

Advocates argue that this approach is valid because of the wide variety of unoccupied facilities available for lease on short notice in most metropolitan areas. Even a conference facility at a hotel could be turned into a temporary operations center within a short time.

Although a warehouse, hotel conference center, or even office space could be located quickly in the event of a localized disaster, such as fire or flooding, this approach offers little confidence in the case of a regional disaster. If the facilities location team must look for new user quarters in unfamiliar territory, a significant amount of recovery time could be lost.

Time would also be lost while cabling and jacking the recovery facility, communicating with vendors and storage facilities to arrange drops of needed supplies to a new address, redirecting long distance and local telecommunications traffic to the new facility, and notifying employees where and when to come to work.

A second approach to facility planning, one which provides only a slightly higher confidence level, is to plan for an "either/or" alternative. That is, if the disaster is localized, plan to locate recovery facilities at that time, but if the disaster is regional in scope, plan to relocate employees to a known facility at a remote location.

It can be argued that it is easier to notify employees, redirect telephone traffic (not always true depending on the facilities of the local carrier and long distance service used), find suitable quarters, and obtain sources of supply in local relocations than in remote relocations. Thus, to safeguard against the difficulties inherent in remote relocation, a "hard" site is designated for remote relocation.

While this approach goes part of the way toward preplanning facilities for user recovery, it still leaves room for delays that a more defined plan might prevent. In fact, the cost savings accrued by designating a remote recovery facility (and presumably preparing it for use in an emergency), and not a local one, are minimal at best.

A third option is to designate a single site—not as remote perhaps as a hot site, but not within a predictable disaster perimeter either—to serve as the emergency work area if a disaster occurs. The costs of maintaining such a facility in a ready state may be high, including costs of leased telephone lines that terminate in the backup operations center, rent, wiring and cabling, etc., but the payoff may be substantial in the event of a disaster.

Having a hard relocation site can ease the transition of critical and vital operations in an emergency as well as provide a location for storing emergency supplies of preprinted forms, office supplies, hardware, etc.

A fourth approach to this issue is being discussed more and more at the present time. A number of vendors, both of off-site storage and of hot site facilities, are exploring the idea of a "shared commercial backroom operations center." For a single monthly fee, companies could subscribe to the facility much in the way they do for a hot site or shell site. Presumably, this fee would be substantially lower than the cost to the company of renting, preparing, and maintaining a private user relocation site.

The determination of which of these approaches will best meet the needs of a specific company has to be made by the disaster recovery coordinator after reviewing all relevant options. However, some provision for a user backup facility should be made in the plan.

• **Employee notification procedures.** Depending on the selected approach to facility replacement, special procedures will need to be developed to ensure that employees who are vital to the recovery are notified in the event of a disaster. Recovery teams and operations staff will need to know when and where to report for work. (This topic is treated in greater detail in Chapter 7.)

• **Employee transportation arrangements.** The disaster recovery coordinator also needs to make provisions for the relocation of users to the user recovery site. Preparations may be as extensive as establishing a provisional service contract for private air transportation or as limited as designating a recovery team to hire buses at the time a disaster occurs. Here, as in any dimension of disaster preparedness, the coordinator may face tradeoffs between the certainty of advance preparation and the cost-savings of a more open-ended approach. (This topic, too, is treated in Chapter 7.)

• **Redirection of telecommunications traffic.** For many businesses the loss of telecommunications for any period of time is tantamount to the loss of business functions. For this reason, user recovery strategies must account for the recovery of telecommunications capabilities as well. Another factor making restoration of telecommunications at the user facility extremely important is that this provides the conduit for connecting users to remote hot site facilities. Chapter 6 treats network (including both voice and data communication networks) recovery strategies in considerable detail.

• **Supply logistics.** Once a facility is designated for user recovery and provisions have been made for notifying and transporting users to the location, the disaster recovery coordinator must determine what supplies users must have to perform productive work. Some supplies, identified in the risk analysis, may have been stored off-site as part of the off-site backup plan. Arrangements have to be made to ensure that they are retrieved and delivered to the user recovery site.

If some supplies (i.e., office supplies) are to be acquired from extant sources, the disaster recovery coordinator should so state in the recovery plan.

For items that may be somewhat more difficult to obtain—including computer terminals, PCs, peripheral devices, portable photocopiers, FAX machines, printer paper, diskettes, ribbons, and other computer-related supplies—advance planning may help minimize recovery time delays. The coordinator should compile a list of all necessary items and then identify possible sources for them in the general vicinity of the recovery site (if known in advance). For electronic equipment, the coordinator may be able to make an arrangement with the vendor, a value added reseller (VAR), or retailer to deliver replacement hardware within 24 hours. If this time frame is unacceptable, either to the company or to the supplier, the coordinator should explore the possiblity of purchasing needed hardware and storing it off-site with other critical supply items.

It is also highly recommended that at least two suppliers be identified for any critical item. Redundant supply arrangements can safeguard against the possibility that a critical item or a supplier will be unavailable when needed.

Where possible, emergency purchase orders should be completed so that only a signature is needed to activate them. Suppliers may require this and may wish to have copies of the purchase orders in their possession as a part of an emergency supply agreement.

Of course, all suppliers and the items they will provide must be listed, together with office and emergency contact telephone numbers. These contact lists will be included in the disaster recovery plan, kept up-to-date through regular plan maintenance, and included in the notification procedures set forth in Chapter 7.

• **Employee accomodations.** If a user recovery site is preplanned, it may be possible to make advance arrangements with an hotel or motel in the site's vicinity to accomodate recovery personnel in an emergency. At a minimum, an inventory of hotels and motels should be made prior to selecting a recovery site if the site is located too remotely for users to commute from their own homes.

Strategies for the Backup of Nonmainframe Computers

Hot sites are generally available for large mainframe backup and recovery. As noted previously, some vendors of minicomputers have made available hot site and service bureau facilities for their users in the event of a catastrophe. Generally, however, the recovery of mini- and microcomputer-based systems (and LANs, too) requires one of the following strategies to be adopted by the disaster recovery coordinator:

- **Replacement.** Similar to the "next box off the line" strategy for mainframe backup, this approach is somewhat more reliable in the case of minicomputers since availablity of hardware may be greater. Mainframes are not typically shelf items in value added reseller (VARs) or retailer inventories due to physical size and storage requirements. Minicomputers, on the other hand, are often stocked and available for immediate delivery.

As with PCs and even small private branch exchanges (PBXs), some suppliers will accept provisional orders for hardware that can be activated in an emergency for delivery within 24 hours. If data has been backed up and is recoverable from off-site storage, and software is either backed up or may be readily purchased, implementation of critical mini-, PC-, or LAN-based applications may be feasible at the user recovery center.

- **Redundant hardware.** Another strategy for mini-computer backup is to purchase equipment by twos. Until a disaster occurs, one unit can serve as a spare for the other in case of malfunction. In some MIS shops, the redundant unit may be employed as a test machine, where applications are written and debugged prior to release in the primary or production unit. Of course, if both units are located in the same facility, both are susceptible to loss from the same disaster. To safeguard against this possibility, one of two scenarios may be envisioned.

The first scenario holds that, with the onset of disaster conditions, the redundant unit will be evacuated from the facility. Because of the comparatively small size of many minicomputers, this may be practical in all but the most sudden disaster situations.

The second scenario places the redundant unit off- site, preferably at the hot site, user recovery site, or an off-site storage facility. This would provide more protection for the redundant unit, but also limit its usefulness in normal operations.

In either scenario, the coordinator will need to develop appropriate documentation and procedures to support the strategy. Be sure to include cabling, UPS, and other requirements in the description of items to be included in both evacuation and recovery of the hardware.

- **Consolidate applications.** Applications residing on minicomputers may often be accomodated on larger processors. Where direct operating system and software compatibilites exist, the coordinator may consider moving critical, miniresident applications onto the mainframe in the event of a disaster.

There are also a number of software companies that compile their programs for use on a variety of CPUs and with a variety of operating systems. Where this is the case, data files from one system, although compiled for a different processor, may be ported to the same software running on a different processor. Disaster recovery coordinators may wish to encourage the acquisition of these software packages as well as the use of "portable coding" for applications written in-house to facilitate a strategy of consolidation in disaster recovery.

The above strategies apply to a host of critical hardware requiring backup and recovery. LAN control units, and even PCs, may be effectively backed up through a strategy of replacement, redundancy, or consolidation.

R E F E R E N C E S

1. Francis Dramis, senior vice-president for corporate information processing centers, AT&T, from a speech delivered at the University of South Florida, Tampa, FL, September 18, 1986.

2. According to Datapro's special report, *All About Disaster Recovery Planning,* (1986), most mainframe vendors reported customer inquiries about hardware replacement in an emergency. Some vendors indicated a willingness to work with customers on a case-by-case basis in making arrangements for special shipments in the event of a declared disaster.

3. Toni Fish and Douglas Morrissey, "DP Backup and Recovery Alternatives," *Data Security Management* (New York: Auerbach Publishers, 1984).

4. "Guidelines for ADP Contingency Planning," Federal Information Processing Standards Publication 81 (Washington, DC: U.S. Department of Commerce, March 27, 1981), p. 15. The National Bureau of Standards issued the following position on mutual backup agreements: "While [these] agreements are conceptually feasible, they rarely, if ever, prove to be totally reliable. The penalty to the shop needing support of discovering in time of need that backup is not available is generally too great to warrant confidence in this strategy."

5. "Computers in Banking," CHI/COR Information Management, Inc., internally-conducted survey, 1986.

6. Phantom hotsites are referred to in correspondence received from HOTSITE®, and in a Diaster Avoidance and Recovery Information Group (DARING) panel discussion in Clearwater, FL, in November 1986. Representatives from COMDISCO Disaster Recovery Services, CompuSource, HOTSITE®, and Sungard Recovery Services served as panelists.

7. Information for this section obtained through correspondence and telephone conversations with hot site vendor representatives Kevin Hephner, HOTSITE®, and James Hunter, Sungard Recovery Services, who also provided sample contracts to the author.

Chapter 6

Strategies
for Network Backup

Planning for business recovery entails more than developing strategies for the backup of computer hardware, critical applications, and data. It must also consider computer sysytem users who produce information assets and users of the end-products of information processing who provide critical and vital business functions.

This community of users may be quite vast. It may include employees and managers of the company (the classic definition of the user community) as well as a host of others who trade with the company, monitor or regulate its activities, or consume its products and services. Facilitating business recovery following a disaster, therefore, requires that business functions be rigorously analyzed and thoroughly understood. The coordinator needs to know what and how information enters the business (inputs), how the information is used and manipulated (processes), and where or to whom the information product (output) is directed.

The disaster recovery coordinator must examine not only computer systems that provide information processing functions, but also the communications capabilities that provide the conduits for user access to processors and data products. In short, the coordinator must understand the communications networks that surround processors and make their work purposeful.

There are basically three types, or layers, of communications networks in modern business information systems.[1] These may be viewed as three concentric circles with a processor at their hub (see Figure 6.1).

The innermost layer consists of internal networks—networks that exist within the physical confines of the company itself. Included in this layer are peripheral devices, such as terminals and printers, connected by various means directly to a CPU, which exchange data over short distances with the processor. This layer also contains local area networks (LANs) that may be used to provide shared access to a central database, to optimize the capabilities of connected devices, substitute distributed for centralized information processing functions, or facilitate interoffice communications. Finally, the internal network layer commonly includes a voice and/or data communications network, often consisting of a Private Branch Exchange (PBX) and numerous communications devices—telephones, modems, teletypes, data communications terminals, FAX machines, and various traffic measurement/ accounting/troubleshooting devices.

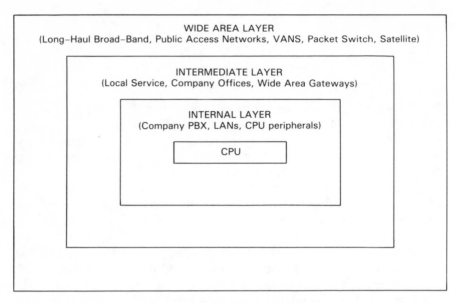

Figure 6.1   Three Network Layers.

The second, or intermediate, layer of networks has become of more practical significance since the divestiture of AT&T. Intermediate layer networks are those of local and regional telephone and communications companies. Local-area vendors control communications traffic that originates and terminates within the local vicinity by means of company offices (COs), which are outfitted with traffic switching equipment. In many cases, local COs also provide the gateway to the third layer of wide-area or long distance networks, although there are now a number of options for circumventing the local CO in accessing the third network layer.

The third layer, then, consists of wide area networks that handle the movement of voice and data traffic across great distances. These networks range from public access networks, to value-added networks (VANs), packet-switching networks, and satellite communications networks.

Preliminary Activities in Network Recovery Planning

It is the disaster recovery coordinator's job to identify the dependency of business functions on the proper operation and the availability of each type of network service. The coordinator must next assess the impact of a loss of service on the company. Finally, the coordinator must develop strategies to prevent avoidable losses and minimize the impact of losses that cannot be prevented. Figure 6.2 is a data flow diagram showing the generic components of a process that may aid in the development of effective network backup and recovery strategies. A discussion of some of the preliminary activities follows.

1. Review the risk analysis document. The risk analysis document, created at the outset of the disaster recovery planning project, contains information about critical business functions and the automated systems and networks that support them. The risk analysis should be reviewed to identify dependencies on networks, the criticality of network services, and the minimum service levels that will be required for business continuation.

2. Obtain network configuration documentation. In addition to the insights obtained through risk analysis, the coordinator may need to solicit the assistance of a company telecommunications manager, network administrator, and/or network security manager to develop a network configuration diagram[2] depicting network operations under normal business operating conditions (see Figure 6.3 for an example of a simplified network configuration diagram).[3]

    Subordinate diagrams may also have to be compiled showing specific characteristics of internal networks, including LAN topologies and protocol architectures, characteristics of transmission media between network nodes, and traffic patterns, loads, and transmission rates.

    If the networks used by a company were developed using a planning methodology, such as the one illustrated in Figure 6.4,[4] much of the needed documentation may already exist. However, if networks evolved over a period of time—in response to company needs rather than in anticipation of them—documenting the current configuration may be a considerable undertaking.

    Either way, good network documentation is prerequisite to the task of relating critical business functions and applications to specific communications services. It provides a framework that the disaster recovery coordinator can use to analyze what effect the loss of a particular network service will have on the company. This, in turn, can guide the disaster recovery coordinator in planning measures to safeguard against network failures that threaten critical functions.

3. Build disaster scenarios. Once network configuration documentation has been prepared, the disaster recovery coordinator may find it useful to develop scenarios to account for failures within networks that could lead to unacceptable network service levels for critical

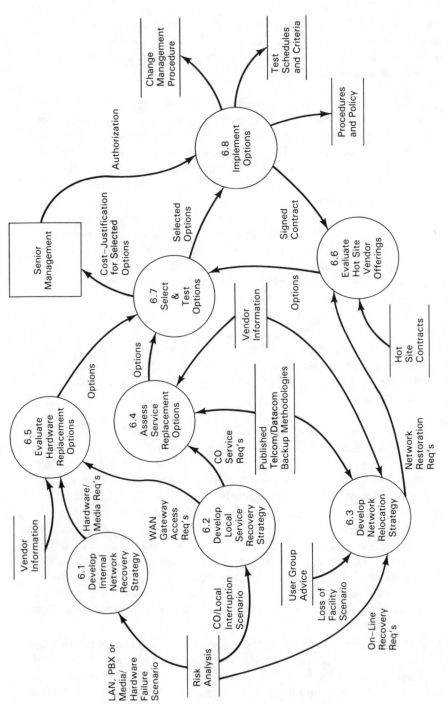

Figure 6.2 Network Recovery Plan Development.

134

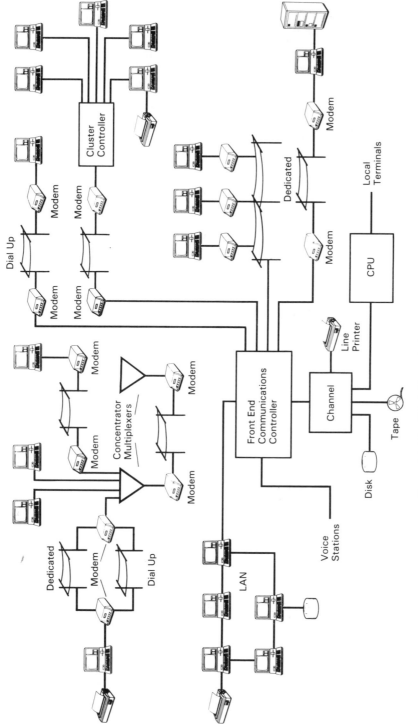

Figure 6.3 Simplified Network Configuration Diagram.

135

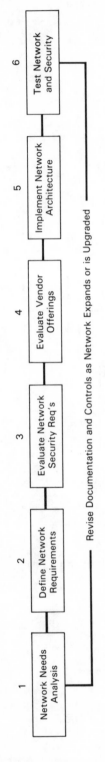

1. Set up planning team; identify user network requirements; determine loads; survey technology.
2. Specify network requirements; identify pertinent environmental considerations; develop selection criteria; select target vendors.
3. Evaluate threats and risks; plan security measures and controls; draft corporate communications policy.
4. Analyze vendor proposals; select vendors.
5. Document network architecture; plan installation; implement network.
6. Test integrity and security of system; obtain user sign–off; monitor and log utilization, MTBF, causes of downtime; plan hardware maintenance.

Figure 6.4 Network Planning Process Model.

business functions. Often scenario building begins with an examination of internal networks. The disaster recovery coordinator assumes that a fire, flood, or other event has destroyed a critical network device, or that software (application or system) has been corrupted. The coordinator then develops strategies for recovering these networks.

Such a device failure within an internal network is just one type of disaster that may confront a business. There are variants in this scenario that may also need to be considered in network recovery planning. For example, a fire which devastates the data center might leave a PBX or a LAN, distributed throughout user work areas, intact. It follows then that a scenario needs to be developed to reflect how the overall configuration of company networks would be altered to accommodate new communications requirements of running data processing operations from a hot site.

Another risk that needs to be addressed is a loss of service resulting from a local CO failure. A brief summary of recent events helps to illustrate this disaster recovery requirement.

- In February, 1987, a switching computer for AT&T communications failed, isolating the 214 area code (incoming and outgoing calls) for five hours, blocking more than two and one-half million calls.
- A Dallas-based mortgage company, serving over 100 branch offices and client companies, sustained four devastating cable cuts in an 18-month period.
- In February, 1986, an AT&T fiber optic cable was hacksawed during a company strike, disrupting a significant amount of West Coast traffic.
- In February, 1987, fire damaged a Bell central office in New York City, cutting service to 40,000 customers for up to a month.[5]

Whether caused by a cut line, a union strike, a hurricane, or a terrorist event, CO failures can cut communications within the local area as well as close access points or gateways to wide area network services. Thus, a CO failure needs to be considered in the scenario-building process and alternatives to CO-provided services developed.

Still another network-related disaster scenario considers the loss of both company data processing and network facilities. In this case, plans need to be developed for recovering network service levels at both the system and user recovery sites and for restoring communications between them.

Depending on the company, additional scenarios may need to be developed to address specific network vulnerabilities. For example, companies located on the shores of the Gulf of Mexico or along the Atlantic seaboard may need to make special provisions for the threat of hurricanes, while this may not be a concern for companies located inland.

Strategies for Network Backup and Recovery

Once the above preliminary steps are completed, the disaster recovery coordinator will be able to address specific network recovery issues. At first glance, the multiplicity of scenarios might seem overwhelming. In the face of such diversity, disaster recovery coordinators may be inclined to forego the headache of planning for network failures, except in their worst case manifestation (i.e., total loss of company facilities). Indeed, attempting to plan for every conceivable contingency would prove an unmanageable task.

Fortunately, the principles of redundancy and backup can be successfully applied to creating strategies to cope with most network failures. By making plans for less-than-worst case scenarios, the coordinator may also find that a pattern of problem escalation emerges that will support emergency management decision making.

Several generic options for recovering failed networks are presented in the following sections.

- **Internal communications systems.** Planning for the recovery of internal communications networks must consider two aspects of the network: station failures and PBX failures. In most modern PBX-based voice and data communications networks, the failure of a station or group of stations will not cause the PBX to fail. Indeed, station failures, due to media faults or hardware malfunctions, are often treated as maintenance issues rather than disaster recovery issues. It is conceivable, however, that the loss of network wiring integrity could create an emergency for the affected operational area of the company. Thus, line redundancy may be a valid measure to insure network integrity for critical business functions. It is also important to acquire appropriate network diagnostic and troubleshooting software and to train technicians in its use so that sources of trouble within the network can be rapidly localized, identified, and repaired.

In the event of a PBX failure, two alternatives may speed recovery. First, sufficient private or dedicated lines (i.e., analog or digital lines that do not have to operated through the switch itself) may be installed for critical, telecommunications-dependent functions. These lines can be used to handle critical traffic until the PBX malfunction can be resolved or the unit replaced.

However, in addition to leasing private lines, companies having a very high level of dependence upon telecommunications can employ another alternative. For some companies, leasing sufficient private lines to sustain critical functions may be more costly than purchasing a second switch and programming it in advance with the network control programs that are resident on the primary unit. In such a case, purchasing or leasing a backup PBX may provide a cost-effective recovery option.

If a second PBX is obtained, common sense dictates that it be located in a different area than the primary unit within the company facility. In this way, the second unit may be insulated from disaster conditions that effect the primary switch. Both the primary and secondary PBX installations should also be backed up for power (via UPS), have appropriate climate control, and be equipped with a suitable fire detection/suppression capability.

Many modern PBXs are programmable. Station services and capabilities (i.e., call pickup, call forwarding) may be defined in a series of program statements or "translations." It is important to ensure that these programmed instructions are backed up regularly to portable media, and a copy of the backup stored off-site for recovery purposes.

- **Computer peripherals.** Computer input and output devices, together with the CPU to which they are attached, make up a straightforward (though often complex) data communications network. As with PBX stations, hardware failures can generally be readily detected, and redundant hardware stocked for immediate replacement of failed critical devices.

  Cabling is another vulnerable aspect of these networks, but exposures to severe loss due to cable cuts or other problems can often be predicted and limited. Proper up-front planning for long cable runs will help ensure that obvious hazards are avoided. Careful attention to proper grounding and surge protection can prevent lightning and other surges from being conducted back to the CPU or attached device resulting in damage.

  Furthermore, until a cut cable can be repaired, it may be possible to utilize alternative media to handle data traffic. Balun™

adapters, for example, may be employed with some systems to convert coaxial cables for use with PBX station wiring.[6]

- **LANs.** Local Area Networks (LANs) pose a complicated problem for disaster recovery planning because of the diversity of types, functions, transmission media, and topologies currently in use. PC LANs have grown from 33,000 installations in 1984 to a projected 521,960 installations in 1990.[7] Driving the growth has been the desire of companies "to consolidate PC resources into manageable work groups around functional or common application areas." The average number of PCs connected to a LAN in 1987 was eight, or nearly 1.3 million PCs installed in LAN configurations alone.[8] Unlike conventional mainframe computer terminals, workstations may actually participate in the processing of data, creating the need for multiple backups of data, multiple uninterruptible power supplies, and multiple physical security capabilities.

Despite these factors, some types of LANs can be readily protected against catastrophic loss due to the failure of a node (an individual workstation), loss of media integrity, or software-related factors. The solution resides in the software used to create and control the LAN.

LAN communication may be viewed as a multifaceted programming problem. It is depicted as such by the International Standards Organization in their open systems interconnection (OSI) model of data communications.[9]

Figure 6.5 illustrates the OSI model as it applies to peer communications within a LAN.

As the model suggests, there are seven levels, or layers, of data communications between two computers. These layers correspond to software components imbedded in the computer's operating system. The following summary describes the layer functions taken from preliminary documentation on the OSI model.[10]

Layer 7: Application—The application layer provides the commands or functions, such as file transfer, document printing, or electronic mail, by which the workstation communicates with other available or open workstations and peripherals on the network. The command will not result in the actual performance of the function, however, until it has been interpreted by other protocol layers.

Frequently, common application service elements (CASE) defined in the application layer allow application programs to find each other and exchange information without requiring special user intervention and guidance.

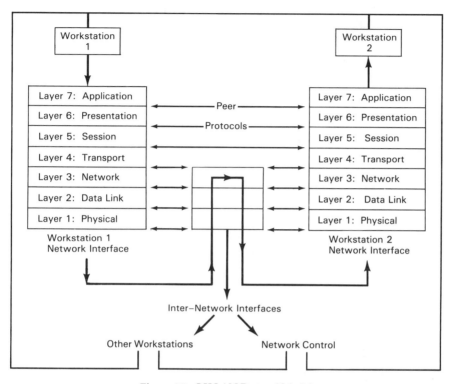

Figure 6.5   OSI LAN Protocol Model.
Source: Lorne A. Dear and Fred Gallegos, "Planning for the Security of Local Area Networks,"
Data Security Mangement (New York: Auerbach Publishers, 1986).

Layer 6: Presentation—This layer provides translation, and sometimes encryption and compression, functions in intranetwork communications. The presentation layer thus provides communication
between workstations with disparate internal codes as well as
security in network communications.

Layer 5: Session—The session layer is responsible for handling conversations between network nodes. In addition to managing node
interaction, the session layer oversees network operating conditions
and can reestablish communications after temporary disruption of
network connections. The session layer also provides a means for
mapping network node addresses to names, thus minimizing the
impact to application programs of hardware changes within the network.

Layer 4: Transport—The transport layer provides error checking between nodes during communication. In the event of an erred trans-

mission, layer four may generate error messages and requests for retransmission of data.

Layer 3: Network—This layer provides internetwork communications as well as the translation of logical addresses (node names) into physical addresses. It also serves as a traffic controller, selecting the best route on the network for communications between two nodes.

Layer 2: Data Link—The data link layer handles the packaging of data to be communicated and its successful entry onto the network. Data may be packaged as frames or packets and, depending on the network software, may conform to certain packaging standards such as those articulated by the Institute of Electrical and Electronic Engineers (IEEE). If packets arrive at their destination in a corrupt or improper form, layer two may notify layer four to signal an error and request retransmission.

Layer 1: Physical—This layer consists of the hardwired instructions of the network—cabling and physical circuitry. Depending on the media, this layer defines the signaling method that is to be used to represent on and off bits.

It is important to understand clearly the functions provided by the network software used in the LAN that is to be safeguarded against disaster. Network products differ widely in their adherence to the OSI model, with some software packages providing the functions of several layers in a single layer. Generally, the functions of layers one and two are provided by network interface cards and cabling. The functionality of layers three through five is usually provided through network software. The functions of layers six and seven may be provided by workstation operating systems, application software, or both.

Knowing how the OSI model functions with company LANs may help the disaster recovery coordinator in several ways. First, the coordinator can use the information collected about the LAN to determine how network nodes are identified (i.e., by name or physical address). If nodes are identified by name, hardware comprising nodes may be able to be changed readily in the event that a workstation fails, or different workstations need to be used to restore the LAN at a recovery site. If hard coded addresses are used to identify nodes (i.e., firmware associated with specific network interface cards), replacement of node hardware and restoration of network operations may be more complicated and time consuming.

Security-related factors are also of importance in network software. Generally, layers six, four, three, and two are utilized to provide security for data and applications on the LAN. The disaster recovery coordinator needs to understand the security measures being employed to determine the extent to which they might interfere with node or network recovery.

LANs need not always be recovered in their original topology. In certain cases, the applications and data that are being shared across the LAN are portable to a mainframe or other central processor. If LAN applications are critical, it may be possible to plan to move them in an emergency to a central CPU. There, the programs and data can be accessed, in a dial-up mode, by users from a recovery site.

Because of the flexibility of most LANs and their ability to communicate with workstations, processors, and other devices that are outside the network topology, it may be possible to back up LAN data to a remote storage device. The use of such a centralized storage device may provide a valuable alternative to backing up data at each and every node of the LAN.

If access to a central storage device is not forthcoming, LAN software may be harnessed to facilitate disaster recovery by notifying users at regular intervals that their data needs to be saved and backed up. Software may go further to deny general network access to a user who has not backed up data according to network policy. Thus, a LAN can provide administrative controls that will help safeguard network data against loss.

In addition to an internal network failure scenario, the disaster recovery coordinator also needs to consider how networks will be reconfigured to accommodate data center recovery in the event that the company's data center, but not its internal networks or user work areas, is lost. To accomplish this, the following factors may need to be considered:

• **Availability of wide area communications lines.** The disaster recovery coordinator needs to examine the company's long distance telecommunications service. Lines that handle incoming data communications traffic to the mainframe may need to be switched to a hot site or other mainframe recovery location. If the lines themselves cannot be readily switched, a procedure must be developed to notify those who must communicate with the company host about the changes in dial-up modem numbers.

Some of the major long distance carriers offer rerouting services[11] that can be used to redirect traffic to a predefined location within minutes of a customer directive to do so. Rerouting traffic over private networks may be similarly prearranged. Rerouting services however can be expensive, consisting of a monthly charge and a hefty initial setup fee. Thus, if the number who must communicate with the company mainframe is few, the disaster recovery coordinator may elect to notify them individually of a telephone number change and make use of public or private long distance services available from the relocation site or service bureau.

Besides the need to reroute incoming traffic aimed at the mainframe, there is also a need to reestablish user contact with the mainframe so that work can be performed. Most hot sites, service bureaus and even commercial cold sites provide strategies and/or capabilities to the customer for reestablishing user-mainframe communications. Figures 6.6 through 6.14 are network recovery offerings from two vendors of hot site backup facilities.

Coordinators should be aware that there are a host of available alternatives, but that these strategies may not be suitable for every facility. Strategies should be based upon the following considerations and practices.[12]

1. **Terminal Activity Profile.** Before a network backup strategy can be developed, the coordinator must know the activity level for each terminal that will have to access the remote processor. Since only critical applications will be available at the remote processing site, it is probable that not all users will need to have access.

   For those who do need access to the restored system, the coordinator must know the characteristics of their terminal use. If the terminal usage will be high in terms of both the amount of time on-line and/or the frequency of transactions, the associated telecommunications connection will have to accommodate this high volume. If terminal usage is low, the coordinator may wish to concentrate the data communications of several low-volume terminals using multiplexing or related techniques.

   The purpose of this analysis is to identify the minimum number of long distance lines (and related hardware) that will be needed to connect critical terminals to the mainframe recovery site via telecommunications.

2. **Minimum Acceptable Service Levels.** Factors such as response time in on-line applications and throughput for batch applications also need to be considered in evaluating minimum number of lines and concentration techniques to be employed.

3. **Line Requirements and Alternative Recovery Methods.** Once a minimum number of lines and related hardware requirements have been identified, alternatives for obtaining the required capabilities

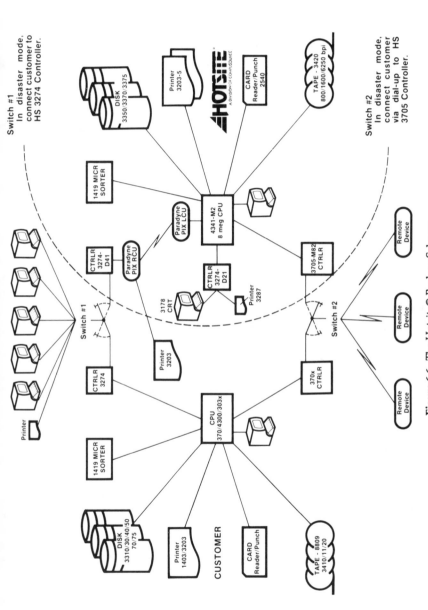

Figure 6.6 The Hotsite® Backup Scheme.

Source: Hotsite®, Division of RMI Company, Niles, Ohio. Reprinted by permission.

145

IMPLEMENTATION ALTERNATIVES
TWO-WIRE DIAL

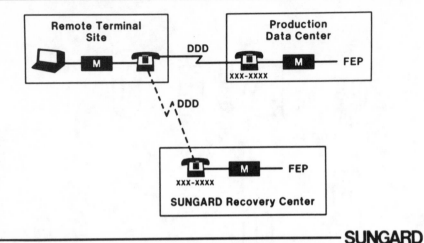

Figure 6.7 Implementation Alternatives: Two-Wire Dial.

IMPLEMENTATION ALTERNATIVES
FOUR-WIRE DIAL BACKUP

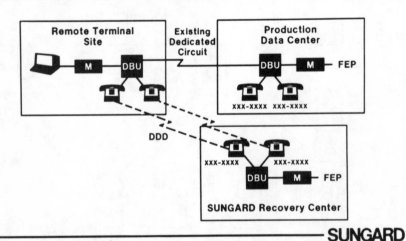

Figure 6.8 Impementation Alternatives: Four-Wire Dial Backup.

IMPLEMENTATION ALTERNATIVES

CIRCUIT EXTENSION (ANALOG OR DIGITAL)

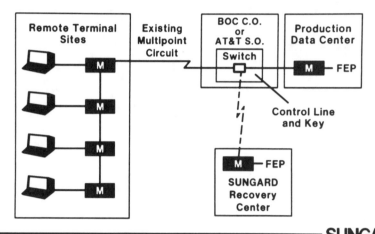

SUNGARD

Figure 6.9 Implementation Alternatives: Circuit Extension (Analog or Digital).

IMPLEMENTATION ALTERNATIVES

MULTIPLEXING CENTER (USING FOUR-WIRE DIAL BACKUP)

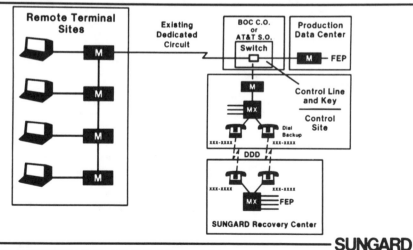

SUNGARD

Figure 6.10 Implementation Alternatives: Multiplexing Center (Using Four-Wire Dial Backup).

IMPLEMENTATION ALTERNATIVES

MULTIPLEXING CENTER (USING SWITCHED DIGITAL FACILITIES)

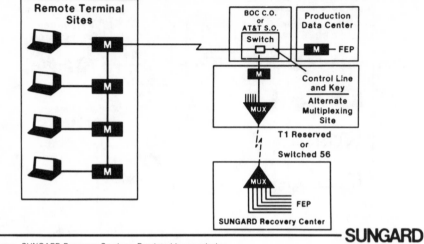

Source: SUNGARD Recovery Services. Reprinted by permission.

Figure 6.11 Implementation Alternatives: Multiplexing Center (Using Switched Digital Facilities).

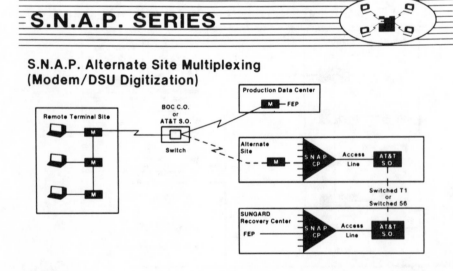

Source: SUNGARD Recovery Services. Reprinted by permission.

Figure 6.12 S.N.A.P. Alternate Site Multiplexing (Modem/ DSU Digitization).

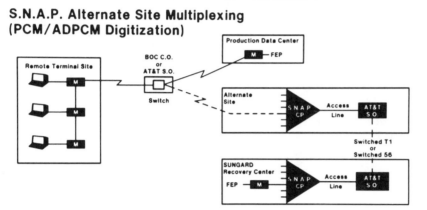

S.N.A.P. Alternate Site Multiplexing (PCM/ADPCM Digitization)

Source: SUNGARD Recovery Services. Reprinted by permission.

Figure 6.13 S.N.A.P. Alternate Site Multiplexing (PCM/ADPCM Digitization).

Serving Office Multiplexing / S.N.A.P. T1 S.O.

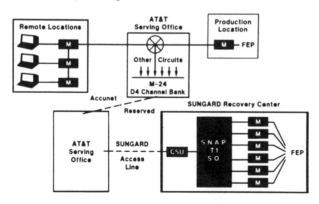

Source: SUNGARD Recovery Services. Reprinted by permission.

Figure 6.14 Serving Office Multiplexing/S.N.A.P. T1 S.O.

need to be examined. There are several options for providing the necessary transmission lines for data communications, including the use of current outgoing wide area services.

If sufficient data-grade long distance lines are available in the current PBX configuration to accommodate both user terminals and critical company activities, reassigning lines to accommodate individual and clustered terminals is a fairly straightforward operation. If there are insufficient available lines, additional lines may need to be installed either at the time of the disaster (entailing considerable delays) or as a redundant capability prior to their need.

If redundant lines are leased, or if sufficient capability exists to reterminate existing lines, the recovery coordinator should perform the following steps where feasible.

  (a) Document the recovery network configuration. A schematic of how the network should look once the recovery strategy is implemented is worth a thousand words.

  (b) If applicable, provide a patch panel change form to show in which blocks patch cords that need to be moved will terminate. Also, where applicable, prepare a diskette or tape containing new translations for the recovery configuration. This will save time that might otherwise be lost by having to program new translations at the time of the disaster.

  (c) Verify that necessary equipment to be used for recovery (i.e., multiplexers, cluster controllers) is available from the hot site vendor, or can be acquired from company stock or local suppliers on short notice. If prearrangements cannot be made to obtain hardware, document the names of suppliers who will be contacted to supply hardware on an emergency basis.

In addition to a network failure, or data center failure, another contingency scenario that the disaster recovery coordinator may need to consider is that of a failure of the local telephone company. The local CO provides local area telecommunications service and, more often than not, is the gateway to wide area or long distance networks.

Strategies for recovery of local and wide area network services in the event of a local CO outage are costly, and must be justified against the costs to the company of an outage of this kind. During a problematic changeover from relay to digital switching in 1986 at a local CO in Florida, customers experienced intermittent outages in long distance service. One company, the national telemarketing concern Home Shopping Network, experienced dollar losses amounting to $3,000 per minute over the three week period.[13] If substantial losses can be demonstrated from CO outages, this can strengthen the case that options for CO-provided services are needed, however expensive they may be.

What are the options? Basically, they are twofold and selection depends on how critical local or long distance services are to the company. For local services provided by the CO, a company may elect to obtain services from a second CO in the general vicinity of its offices. The expenses involved in running lines to a company that is not located in the operating area of a given CO can be quite high, although the costs of having this capability can be minimized by using alternative circuits for testing only, until an outage at the primary CO occurs.

If the major risk entailed in an interruption of local CO operation is the loss of a gateway to long distance networks, there are a number of alternatives that the coordinator should explore. One alternative that a number of national banks have already installed is a company-owned microwave uplink. In the absence of CO gateway services, the banks can switch their mode of long distance access to satellite. Disaster recovery coordinators should be aware, however, that there are some legal ramifications when satellite and microwave transmission are utilized to communicate certain financial and private credit information. Coordinators who are considering the satellite alternative should explore this issue in greater detail with auditors and lawyers as well as technical experts before proceeding.

It should also be mentioned that a movement is afoot to utilize satellite communication to provide remote storage of backup data at vaults that are equipped to receive it. This concept—*data vaulting*—holds much promise for the secure storage of critical data at remote off-site facilities in the future, but is beset by the same legal and technical problems confronting companies that wish to transmit private credit information to networks by this means.

Another alternative to local CO service may be found in the form of independent cable, radio, or microwave links to private-access networks or privately-operated network gateways. Figure 6.15 shows one such configuration offered by a network disaster recovery vendor.

Besides private vendors, however, several well-known telecommunications carriers offer companies that demonstrate sufficient need and potential use the ability to circumvent local COs by running private lines directly to a local network access point, or point-of-presence. Media, access fees, and special line runs are costly, but if a company already has a substantial stake in uninterrupted access to wide area networks, the cost of ensuring that access may be viewed as a means of protecting its investment.

TYPICAL PREMIERE TELECOMMUNICATIONS RECOVERY
ASSEMBLY
(DALLAS AREA CLIENT)

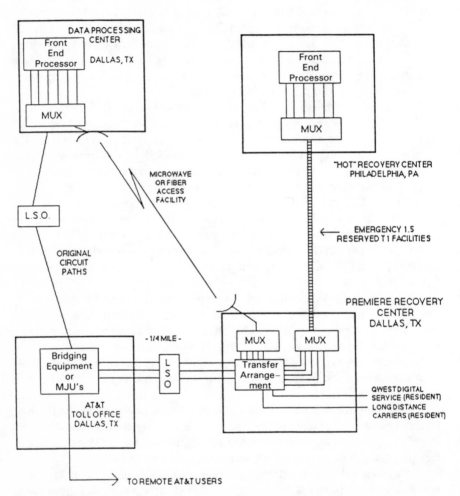

Figure 6.15 Typical Premiere Telecommunications Recovery Assembly.
Source: Premier Network Services, Inc. Reprinted by permission.

Recovery Strategies for a Total Loss of Corporate Facilities

The scenario that is the subject of the most discussion in disaster recovery
planning is the one envisioning the total loss of company facilities.

Recovery strategies must provide for restoration of data communications at acceptable levels between the user recovery facility and the computer recovery facility (hot site, cold site, service bureau, redundant data center, etc.). The principles and techniques discussed in the previous sections are portable to recovery strategies for total facility loss.

For example, before any of the following recovery strategies can be employed, terminal usage profiles and other up-front analyses must be conducted to determine how many and what types of communications services will be required at the recovery sites. In addition, essential communications hardware, needed to support the recovery, must be identified and acquired (or suppliers identified and arrangements made to provide hardware within an acceptable time frame). Finally, a new configuration for networks operating under total disaster conditions needs to be developed.

The disaster recovery coordinator must perform the above preliminary steps before engaging in discussions with vendors and suppliers to decide upon the specific components of a network recovery strategy. The following components are typical of such a strategy:

* **Redirection of incoming communications traffic.** Redirecting incoming long distance and local communications traffic to alternative user and data center recovery sites is primarily a technical problem. A number of good technical sources are available to the coordinator who is exploring this problem. Summaries of some of the redirection techniques that may be appropriate follow.

  Vendor-provided rerouting services—A number of long distance carriers provide automatic long distance rerouting services to their customers on a fee-paid basis. For this service to be worthwhile, however, the customer must know where users will be relocating and what communications hardware will be available at the user relocation site. If these facts are known, rerouting can be accomplished within minutes of a customer request.

  Local lines can also be redirected to a predetermined recovery site by arrangement with a local CO office. This service can be provided by bridging incoming circuits and switching them to a prearranged path. For large numbers of circuits, this service can be very expensive, and the service itself is available only for circuits that pass through the local CO.

  If the location (and telephone numbers) of hot sites or other data processing backup facilities are known in advance of a disaster, the above rerouting methods may be used for data communications lines as well.

The benefits of these rerouting services are that they can be implemented quickly and are evident to those who need to communicate with the company.

Other rerouting methods—While considerable attention is often paid to planning for the recovery of data processing operations, user recovery is often less well planned. If a user relocation site has not been designated in advance, vendor rerouting services may be inappropriate or unavailable. Where this is the case, the following steps will need to be taken at the time of the disaster.

First, a user recovery site will have to be located and sufficient telecommunications-handling equipment acquired and installed. Next, if telephone service is not immediately available at the recovery site, it will have to be installed. Finally, those who need to communicate with the company will have to be notified, either individually or via a recording, of the new telephone (and modem) numbers, until traffic can be rerouted directly to the recovery site.

Locating a facility and connecting communications service can be time-consuming. For companies that have assigned a dollar value to the cost of downtime, the maximum allowable time frame for accomplishing these tasks may be as short as a few hours. In reality, the tasks may take a few days, or even weeks, depending on the scope of the disaster and the number of companies (including the local CO) that have been affected. For effective network recovery in companies that are highly network-dependent, therefore, prearranged recovery sites are a practical necessity.

The fact remains that an overwhelming number of companies have no fixed user recovery site. Thus, assuming that the company is not lost in the time that it takes to find and outfit a site with the prerequisite hardware and lines, the following steps may be taken.

1. Plan to have the local CO or long distance carrier "busy" incoming lines to the company.

2. Either activate rerouting services that have been prearranged or notify communicators of the new modem number by calling them individually or via a recording. This can be done only if data processing has been relocated to an alternate site and is ready to receive data communications.

3. Notify users of the new numbers by the best possible route once the user recovery site is prepared, and coordinate the rerouting of incoming traffic on the old circuits to the new location by the most expedient means.

- **Establishment of the terminal to mainframe link.** Reestablishing communications between users and a remote CPU is the second of the twin goals of network recovery. This objective requires the fulfillment of the following tasks:

Obtain Hardware and Software—If prior arrangements were not made for a user recovery site, one of the first tasks in reestablishing the user-mainframe link may include the acquisition of terminals, terminal emulation software, controllers, and communications hardware. Suppliers for these items (and backup suppliers) should be identified by the disaster recovery coordinator and contact names recorded in the disaster recovery plan. If a hot site is used for CPU recovery, the hot site will probably be providing some of the communications hardware that is required.

Configure Hardware—Once hardware is acquired, it must be installed according to the disaster recovery configuration developed and tested in the planning stage.

Link Users to the Remote CPU—This task is dependent upon the successful completion of communications network restoration. Disaster recovery plans should include routines for testing hardware and communications lines before the system is made available to users for actual work.

Special consideration should be given to the security and integrity of data communications in the new network. Data that is deemed sensitive in normal operations remains sensitive in a recovery operations mode. All levels of program and database security should be rigorously tested both at the CPU recovery site and at the user recovery site to ensure that one disaster does not lead to another.

Integrity in data communications refers to the susceptibility of the data being transmitted to corruption due to a hostile communications environment. If data is being transmitted over new routes, there may be new environmental factors that can corrupt it. It is therefore important to obtain the "cleanest" media possible to handle communications between the user backup facility and CPU backup facility. Coordinators may also wish to consider installing new error-checking software to facilitate detection and correction of data communications errors due to line noise and other environmental factors.

REFERENCES

1. The concept of a three-tier or tri-layer business communications network appears in the literature of major vendors of network hardware and software, and is referred to in Robert P. Campbell, "Survivability: More than

Redundant Lines and Hardware," *Telecommunications Products and Technology*, Vol. 4, no. 12 (December 1986).

2. Ibid.

3. Jerry FitzGerald, "Security and Control in Data Communications Systems," in *Data Security Management* (New York: Auerbach Publishers, 1986).

4. Lorne A. Dear and Frederick Gallegos, "Planning for the Security of Local Area Networks," in *Data Security Management* (New York: Auerbach Publishers, 1986).

5. From a listing of CO failures prepared by Premier Network Services, Inc., Dallas, TX, 1987.

6. *The Promised LAN: Integrated Networks*, attendee booklet, AT&T Information Systems, Central Region Customer Education Center, Denver, CO 1986.

7. Dana Richens, ed., *Local Area Networking Sourcebook*, 4th ed. (Potomac, MD: Phillips Publishing Co., 1987), pp. 314- 328.

8. Ibid.

9. Eric Spiewak, "Networking Schemes Integrate Islands of Automation," *Telecommunication Products Plus Technology*, Vol. 4, no. 2 (February 1986).

10. Material on the OSI model is drawn from the following sources: Dick Lefkon, "The OSI Model: A Seven-Layer Cake Made Simple," *LAN Magazine* (February 1987); Spiewak, "Networking Schemes"; Dear and Gallegos, "Planning for the Security of Local Area Networks."

11. See AT&T, "Advanced 800 Service Command Routing," 1985 brochure.

12. Thomas J. Murray and James M. Domanico, "Network Disaster Recovery Planning-Part II," *Data Security Management* (New York: Auerbach Publishers, 1987).

13. Home Shopping Network, in 1987, filed suit against General Telephone of Florida for dollar losses accrued to excessive call blockage by the local CO. The outcome of the suit could decide several interesting issues that touch the core of disaster liability in CO-related network failures.

Chapter 7

Emergency Decision Making

One aspect of disaster recovery that is particularly elusive and difficult for many disaster recovery coordinators to treat adequately in their plans is emergency management. Emergency management planning aims at the management of three projects that are intrinsic to disaster recovery: evacuation, recovery, and relocation or reentry.

An emergency management plan provides the skeleton of a disaster recovery plan—the organizational and policy structure that will be referenced to determine whether and by whom the disaster recovery plan will be invoked and who will do what when. Development of the emergency management plan (see Figure 7.1) requires the disaster recovery coordinator to (1) designate recovery teams and assign responsibilities; (2) work with other managers to staff the teams; and (3) develop timelines and flowcharts identifying the sequence of—and interrelationships among—various disaster recovery tasks. The third aspect is often the most difficult for several reasons.

First, most disaster recovery coordinators have never directly experienced a company disaster. Those who have offer mixed reviews of the performance of flowcharts portending to map crisis decision making. Efforts to predict and chart every conceivable decision are usually inadequate in real life situations, and procedures that spell out too rigidly what each recovery team member will do—step-by-step, thought-by-thought—are often set aside in the frantic, urgent, and imperfect world of disaster recovery.

That coordinators sometimes provide too much detail is only one of the problems in emergency management planning. In some cases, emergency management is viewed as a mere extension of normal management practices and little thought is given to how managers will perform their duties in an actual disaster situation. However, experience dictates that, in the absence of such a plan, there can be little coordination of recovery strategies, particularly intricate and detailed strategies for system and network recovery.

The message from those who have experienced disasters is that, without an emergency management plan that provides for top-down direction and coordination of recovery tasks, inefficiencies can result that will extend the length of downtime. If the business is out of operation for too long, regardless of the integrity of plan components, the plan itself will be ineffective in supporting business recovery.

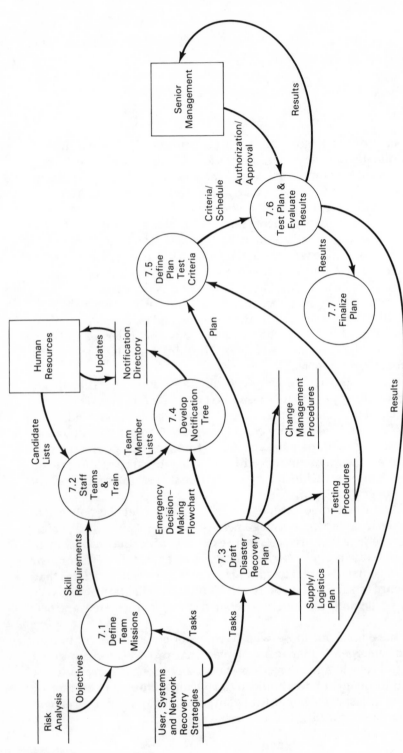

Figure 7.1 Plan Staffing, Testing, and Management.

Thus, coordinators need to develop an emergency management plan that will formalize certain aspects of the management process and provide guidance for managing situations that cannot be anticipated prior to a disaster. Such a plan is less than a script for emergency management from which actors dare not stray, but it is also more than a collection of platitudes.

The following discussion aims to clarify emergency management planning by detailing its several dimensions and typical components.

Designating Teams

One of the first steps in emergency management planning is to identify where personnel will need to be allocated in order to implement the strategies that have been developed for business recovery. Of less importance at this stage is the task of assigning individuals to each team based on their skills and knowledge. Team assignments will be discussed in greater detail later this chapter.

Teams should be created in response to a critical recovery function or task defined in the plan. With properly organized plan documents, the coordinator should be able to look to the plan's table of contents for an overview of plan functions. The reason for this is simple: Most plans are compiled as procedures are developed to accommodate system, user, and network recovery strategies. There is usually a section devoted to each of the following subjects.

SECTION 1.   Emergency Action—Procedures for reacting to crises, ranging from Halon activation procedures to emergency evacuations.

SECTION 2.   Notification—Procedures for notifying relevant managers in the event of a disaster. A contact list of home and emergency telephone numbers is typically provided.

SECTION 3.   Disaster Declaration—Procedures pertaining to the assessment of damage following a disaster, criteria for determining whether the situation *is* a disaster, and procedures for declaring a disaster and invoking the plan.

SECTION 4.   Systems Recovery Procedures—Procedures to be followed to restore critical and vital systems at emergency service levels within a specified time frame in accordance with the systems recovery strategy defined in the plan.

SECTION 5.   Network Recovery Procedures—Procedures to
reinstate voice and data communications at emergency service levels within a specified time frame
in accordance with the network recovery strategy
defined in the plan.

SECTION 6.   User Recovery Procedures—Procedures for
recovering critical and vital user functions within
a specified time frame in accordance with
planned strategy.

SECTION 7.   Salvage Operations Procedures—Procedures for
salvaging facilities, records and hardware, often
including the filing of insurance claims and the
determination of the feasibility of reoccupying
the disaster site.

SECTION 8.   Relocation Procedures—Procedures for relocating
emergency operations (system, network and
user) to the original or a new facility, and the restoration of normal service levels.

When viewed from the perspective of three distinct disaster
recovery projects, the procedures in sections 1-3 pertain to the evacuation
project; sections 4-7, to the recovery project; and section 8 to the relocation or reentry project. Teams are developed to fulfill the requirements of
each project.

What are the functional requirements of the evacuation project?
Basically, there are three. First, the emergency must be met with an appropriate response. Responses range from use of an extinguisher to suppress a small fire, to evacuating hardware in the hours before a hurricane,
to evacuating personnel in a bomb threat.

The second function is assessing damage caused by the disaster and
determining whether disaster declaration criteria have been met. If the
coordinator has determined that 24 hours is the maximum length of time
that the company can be without critical or vital operations, this might be
established as the criterion for declaring a disaster. If the affected site will
be out of service for more than 24 hours, it may be necessary to declare a
disaster and activate the plan. However, to make this determination, site
damage will need to be accurately assessed and realistic recovery time
frames estimated.

The third function is to declare a disaster and invoke the plan. The
plan may need to be activated in whole or in part, since a data center disaster may not affect user facilities, or a telecommunications switchroom

fire may leave both DP and user work areas intact. Activating the disaster recovery plan also entails certain risks from a public relations standpoint. A bank, for example, may experience panic withdrawals by customers if a disaster declaration is perceived as impending bank failure.[1]

This list is not exhaustive and there may be other functions within the evacuation project that are specific to a given company. However, to fulfill the three basic requirements for evacuation, the following teams may be developed:

1. Emergency action teams. Sudden emergencies rarely lend themselves to team efforts. However, in some companies, there are designated fire wardens and "bucket crews" whose function is to deal with fires.

This team would be trained in its function and drill regularly. It could also handle evacuation of personnel or provide informational support to local fire fighting officials, explaining security systems or structural features of the facility.

Other than specialized fire fighting teams, the emergency response function is typically provided by individuals rather than teams. A night operator may report a fire, then evacuate himself from the danger area. A late working employee, detecting water leakage, would safely power down electrical equipment and notify management. These individual responses can be expected only if reaction procedures are developed and employees are trained in them.

The point is that response may be a function that does not require a team (except in the sense that every employee is a member of the team). Effective response may be provided by an individual, or it may be automatic, as in a water sprinkler or Halon system. In some cases, there may not be an available response for a sudden emergency.

Besides sudden emergencies, some companies are subject to phased disasters. Phased disasters are disaster potentials that are known well enough in advance to allow for the implementation of planned response procedures.

One example of a phased disaster scenario, familiar to businesses near the coastlines of North America, is the hurricane or typhoon. Warnings of a storm landfall (or associated tidal surges, tornadoes, etc.) may be issued well in advance of an actual disaster.

Procedures can be developed as part of the disaster recovery plan to make the best use of this advance warning. Reaction to a phased-disaster scenario may include such functions as evacuation of backup hardware and supplies, last minute data backup, notification of hot site and off-site storage vendors, and advance notification of personnel about recovery site relocation. Emergency action teams can be formed to provide these functions, or the functions can be performed at the direction of company managers without the formal designation of teams.

2. Damage assessment team. The second function of the evacuation project is to assess the extent of damage following the disaster. The team should be comprised of individuals who are qualified to assess damage and estimate the time required to recover operations at the affected site. This team should include persons who are skilled in the use of testing equipment, knowledgeable about systems and networks, and trained in applicable safety regulations and procedures. The team's product is a report identifying possible causes of the disaster and, more importantly, its impact in damage and predictable downtime.

3. Emergency management team. One team that is common to nearly all disaster recovery plans is an emergency management team. This is the group that will coordinate the activities of all other recovery teams and which will provide a key decision-making role. In the context of the evacuation project, the emergency management team receives the report of the damage assessment team and makes the decision to activate the plan, in part or in toto.

Other functions of the emergency management team in the evacuation project may include arranging the finance of the recovery, handling legal matters evolving from the disaster, and handling public relations and media inquiries. The roles of the emergency management team may be defined in sufficient detail to assign functions to specific members of the team.

Thus, the functions of the evacuation project define the missions, skill requirements, authority requirements, and activities of the teams that will be active in performing project tasks.

The same is true of the recovery project whose basic functions may include the following:

- Retrieving critical and vital data from off-site storage. Off-site backups may have to be obtained from off-site storage, if the company has contracted for this service, and shipped to the systems, network, and user recovery facilities.
- Installing and testing systems software and applications at the systems recovery site (hot site, cold site, service bureau, etc.). Depending on the recovery strategy that has been developed, a number of tasks will have to be performed in order to recover critical and vital system operation. Restoration of software functions is usually a large component of any strategy.

- Identifying, purchasing and installing hardware at the system recovery site. If a system recovery option has been selected that does not provide access to installed hardware, another recovery function may be to locate a supply of equipment, lease or purchase that supply, arrange its delivery to the systems recovery site, and install it.
- Operating from the system recovery site. Once hardware and software are prepared, it will be necessary to ensure that minimum acceptable service levels are established and maintained. The function of system recovery, after all, is not to restore systems, but to operate them over the duration of the disaster to process data.
- Rerouting network communications traffic. Network recovery is another typical function of a disaster recovery plan. Rerouting incoming traffic to a user recovery site and data communications to a system recovery site may be more or less complicated depending on the strategy settled upon in the plan. As with systems recovery, additional functions may include the acquisition and installation of new hardware as well as programming and software installation.
- Reestablishing the user/system network. Related to the rerouting function above is the reestablishment of data communications between the user recovery site and system recovery site. This function should be provided as a strategy within the recovery plan, and may include the lease or purchase of user terminals and peripherals, modems, front-end controllers, terminal controllers, and even leased lines or private network services.
- Transporting users to recovery facility. Depending on the user recovery strategy that has been developed, it may be necessary to provide transportation and housing for employees at the user recovery facility. If prior arrangements have not been made for a user facility, a preliminary function may be to locate a suitable workplace and equip it with the basic furniture, telecommunications capability, workstations, etc., required. Another preliminary step may be to notify all employees of the new work location, transportation schedules, and emergency accommodations that will be provided.
- Reconstructing databases. If data is lost in the disaster, it may be necessary to restore or reconstruct production databases using any available documents. Where reconstruction is possible, this function may be performed prior to the release of the system for general use. In addition to company personnel, outside contractors may be brought in to aid in the data entry effort. The training and oversight of these personnel may also be viewed as a recovery function.

- Supplying necessary office goods. Yet another function of the recovery project involves the requisition, delivery, and distribution of office supplies and other items, such as computer paper and printed forms, needed to perform useful work. Vendors must be contacted, logistics coordinated, costs and inventory monitored, reorder points established, etc.
- Coordinating systems use and employee work schedules. To utilize minimum system configurations efficiently, it may be necessary to schedule system use rather tightly. The scheduling of user input, processing, and output periods may be necessary, and implementing a regimen of shift work is not uncommon.

It is self-evident that sustaining operations under these conditions requires considerable supervisory skill. Moreover, preventing and resolving technical and operational problems before they reach disastrous proportions are vital for business recovery.

The above list, which is partial at best, suggests the multiplicity of functions that may be undertaken during the recovery project. The emergency management team has a continuing role—coordinating team efforts, financing the recovery project, and maintaining a focal point for business planning and public information. However, to provide the functions required for the recovery of critical operations the following teams may also be created.

4. Off-site storage team. This team would obtain, package, and ship media and records to the recovery facilities as well as have an ongoing role of establishing and overseeing an off-site storage schedule for information created during operations at the recovery sites. The off-site storage team may also assist in records salvage and storage efforts as described below.

5. Software team. Some companies designate a special team whose mission is to restore system packs, load and test operating system software, and resolve system level problems when they arise.

6. Applications team. Applications teams, together with the software team and emergency operations team, (see number seven), travel to the system recovery site and restore user packs and applications programs on the backup system. As the recovery progresses, this team may have the responsibility of monitoring application performance, security, and database integrity.

7. Emergency operations team. The emergency operations team may consist of shift operators and a shift supervisor who will reside at the systems recovery site and manage system operations during the entirity of the disaster and recovery projects. They may also be called upon to coordinate hardware installation if a hot site or other equipment-ready facility has not been designated as the recovery center.

8. Network recovery team. This team is responsible for rerouting wide area voice and data communications traffic and reestablishing host network control and access at the system recovery site. This team may travel to the system recovery site where it will provide on-going support for data communications and oversee security and communications integrity.

9. Communications team. This team travels to the user recovery site where it works in conjunction with the remote network recovery team to establish a user/system network. The communications team may also be responsible for soliciting and installing communications hardware at the user recovery site and working with local COs and gateway vendors in the rerouting of local service and gateway access.

10. Transportation team. This team, which may also serve as a facilities team to locate a user recovery site if one has not been predetermined, is responsible for coordinating the transport of company employees to a distant user recovery site. Transportation may also assist in contacting employees to inform them of new work locations and schedules and arranging employee lodgings.

11. User hardware team. In addition to locating and coordinating the delivery and installation of user terminals, printers, typewriters, photocopiers, and other necessary equipment, this team may also support the communications team, and ultimately the hardware salvage team in their functions.

12. Data preparation and records team. This team updates the applications database, working from terminals installed at the user recovery site. The team may oversee contract operators and support records salvage teams in acquiring primary documents and other input information sources.

13. Administrative support. This team may provide clerical support to the other teams and serve as a message center for the user recovery site. Accounting and payroll functions as well as on-going facility management issues may also be controlled by this team.

14. Supplies team. The supplies team supports the efforts of the user hardware team and contacts vendors and coordinates logistics for an on-going supply of necessary office and computer supplies.

Some of the teams may, in actuality, perform functions that can be handled by one person. Again, the complexity of the disaster recovery plan for a specific business will determine whether functions require a team, or a single, properly-trained individual. Conversely, coordinators may find that additional teams are needed or that some of the listed teams need to be combined into a larger conglomerate. Business recovery needs will dictate these adjustments.

Teams are not static entities and they may dissolve after performing their function. Teams may also change and their members may be shifted to other responsibilities as the recovery project gives way to the relocation or reentry project.

Relocation or reentry refer to the two options that may confront a business following a disaster. If the original facility is salvageable, it may be possible to reenter it once cleanup and refit activities are completed. If the facilities are uninhabitable, or prohibitively expensive to reconstruct, the business may choose to relocate to new quarters. In either case, there is usually an interest in salvaging whatever can be, especially when expensive hardware, critical documents not off-site, and other company assets are involved.

Functions commonly associated with the relocation or reentry project include:

- Facility and hardware salvage. This function of the relocation and reentry project is to make a more detailed assessment of the damage to facilities and equipment than was performed immediately after the disaster. The purpose of this assessment is twofold. First, it will provide the emergency management team with the information it requires to determine whether planning should be directed toward reconstruction or relocation; second, it will provide a basis for certain insurance claims—a potentially vital component of the funding for recovery activities.

  If salvage is determined to be economically desirable, salvage operations may be undertaken concurrently with recovery project activities. As teams complete recovery tasks, they may be reassigned to aid in salvage operations.

  If facilities are not salvageable, teams may be directed to the task of identifying comparable facilities and preparing them for company occupancy.

- Records salvage. Important paper records and documents, damaged by smoke and water, require immediate attention if they are to be salvaged. They need to be cleaned of visible debris, logged and packed, and then moved to a cold storage environment to forestall loss to fungi and mold. Following packout and cold storage, they may be recovered through a vacumn freeze-drying process available through records reclamation vendors. Excellent publications are available from federal and private sources describing all facets of this process that can produce amazing results.

- Relocation. Many of the same activities that were involved in the recovery of systems, networks and users immediately following a disaster may be repeated for the purposes of relocating data processing, communications traffic, and user operations to the new or restored business facility.

- Transition to normal service levels. The final function of disaster recovery is to provide a smooth transition from emergency service levels to normal service levels. Although important to full recovery, this function is not generally documented in detail within a disaster recovery plan. It is typically a function of planning undertaken following successful recovery and while salvage or site preparation activities are underway.

To provide these functions, many of the teams previously defined are reassigned to relocation or reentry project duties. However, there are a few specially trained teams, such as a facilities salvage team, hardware salvage team, and records salvage team, that may perform critical tasks depending on the nature and impact of the disaster and the consequent decisions reached by the emergency management team.

Staffing Teams

Once teams are defined by the disaster recovery coordinator, it is important that their tasks be clearly documented in written procedures. If teams are organized by recovery *functions*, they need to understand in detail only those procedures that pertain to their functions. Thus, they will be trained to perform only the procedures in one section of the well-written plan.[2]

However, someone in the team, such as a team leader, must know how the team's work affects and is affected by other teams. A team leader may also be given the responsibility of reporting on the progress of tasks that his or her team has been assigned and maintaining records of costs associated with team activities.

Staffing teams, then, requires the identification of personnel who have the prerequisite skills and knowledge to perform the technical tasks that are assigned them. Moreover, it is vital to select one person—a team leader (and an alternate)—who has the supervisory and communications skills required to manage team activities effectively.

Staffing efficient teams is a challenge for the disaster recovery coordinator. The coordinator can develop a fairly comprehensive list of skills and knowledge needed for each team. However, the fact that team members possess the listed requirements may offer little indication of how the team will perform in an emergency. The skills and knowledge possessed by a team member cannot guarantee that the person will remain calm in an emergency, think creatively, or handle stress. In the end, team selection may come down to judgment calls by a department manager, and be based on political or personal (as opposed to objective) criteria.

The experience of several companies that have recovered from disasters offers little guidance about the best method of selecting team members and team leaders. For this reason, the following points should be considered in establishing evaluative criteria rather than blueprints for selecting individuals:

• **Worker performance.** An employee's performance record may not be the best criterion on which to judge suitability for team membership or leadership. That the employee is not punctual, or that he or she always comes to work early and stays late may be meaningless in the context of recovery. The same is true of a worker's motivation and attitude. Disasters can reveal surprises about personal mettle.

There are, however, some important dimensions to work performance that should not be ignored. A worker who requires a considerable amount of structure and supervision is probably not the best candidate for a leadership position where some creativity and self-direction are desirable. Also, a worker who is technically astute, but who cannot communicate ideas, is probably a poor choice; or one who has great difficulty in reaching decisions or reasoning to conclusion.

The difference between the ideal team leader and the marginal candidate is the difference between a troubleshooter and a technician. The troubleshooter has added analytical thinking to technical skills. Teams need both technicians and troubleshooters, but the troubleshooter is the person who should lead the team.

• **Worker tenure.** Tenure is another factor that may be considered in staffing teams. Tenured workers may understand the business better than novices. They may have a greater stake in business survival (higher salary, well-developed pension, etc.). They may also command greater respect from fellow, less-senior employees.

On the other hand, tenured workers may lack the exposure to alternatives that would be the forte of a worker who may be new to the company, but not the workplace.

Since some team leaders will necessarily be privy to security information (passwords, filenames, etc.), tenure may also be a consideration in this regard. While there is no correlation between tenure and trustworthiness, a more senior employee is often perceived as a better security risk than a new hire.

• **Worker marital status.** There is little data to establish that a married worker will handle disaster recovery responsibilities any better or worse than an unmarried one. However, many coordinators still assert that married persons are less reliable due to the distraction factor. In the event of a regional disaster, so the argument goes, the married employee is going to be more worried about the well-being of his/her family than about the company. This distraction could affect performance.

This argument has little merit as even unmarried persons can have parents, siblings, or significant others to distract them. In acknowledgement of this fact, some Florida companies have gone so far as to have their facilities approved as evacuation shelters. In the event of a hurricane, employees and their families and friends are urged to utilize the shelter. Thus, recovery team personnel will know that their relatives and friends (though not necessarily their property) are safe as they proceed in their recovery tasks.

• **Residence of recovery personnel.** One factor that may be important in the consideration of candidates for recovery teams is the location of their residence in relation to the company offices. Employees who must travel two hours (in good traffic) to reach the workplace may be less suitable for critical disaster recovery roles than those who reside in the company's back yard.

Even when travel time is not an issue, there may be compelling reasons to select employees who are located in the general vicinity of the facility. The main reason is that in some disaster scenarios, including natural disasters and civil disturbances, there may be restrictions imposed on movement into and out of the affected region or area.

For example, following the passage of Hurricane Elena in September 1985, along the shores of southwestern Florida, the police cordoned off Pinellas County. Until damage could be assessed, no one from neighboring Hillsborough County was allowed in or out of Pinellas County. Following cessation of disaster conditions, many hours passed during which only those who could *prove residence* in the county to which they wished to travel were allowed into that county. Thus, employees who resided in one county were not permitted to travel to their workplace in the neighboring county for a protracted period of time. Had significant damage been sustained by the Tampa Bay area, it is doubtful that companies could have activated their disaster recovery plans very effectively.[3]

The above considerations illustrate that there is a lack of hard, experiential data available to disaster recovery coordinators to guide them in team staffing. Coordinators may find themselves completely dependent upon the judgment of the department managers whose aegis extends over the teams and functions in question. Since there are no objective grounds for challenging department management decisions, the only hedge that the coordinator may have against seemingly poor choices is procedural.

Coordinators should strive to portray the role of team leader or member as nonglamorous, even clerical. This may be accomplished by requiring team leaders to be responsible for maintaining the integrity of "their" section of the disaster recovery plan according to a plan maintenance schedule. It should also be made clear that plan testing may interfere with off-work activities of those who are designated to play recovery roles. For some, the added responsibility and interference in their personal lives will dissuade them from lobbying for the position of team leader.

If a seemingly inappropriate selection of team leader is made, regardless of the above procedural checks, another hedge against incompetence is to train an alternate person to lead the team if the primary candidate is unavailable. The selection of an alternate may be the coordinator's call if the department manager is appeased by his or her selection of the primary team leader. Where this is not the case, and the coordinator's confidence in both primary and alternate team leaders is low, *all* team members may need to be cross-trained in recovery team operation and management.

This is not intended to imply that department managers will always make bad choices about team leaders and members. In most cases, not only will the department manager identify appropriate candidates, but their insights will be of considerable value, since the coordinator is not in a position to evaluate the personal qualifications of each and every company employee. As a control against team incompetence, teams can be trained and tested in detailed procedures until the procedures become routine.

Develop a Notification Directory

Once recovery teams have been staffed, the coordinator will have most of the information needed to develop a telephone directory of persons to be notified in the event of a disaster. Besides team members and company employees, phone lists may include the numbers for representatives of equipment and software vendors, contacts within companies that have been designated to provide supplies and equipment, contact persons at recovery facilities (including hot site representatives, representatives of predefined network communications rerouting services, etc.), and insurance company agents.

Primary and emergency telephone numbers for each critical contact person should be compiled and kept in the back matter of the disaster recovery plan. In the case of company employees who will be called on to staff the user recovery facility (other than teams), the human resources or personnel department is often a good resource for compiling a telephone directory and keeping it up-to-date and off-site.

In conjunction with the directory, many disaster recovery planners develop a notification schema or "tree" to indicate who will be responsible for contacting whom. Sometimes the responsibility for contacting team members is vested in the team leader (and alternate). The team leader or his/her designee may also have responsibility for notifying vendor representatives whose roles relate directly to the team's area of recovery responsibility.

Other branches of the notification tree may provide for the notification of company personnel by a team designated to provide this function. Employees will need to know where and when to report for work once a user recovery facility has been prepared and systems and networks have been restored.

Notification trees may also indicate "triggers," or chronological points, at which a branch of the notification tree is to be activated and contacts on the branch notified of some impending activity or event. A trigger in a notification tree may be the declaration of a "voluntary evacuation order" in a hurricane scenario. Such orders are usually issued one to three hours in advance of a mandatory evacuation order and may be used as a trigger not only for notification trees, but also for activation of other plan components (emergency system and data backups, safe deenergization of hardware, evacuation of redundant hardware, etc.).

The notification tree, with its carefully-defined branches and triggers, is one of several tools that may help emergency managers make order out of chaos following a disaster. Communication is essential for command and control in a disaster situation. Communication of impending disaster conditions can help reduce the impact of the disaster when it occurs, and communication about the extent of damage can be used to determine whether the disaster recovery plan must be invoked, and whether to activate it in whole or in part. Finally, communication between recovery teams and emergency managers—regarding the progress of recovery activity, new strategies and directions, decisions and plans, etc.—will determine how effectively business resumption may be realized. Figure 7.2 summarizes command, control, and communications factors as they relate to the management of the three projects within disaster recovery: evacuation, recovery, and relocation or reentry.

Creating the Emergency Management Flowchart

In addition to the notification tree, most disaster recovery plans contain an emergency management flowchart that graphically depicts the sequence in which recovery tasks will be undertaken. This flowchart can be of substantial value in helping disaster recovery teams and emergency managers understand the disaster recovery plan as a whole.

The following flowcharts are segments of the detailed flowchart which is in Appendix A. To enhance their usefulness to teams, flow chart segments, such as these, may be placed at the front of the sections of the plan to which they correspond.

The diagrams provided here may be less detailed than those that would be developed for an actual recovery plan, but the coordinator should strive in every case to keep the charts he or she develops clear and straightforward. If possible, the coordinator should relate chart symbols to specific plan procedures using a numbering scheme common to both.

- **Emergency response.** Figures 7.3 and 7.4 are simplified examples of decision-making flowcharts that may be placed at the front of a plan section treating emergency response.

    Figure 7.3 deals with a sudden crisis in which on-site employees may be called upon to take immediate action procedures as outlined in the plan. Since the night operator may not have the luxury of time (or presence of mind) to refer to the manual and perform a written procedure, all operators should be thoroughly trained and drilled in procedures such as interpreting alarms, powering down equipment, dumping Halon, and of course evacuating the facility quickly and safely. While these procedures will probably be conducted without reference to a plan document, it is a good idea to document them in a section of the plan both for use as a training aid and as evidence to the auditors that response procedures have been developed and tested.

    Following emergency actions, the flowchart indicates that the emergency management team is to be notified. Again, the plan document may not be accessible to the evacuated night worker, but all 24-hour personnel should be provided with emergency contact

Figure 7.2   COMMAND, CONTROL, AND COMMUNICATIONS IN EMERGENCY
MANAGEMENT

Phase I Evacuation	Phase II Recovery	Phase III Relocation
Command	**Command**	**Command**
Emergency Response On-site personnel react to situation in accordance to emergency action procedures Emergency management team assesses impact; invokes plan **Phased Response** Emergency management team decides when to evacuate Emergency mamagement team assesses impact; invokes plan	Command of Recovery Phase activities vested in Emergency Management Team supported by subordinate recovery team managers.	Relocation to the evacuated or new permanent operating site will require management oversight and coordination; lines of reporting established by the disaster recovery plan will continue until systems are stabilized and normal service levels are reestablished
Control	**Control**	**Control**
Emergency Response Minimal control over employee reaction to crisis; routine drills in emergency action procedures will help to ensure adherence to procedures **Phased Response** Emergency Management team exercises direct control over last minute backups and evacuation of personnel, equipment, and supplies Management controls disaster declaration	Control of Recovery achieved through management of subordinates performing tested procedures	Control of relocation activities will be accomplished through management channels established by disaster recovery plan; the emergency management team will control the acquisition and preparation of the salvaged or new facility, direct facility preparation teams, and oversee the relocation of systems and networks; the transition from emergency to normal service levels will be controlled in accordance with a management plan

Figure 7.2 continued

Phase I Evacuation	Phase II Recovery	Phase III Relocation
Communication	Communication	Communication
Emergency Response Initial communications conditions uncertain; possible difficulties in locating authorized emergency management team member; possible difficulties in accessing site to perform evaluation; potential for miscommunication of damage assessment if emergency management team member unavailable for site inspection Disaster definition and inspection criteria may aid in prevention of unwarranted disaster declarations **Phased Response** Generally favorable communications conditions may exist at outset of disaster; however, damage assessment may be delayed Evaluation of damage and communication of situation may be enhanced if emergency management team members are present	Voice and data network restoration is a priority; until networks are restored, communication between management and recovery teams may be impaired—thus, activities will be conducted according to tested procedures within an agreed-upon time frame; following network recovery, communications will be normalized, beginning with channels for management reporting	Communication of management plans for preparation of and relocation to the salvaged or new operating site should occur in a stabilized communications environment

Figure 7..2 continued

Phase I Evacuation	Phase II Recovery	Phase III Relocation
Communication	**Communication**	**Communication**
Communication with News Media regarding details of disaster controlled through Emergency Mangagement Team which will designate from among its ranks an individual to serve as media liaison		

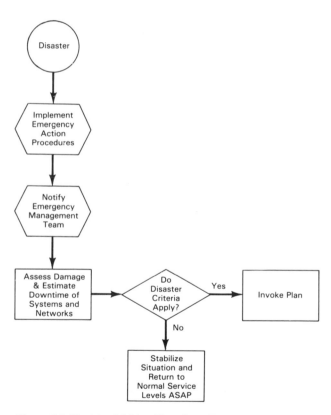

Figure 7.3 Decision-Making Flowchart (Emergency Response).

numbers, possibly on a wallet-sized card, that can be referenced in an emergency. The existence of the card and the telephone numbers listed on it should be documented in the written plan as well.

The next activity denoted on the chart calls for an assessment of the damage caused by the disaster and an estimate of anticipated downtime or inaccessibility to affected systems and networks. If the facility has to be evacuated, it may not be possible to reenter immediately to assess damage. However, even the "best guess" of fire officials or other emergency officials may be sufficient to determine whether a prolonged business interruption is probable.

Thus, the next symbol indicates that a decision needs to be made whether to activate the disaster recovery plan. If disaster recovery criteria, which should be spelled out in the plan document but are usually common sense considerations (i.e., will downtime exceed 24 hours?) are met, a decision is made to invoke the plan.

If the event does not meet disaster criteria, the situation will be stabilized as soon as possible and operations returned to normal service levels. For example, if the crisis is a power blackout, but power company representatives assure the company emergency management team that power will be restored within eight hours, and this time frame is acceptable, the emergency management team may decide to ride out the situation and work to restore operations to normal as soon as power is restored.

Figure 7.4 portrays a different type of emergency response: response to a phased disaster. In a phased disaster scenario, the company has advance notification of an imminent crisis. The plan document may contain procedures for bracing for such an event—a hurricane, a labor strike, or even a possible civil disturbance. These emergency procedures may be activated by a "trigger" event such as a warning issued by the National Hurricane Center in Miami, the tornado center in Kansas City, local TV, police bulletins, or civil voluntary evacuation orders.

Once triggered, planned procedures may include performing last minute system backups to reduce the amount of "catch up" work that will be required later to restore databases to a current form. Redundant hardware may also be deactivated and evacuated to a designated safe location. The hot site, or other system recovery center may be placed on alert. Off-site storage facilities may be contacted and teams sent to retrieve stored backups and prepare them for transportation to recovery destinations. Finally, personnel will be evacuated if the threat exceeds safe levels.

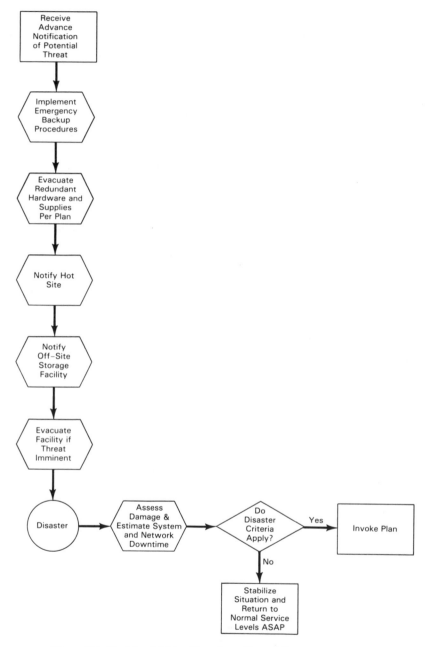

Figure 7.4 Decision-Making Flowchart (Phased Disaster Scenario).

If the disaster then occurs, these prophylactic measures should speed the recovery of the company. However, before a disaster is declared, damage will need to be assessed, disaster criteria will need to be applied, and a decision will need to be reached as to whether the plan should be invoked.

Given the variety of possible disasters that can confront a company, the assumption that one or two simplified decision-making flowcharts can cover all the bases is foolish. Whether the disaster is phased or sudden, the decision to invoke the plan rests on human judgment and is subject to all of its foibles. For example, in August 1987, a major metals distributor in the Chicago area sustained more than $10 million in hardware and facility damage (and an incalculable amount in lost revenue) due to flooding. The MIS Director reported that he held off on declaring a disaster in the early hours of a torrential downpour, expecting the rain to stop and the water level to fall. Twelve hours (and 10 inches of rain) later the plan was finally invoked. Systems went off-line on Friday and were not restored at a hot site until the following Monday. The company's extensive data communications network was out until Tuesday.[4]

Despite his fully tested disaster recovery plan, the director conceded, critical on-line order processing and inventory systems were out of commission for a protracted period—because the plan had not been invoked at the first sign of trouble. On the other hand, added the director proudly, without the plan—although implemented late—the company would never have survived.

The story illustrates one of the major flaws with the expectation that emergency management flowcharts will be implemented without delay or modification in an actual disaster. It doesn't fit the facts. However, these charts do provide the means—for testing purposes at least—to "black box" the disaster and superimpose rationality upon a complex, multifaceted, and irrational phenomenon.

Once the initial response to a disaster has been made, Figure 7.5 begins the project of recovery from the disaster.

- **Situation assessment and response.** Once the plan is invoked, a number of plan components come into play automatically. As seen in Figure 7.5, recovery teams are notified by the emergency management team. Two teams—damage assessment and salvage—go directly to the disaster site, if this is possible, to make a more comprehensive, less-hasty evaluation of the situation. Meanwhile, an emergency command center is set up (impressive as the term command center may seem, it is often nothing more than a meeting of

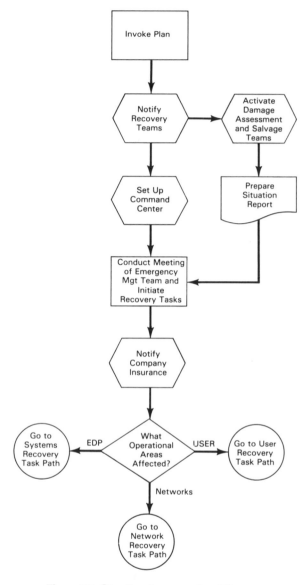

Figure 7.5 Situation Assessment and Response.

the emergency management team at the home of one of its members). The team—often headed by a senior corporate officer—holds a meeting, and using the reports of the damage assessment and salvage teams, determines which parts of the disaster recovery plan must be implemented. If the data center has been rendered unusable, but user work areas and the telecommunications switch are intact, the decision may be made to implement only the systems recovery section of the plan, and so forth.

It should be noted that damage assessment and salvage teams may have some critical tasks to perform. They may tour the facility with electrical contractors and facility reconstruction vendor representatives and obtain cost and time estimates for repair work. If damage has been done to user areas, there may still be working hardware that can be salvaged, tested and relocated to the user recovery site. They may also obtain eyewitness accounts from persons who were in or near the facility when the disaster occurred. Finally, an insurance claims adjuster, contacted by the emergency management team, may need to be escorted through the damaged area to initiate the claims adjustment process.

The disaster recovery plan should indicate, generally, what tasks are to be performed by the recovery teams at the disaster site. If eyewitness accounts are to be gathered, the plan may provide a form for gathering this information and instructions for using the form, possibly developed with the assistance of an attorney. In addition, hardware testing routines may be summarized in the plan, although it would be wise to have someone on the salvage team who is thoroughly conversant with the procedures for testing hardware. The plan should also contain safety guidelines to instruct teams in avoiding personal risks.

Based on the decision of the emergency management team using the best available information, the recovery sections of the disaster recovery plan may be activated in whole or in part. Figures 7.6 and 7.7 depict events in the recovery of systems. In these flowcharts, systems recovery will involve the use of a remotely-located commercial hot site. Be aware that the systems recovery strategy will probably already have been implemented if a decision has been made to activate the plan. If after further examination the original center is found to be inhabitable, the systems recovery plan may advance quickly to the reentry phase.

- **System recovery task path.** In Figure 7.6, the need to activate the systems recovery plan has been acknowledged by the emergency management team. The emergency management team issues a formal disaster declaration to the hot site and the systems recovery team leader assembles the teams.

  The off-site storage team retrieves backups from the storage facility, crates or otherwise prepares them for transportation, and

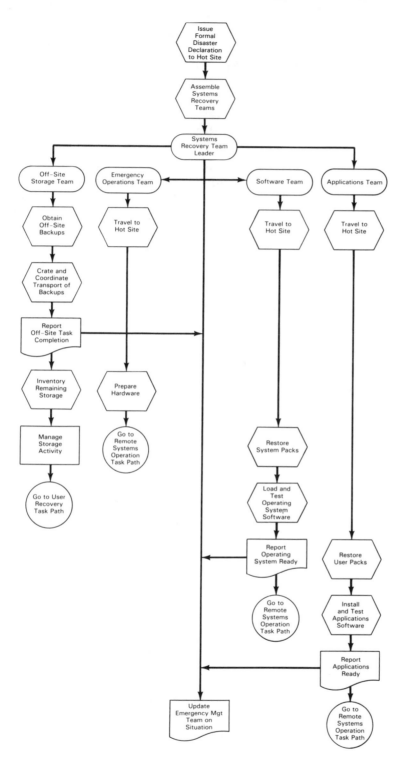

Figure 7.6 System Recovery Task Path.

transports them to the hot site. (This may already have been done if it is a phased disaster.) The team may also arrange for the pickup of deliverables at the destination and transport them to the hot site. Once these tasks are completed, the off-site storage team so reports to the systems recovery team leader.

The off-site storage team then inventories remaining storage and, if necessary, prepares stored documents, preprinted forms, and other user supplies for transport to the user recovery site. The team will then coordinate new storage arrangements for vital and critical records generated during recovery operations. An off-page connector indicates that the reader should go to the user recovery task path in Figure 7.9 to see additional off-site storage team tasks.

Meanwhile, the emergency operations, software, and applications teams travel to the hot site. Once there, the emergency operations team prepares system hardware and the software team restores system packs, loads system software, and reports task completion to the systems recovery team leader. The applications team restores user packs, installs and tests application software, reports task completion to the team leader. Off-page connectors direct the reader to go to the remote systems operations task path in Figure 7.7.

With systems fully prepared, the systems recovery team leader so reports to the emergency management team.

In actuality, a host of additional steps may be required and each should be thoroughly documented in the disaster recovery plan and regularly tested at the hot site. Also, in point of fact, systems are not restored until databases are current, communications have been reestablished with users and data communicators, and users are on the system performing work. Network and user recovery tasks occur concurrently with systems recovery, as the combined flowchart in Appendix A clearly indicates.

- **Remote systems operation task path.** In some disaster recovery plans, procedures for operating restored systems from a hot site are documented in broad sweeping strokes. Specific attention may be paid to cost-accounting responsibilities and performance reporting requirements. In Figure 7.7, the on-going responsibilities of systems recovery teams during operations at the hot site are set forth.

  Basically, the emergency operations team is responsible for operating systems at emergency service levels, scheduling jobs, performing backups, and maintaining system recovery team time and payroll records, and records of other accrued expenses. Expenses are

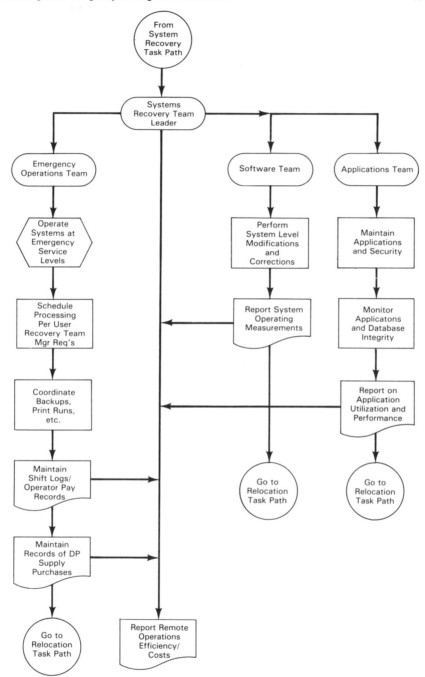

Figure 7.7   Remote Systems Operations Management (Remote Systems Operation Task Path).

reported on a regular basis to the systems recovery team leader who includes them in his/her regular reports to the emergency management team.

The software and applications teams monitor system performance, work to resolve problems, maintain applications security and data integrity, and report performance and utilization measurements to the recovery team leader. Presumably, the team leader will advise the teams of changing requirements and the decisions of the emergency management team which pertain to their activities.

These tasks are ongoing until the recovery phase gives way to the relocation of systems to the original or newly constructed facility.

With some hot sites, facility use in excess of 60 days is not permitted. The hot site may be used only until a cold site at or near the vendor location can be fitted with necessary hardware. Then, the client is moved to the cold site. This opens the hot site for use by other subscribers wishing to test their plans or needing a recovery facility in a disaster.

Rather than proceeding to the relocation task path for the system recovery teams, Figure 7.8 considers the network recovery enterprise, which may be undertaken concurrently with the system recovery and remote system operation task paths. In this flowchart, it is assumed that the company has contracted with a wide-area network service vendor for rerouting long distance communications along a preplanned circuit path. For plans where this is not the case, additional procedures may be needed to accommodate the rerouting of long-distance lines from the original facility to system and user recovery facilities.

If the company data center, but not the user work areas or company telecommunications capability, has been damaged by a disaster, it may not be necessary to reroute all wide area circuits. Instead, only those circuits that terminate at the CPU may need to be redirected to the system recovery site. In Figure 7.8, the flowchart deals with a total loss of both user work areas and systems. Hence, a network recovery team located at the hot site and a communications team located at the user recovery site are presented. Another flowchart may need to be developed to reflect a partial disaster scenario.

- **Network recovery task path.** As Figure 7.8 indicates, once the network recovery section of the disaster recovery plan is invoked, the network rerouting service vendor is contacted and communications are rerouted along predefined paths. The network recovery team leader notifies his/her teams and each team travels to its intended destination. (Subsequent plan tests will determine whether the recovery team leader should travel to the hot site with the network

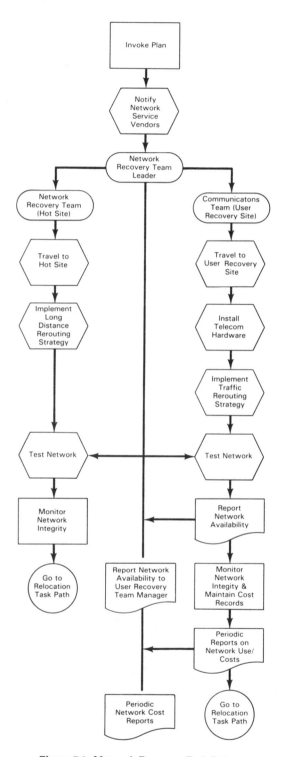

Figure 7.8 Network Recovery Task Path.

recovery team, or to the user recovery site with the communications team. Considering the task allocation, the communications team appears to be the one with the greater need for personalized direction.)

The network recovery team is responsible for implementing the long distance rerouting strategy, which may include notifying other network nodes of operational changes or installing/preparing communications hardware at the hot site for use in the network. Thorough testing of the network can only be accomplished after telecommunications hardware (including modems, terminal controllers, and front-end communications controllers) have been installed at the user recovery site.

The network team will then monitor network traffic for utilization and data communications integrity. This will persist until systems are relocated to the original or new company facility.

Meanwhile, at the user recovery site, the communications team installs hardware received from prearranged vendor sources and from the hot site. In conjunction with the original CO and the new server, they implement a local traffic rerouting strategy in accordance with the disaster recovery plan and test wide area lines rerouted to the user recovery site.

When network tests are completed (according to a planned testing strategy), the availability of the network for use is reported to the team leader who in turn reports this to the emergency management team.

Until systems and networks are relocated to the original or a new company facility, the communications team monitors network traffic and maintains cost records which are periodically summarized and reported to the team leader for inclusion in his/her management reports.

Again, rather than proceeding to the relocation task path, Figures 7.9 and 7.10 refer to user recovery tasks which are undertaken concurrently with system and network recovery tasks. These flowcharts assume that a user recovery site has been preplanned and designated in the recovery plan. Were this not the case, strategies for the automatic rerouting of communications networks would be difficult to coordinate in advance of a disaster and recovery would be delayed by the need to locate and outfit a user recovery site, and then notifying all necessary parties of the new address.

- **User recovery task path.** As shown in Figure 7.9, once the decision has been made to activate the user recovery section of the plan, the

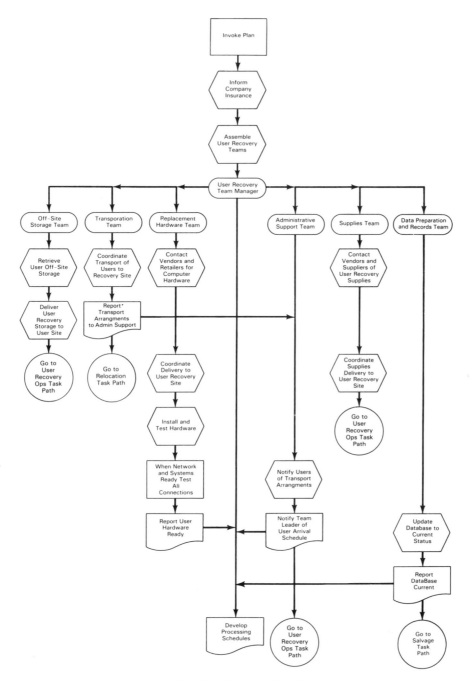

Figure 7.9 User Recovery Task Path.

company insurer is notified so that extra expense coverages for user relocation and above-normal operating expenses can be activated.

User recovery teams are notified by the team leader and given their instructions on how to proceed. Note that the off-site storage team carries additional responsibilities in the context of user recovery. These include retrieving stored materials required by the user recovery site and delivering them to the site.

A transportation team coordinates the transport of users to the recovery site, although this is not done until other aspects of site preparation are completed. Transport arrangements are reported to the administrative support team.

A replacement hardware team contacts vendors and retailers who are identified in the plan to coordinate shipments of terminals, photocopying equipment, FAX, and other office equipment to the user recovery site. This team is then responsible for installing and testing hardware. Once the communications and network teams have completed their work, terminal controllers are connected to communication controllers, multiplexers, etc., per the plan, and a series of documented tests are conducted to ensure network integrity. A report is made to the team leader that systems are ready for use.

As systems are readied, the administrative support team contacts users to staff the facility and advises them of transportation arrangements. When users have confirmed that they will participate in the recovery, administrative support notifies the team leader of their arrival schedule.

Meanwhile, a supplies team coordinates the delivery of office supplies from vendors identified in the plan. Supplies are delivered to the recovery site.

Once systems and networks are ready, a data preparation and records team uses salvaged records and off-site documentation to update the user database. Indices pertaining to user IDs, device identifiers, and other user administration files are updated to reflect the new configuration. Once databases are current, this is reported to the team leader and the user recovery site is ready for operation.

The user recovery task path depicted above assumes that certain capabilities already exist and will not need to be hastily developed. This may not be the case for every business. Additional teams, such as a facility location team, may need to be identified and staffed to handle additional

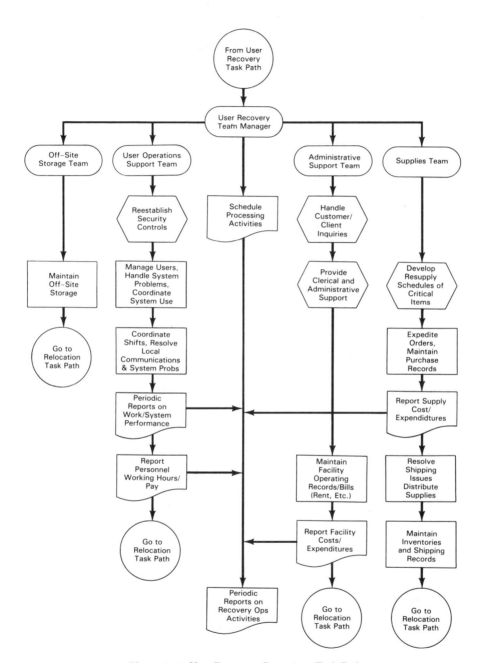

Figure 7.10 User Recovery Operations Task Path.

functional requirements of user recovery. Note also that the data preparation and records team, unlike the other teams in this task path, has continuing responsibilities in the salvage task path; they will assist in records
reclamation and other salvage activities. The on-going activities of the
other teams are depicted in Figure 7.10.

- User recovery operations task path. This task path, illustrated in
  Figure 7.10, includes some of the ongoing procedures for operations
  at the recovery site. The off-site storage team maintains a storage
  schedule for information and data generated at the user recovery
  site.

  A user operations support team oversees premise security,
  manages users, handles system problems, coordinates shifts, and su-
  pervises work. Regular reports of work and system performance,
  personnel time, and payroll are made to the user recovery team
  leader.

  The administrative support team handles customer and client
  inquiries, provides clerical and administrative support for the other
  teams, and maintains facility operating cost records. Reports of
  facility costs and expenditures are made by the team to the user
  recovery team leader on a regular basis.

  A supplies team coordinates the resupply of critical office and
  computer supplies. This team escalates orders, maintains purchase
  and inventory records, resolves shipping issues, and distributes supplies upon arrival.

The activities described above may not have corresponding procedures in the disaster recovery plan document. However, special forms and
report formats may be developed and included in the plan with instructions for their use.

The user recovery team continues its operations until a plan is
developed to relocate the users to the original or a new facility. The
decisions of where and when to relocate are made by the emergency
management team, based in part upon the findings and progress of the
salvage effort.

- **Salvage task path.** Salvage activities may begin the moment that
  reentry is permitted to the disaster-stricken facility. These efforts
  continue concurrently with response and recovery activities undertaken by other disaster recovery teams. Figure 7.11 provides an overview of some of the activities that may be a part of a salvage effort.

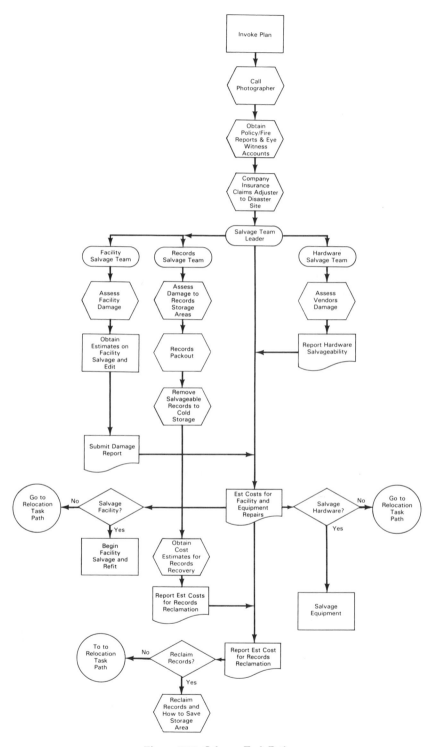

Figure 7.11 Salvage Task Path.

As indicated above, once the plan is invoked, a damage assessment team—possibly comprised of the salvage team leader, a qualified member of the emergency management team, and others familiar with source records and computer hardware—enter the facility. A photographic record is made of the damage by either a team member or a professional photographer on retainer to the company for this purpose. Witness accounts may also be collected at this point.

Some plans provide for a claims adjuster from the company's business interruption insurer to accompany the damage assessment and salvage teams to the disaster site. Since payment on insurance claims may provide part of the financing for the recovery, the quicker that claims can be filed and paid, the better.

Following the initial visit, formal salvage teams go to work in specific damage assessment and salvage functions. A facility salvage team determines whether the environment can be restored and at what cost. It submits an itemized damage report to the team leader. Similar reports are filed by a hardware salvage team.

The records salvage team immediately sets to work. Its job is to rescue what paper and microform records can be saved—to clean, pack, and inventory them—and to remove them to cold storage. This must be done within 24 to 48 hours, before mold and fungi begin to corrupt salvageable documents. The procedure for packout should be set forth in the disaster recovery plan, as should a list of cold storage facilities in the vicinity of the company.[5] Figure 7.12 summarizes some of the media-specific procedures that may be performed by the records salvage team.

Following packout, and when the extent and quantity of damaged records are known, the records salvage team should then obtain an estimate from a records reclamation vendor (also noted in the disaster plan) of the cost for restoring the volume of records salvaged from the company records center. This cost estimate should be reported to the salvage team leader.

The salvage team leader is responsible for reporting cost estimates for facility, equipment, and records salvage to the emergency management team. The emergency management team will decide whether to undertake salvage or to write off the loss and look for new hardware and new quarters for the company.

If the decision is made to salvage and reenter the original facility, the facility salvage team initiates contract work and provides a completion schedule to the team leader. The other sal-

Figure 7.12
Salvage Priority by Type of Media

Type of Media	Color films and photographs	Silver or emulsion films and photographs	Diazo or vesicular (duplicate) films	Bond, rag, or duplication paper	Magnetic media (including tape, disc packs, floppies, audio tape, and video tape)
Priority	Immediate	Immediate	Last	Within 48 hours (depending on temperature and humidity levels at the disaster site, and on the extent of damage)	Immediate
Immediate action	Once wet, keep wet	Immerse totally in water	If time and staff are available, rinse off and lay out flat on clean surface to dry; otherwise, leave until last	Air dry in well-ventilated area. If volume of wet records is large, consider freeze or vacuum drying	Contact vendor
Purpose of Action	To avoid further damage and loss of image	To avoid further damage	To prevent water spotting and curling of films or fiche	To prevent further deterioration of paper materials and eruption of mold and fungus	To obtain professional advice and service
Follow-up action	Within 48 hours, obtain professional advice and/or assistance with cleaning, drying and restoring. Freeze if professional help is delayed longer than 48 hours.	Seek professional assistance with cleaning and drying. Freezing may cause image damage, but much less so than would be caused by delaying treatment. If freezing will be delayed longer than 48 hours, immerse films in 1 percent solution of formaldehyde in cool water.	Wash with liquid detergent and rinse. Dry on flat, absorbent paper towels.	May include freeze- or vacuum-drying. If mold erupts, treat with approved fungicide.	May include special cleaning techniques and professional assistance in retrieving data.

Salvage Priority by Type of Media (continued)

Type of Media	Color films and photographs	Silver or emulsion films and photographs	Diazo or vesicular (duplicate) films	Bond, rag, or duplication paper	Magnetic media (including tape, disc packs, floppies, audio tape, and video tape)
Purpose of follow-up action	Freezing may be required to stabilize color dyes	Use of a formaldehyde solution will help prevent softening or frilling of gelatin or emulsion layer. If films are allowed to dry, they will stick to the surface with which they are in contact, resulting in image loss and other damage	To remove water spots and other contaminants and to restore film	To remove moisture from materials and to reduce exposure to humidity; to eradicate mold	To remove moisture and contaminants from media; to recover valuable data from damaged media
Comments	Color dyes are inherently unstable and should be handled immediately to prevent loss of color and other damage		These films are nearly impervious to water damage and generally clean easily. Diazo films sometimes fade with age, though this and other damage is generally due to poor quality control, rather than to disaster-related causes.	In high humidity, deterioration of wet papers begins within 2 to 3 hours.	Advice on media recovery should be sought well in advance of a disaster. Heat and water damage inspections should be performed on hardware before operating. Proper backup and recovery procedures will help to prevent major data loses.

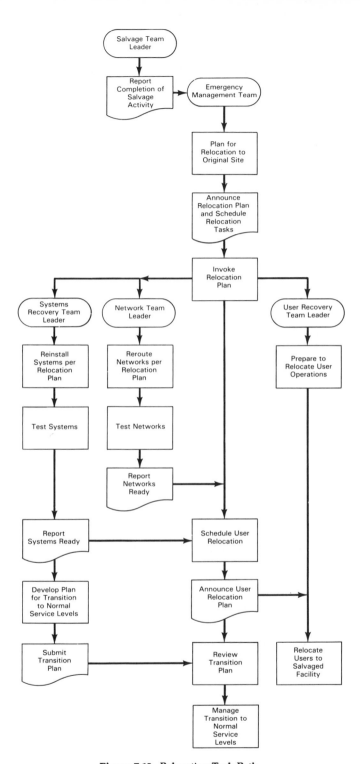

Figure 7.13 Relocation Task Path.

vage teams move forward with salvage activities, identifying task progress and anticipated completion schedules as work proceeds.

Whatever decision is reached by the emergency management team, it is followed up by the development of a relocation plan. The specific components of the relocation plan cannot be predetermined by the disaster recovery coordinator. However, if the relocation plan utilizes the same team structures that were defined in the disaster recovery plan, this may facilitate efficient relocation of systems, networks, and users to the original or new company facility.

In addition, the relocation or reentry plan should provide a scheme for the gradual transition back to normal user and system work levels from the emergency service levels in effect during recovery operations. Presumably, this transition will be scheduled following the successful relocation of critical and vital systems to the company site.

Figure 7.13 summarizes the tasks that may be involved in the relocation of emergency operations to the original (salvaged) facility. The task path mirrors recovery task paths in many respects, except that emergency service levels are gradually replaced by normal service levels per a plan developed by the emergency management team during recovery operations.

REFERENCES

1. Robert Levy, "Crisis Public Relations," *Dun's Business Month* (February 1983).

2. According to Michael Kern, who assisted in the recovery of certain telecommunications capabilities following the fire at Norwest Mortgage in Minneapolis in 1982, teams were provided with only the section of the plan that pertained to them rather than the whole of the multivolume plan created for Norwest. CHI/COR Information Management and other disaster recovery consultancies also create plans that are organized by recovery functions.

3. Jon Toigo, "Storm Warnings Sound," *The Databus*, Vol. 4, no. 7 (July 1986).

4. Richard Sandhofer, "Chicago Not Prepared for a New River," *Disaster Recovery Journal*, Vol. 1, no. 1 (January 1988).

5. Dick Rice, a consultant specializing in the recovery and salvage of paper and microform records, has defined the steps of a packout operation and subsequent records recovery activity in a number of journals and books. He recommends readers obtain Richard Harms, et al., "A Program for Disaster Response in Michigan," Michigan Archival Association, East Lansing, MI, 1981.

Chapter 8

The Recovery Management Environment

As discussed in Chapter 7, the emergency decision-making plan provides the framework of the disaster recovery plan. Its flowcharts and notification directory map the relationships and timing of all of the strategies, tasks, and procedures that have been developed to recover critical business operations in the event of a disaster. However, flowcharts—and the scenarios on which they are built—are only theoretical constructs. Disaster teams may have to deviate from the preplanned path in response to the actual recovery environment.

There is no way to predict every recovery problem or to develop, in advance, suitable responses. However, there are ways to identify potential obstacles to plan implementation, educate team leaders about them, and—in some cases—develop the means for surmounting them.

To understand the recovery management environment and develop means for coping with it, disaster recovery coordinators need to research the experience of other companies that have implemented their plans. Research entails more than reading this book or disaster-related articles in back issues of popular data processing journals. An important part of the research involves conducting interviews with those who have led or served on recovery teams in a business disaster. Research also entails interviewing civil authorities and representatives of local utilities, telephone COs, and governmental emergency management offices.

Disaster recovery coordinators can perform this research themselves, or they may be assisted by team leaders who will profit from direct participation in the research endeavor. The purpose of this research is to learn. Much of what is discovered may not be useful in writing the disaster recovery plan. However, it may help those who will implement the plan to see their environment more clearly, and perceive the parameters within which improvision (in the face of obstacles to recovery) may be successful.

Researching Literature

It is probably a fact that best information about business disasters and recovery projects is locked away in company filing cabinets. Businesses often wish to secrete any information that might indicate instability or vulnerability to investors, customers, stockholders, and auditors. However, accounts of successful (and unsuccessful) recovery projects are increasingly finding their way into the press. Part of the reason, of course, is that some disasters take a large toll in human life (Bhopal, etc.) or are spectacular and visual (Norwest's or MGM's fires). However, even a software malfunction can achieve prominent media attention when it causes the Bank of New York to borrow $22 billion at the Federal Reserve's discount window and destabilizes the securities market.

The point is that more and more information about the problems and pitfalls of disaster recovery is available in the popular media. This information can be helpful in identifying potential obstacles to the implementation of disaster plans.

For example, companies located in Canada with hot sites in the U.S. can learn a great deal from the 1986 Steinberg disaster in Montreal. According to one account, the evening after a fire demolished company headquarters, 25 data processing employees packaged over 10,000 reels of tape containing payroll systems and data (and blank check stock), and formed a caravan headed for a hot site in New Jersey. At the border, however, they were prevented from entering the U.S. by customs agents, who were concerned that the software and checks could be used for illegal purposes.[1] It took the company CEO in conjunction with the U.S. consulate to straighten out the matter.

In addition to procedural formalities, the Steinberg fire also taught Canadian companies about the incompatibilities of certain Canadian networks and those in the U.S. Nearly two days passed before Bell Canada was able to make available compatible lines which allowed the company to reconnect its hot site-based network to its many retail stores.[2]

Still other companies have learned from published accounts of disasters that were worsened by improper management of the media. The results of inept handling of the media in the face of allegations of company wrong-doing or product problems—Star-Kist's "Tunagate," Union Carbide's Bhopal, E. F. Hutton's overdraft scandal—have taught many companies about the need to inform the media of the scope of a disaster up-front in order to convert newspeople from critics to supporters of the recovery project. For this reason, increasing emphasis is being placed on developing company executives' public relations, fully defining legal ramifications of public disclosures during a crisis, and improving executive understanding of the psychological and structural incentives to "black out" or "cover up" disaster information.[3] This literature can teach a great deal to disaster recovery coordinators and can provide the basis for a plan section defining who will speak for the company, when media will be informed, and how media communications will be handled.

It would be impossible for coordinators to gather all of the publications covering all of the subjects that might offer insights into disaster recovery planning. However, vendors of products and services used by the coordinator often read this literature and forward relevant articles to the coordinator's attention. Many marketing representatives review literature and forward clips to customers or prospects as part of their effort to inform and educate clientele or demonstrate their interest in the client's project.

In addition to subscription publications and vendor clips, many hardware and software companies generate their own disaster recovery guidelines. Coordinators can obtain these through marketing representatives for the various companies. While this literature rarely provides a comprehensive treatment of disaster recovery, it may provide useful information about a specific application or device used by the company.

Interviews and Tours

Another way to learn about the environment in which a company disaster recovery plan will be implemented is to conduct interviews with coordinators in other companies, with providers of public services, and government officials concerned with public safety and emergency management. From these discussions, coordinators can identify what measures other, similarly-configured companies are taking in disaster recovery, and how the coordinator's plan will be affected by the plans of those whose plans shape the recovery environment.

In some instances, vendors of disaster recovery products and services can provide the names of contacts in neighboring companies or arrange introductions between coordinators. By discussing everything from how the coordinator for another company cost-justified his or her plan to management, to the technical details of how a certain type of local area network can be backed up, to the other coordinator's evaluation of the performance of various vendors, a great deal of useful information can be gathered.

Coordinators would also be well-advised to interview representatives of public services and utilities and local government officials tasked with emergency management. It would be useful to gather information on the following:

• **The power company's policy on repairs and service restoration.** Most utilities are willing to allow company disaster recovery coordinators to tour their facilities. The coordinator should ask questions and develop a thorough understanding of how the utility goes about localizing and repairing the causes of outages. In addition, the coordinator should identify how a "trouble report" is handled: What is the emergency telephone number for reporting an outage? Is more than a single report required to initiate corrective action? What is the typical length of a power outage? What has been the maximum length of an outage in the past two years? Is there a policy regarding priority of service restoration (who is turned on first, second, third, etc.)?

The answers to these questions can lead into a particularized discussion of the coordinator's company power requirements. Ask the representative to show how the company is supplied and what redundancies exist in the system to supply power along an alternative route should the primary route suffer damage.

Power company representatives can also provide information that will guide further research. For example, an office park or high-rise building may be supplied to a central location by the power company, then fed from this central point using secondary lines, transformers, and other hardware that is owned and maintained by the building management company. The power company can point out where its responsibility (and ability to correct problems) ends, and where the building manager's responsibilities begin. This may lead to a subsequent interview of the building manager to understand problem reporting procedures, job order methods, and power restoration time frames from the management company's perspective.

The coordinator may also wish to identify what hardware the management company is using and whether redundant hardware is available to replace malfunctioning equipment. If the management company is using obsolete or hard-to-find hardware, some tenant pressure may persuade the management company to upgrade to newer, more-readily-obtained equipment.

- **How local telephone COs are configured and how they will handle service restoration in an outage.** Coordinators will find that many of the same questions asked of the power company also need to be discussed with a local telephone company representative: where to report trouble, how to escalate response, what are the restoration priorities in the event of a regional outage, and how long an outage may persist. It would be useful to coordinators, whose companies utilize wide-area gateway services from the local CO, to tour the facility containing these master switches. Find out what redundancies exist and where other COs are located in proximity to the company. This information may be used to determine whether it is necessary, or possible, to obtain local area and gateway services from a second CO.

Find out also what services the CO offers in the areas of line noise suppression, data-grade lines, and automatic rerouting of local traffic. If the coordinator is able to speak with a CO engineer who has helped other companies with their network planning or disaster recovery projects, he or she may be able to obtain useful information about the techniques and strategies others have successfully applied.

• **Local civil emergency management plans.** Due to the threats posed to entire communities by natural and man-made disasters, many state and local governments (as well as the federal government) have developed emergency management plans. These plans provide for the evacuation and relocation of the public in the event of hurricanes, typhoons, floods, earthquakes, or nuclear, biological, or chemical disasters.

While not every disaster experienced by a company will entail government intervention, businesses located in "high-risk" areas (i.e., those located on the coastlines of North America, or near chemical or nuclear plants) need to be aware of the impact that civil plans will have on the implementation of their own plan.

A local administrator is usually responsible for the maintenance of a civil emergency management plan. In some localities, the administrative function is given to a local law enforcement or fire protection agency. It may take some time to sift through the bureaucracy to locate the individual or group responsible for emergency planning, but the coordinator should make the effort and meet with the responsible party.

Many coordinators may view this recommendation as superfluous. The concept of civil defense conjures up images of 1950's planning for bomb shelters, air raid sirens, and emergency broadcasts. This perception aside, residents of disaster-prone regions of the U.S. are aware of the ongoing need and true benefit of emergency management agencies in local and state governments. In the event of a natural or man-made threat such as a hurricane, city, county, and state governments have developed strategies for notifying the people and safely evacuating them.

Following cessation of disaster conditions, governmental emergency management plans often provide for controlled reentry into the evacuated areas. These plans have proven their worth time after time and have probably accounted for saving more lives than the polio vaccine. However, such plans are not without their cost to a business if disaster recovery coordinators have not anticipated how they will impact on their company disaster recovery plans. The following brief story illustrates the point.

In 1985, Hurricane Elena forced the evacuation of metropolitan areas up and down the Florida Gulf Coast. (Later that same season, Gloria forced civil governments to relocate populations away from coastal areas all along the Atlantic seaboard.) The Tampa Bay metropolitan area was evacuated while the hurricane was still more than 21 hours distant and had less than a 30 percent chance of making landfall anywhere near the area. Officials called for the early evacuation because they added a 15-

hour period of "prelandfall hazard" to the 9 to 15 hours they calculated it would take to evacuate the residential populations of all flood-prone areas, (including the Gulf Beaches and low-lying areas). Local and state emergency managers had to take into account the period of sustained gale force winds (40+ miles-per-hour) preceding the storm's landfall during which travel would be extremely hazardous. (The length of this period is determined by the size of the hurricane and its rate of movement.) Because of these factors, civil planners anticipated that up to 15 additional hours should be added to the time requirement for safe evacuation. This, in turn, affected the timing of the evacuation order.

While many business planners expected evacuation orders to be inconvenient whenever they were issued, most did not anticipate being ordered out so long before the storm even appeared on local TV radar. The disaster recovery teams of more than one business were ordered out by local law enforcement officials with system backups only partially completed and other planned procedures implemented haphazardly or not at all.

Responding to post-Elena criticisms of their evacuation policy from area businesses, local officials noted that at the time that the mandatory evacuation for Elena was ordered, the storm had been sustaining a 10-mile-per-hour speed toward Tampa Bay for several minutes. Applying the government formulas for calculating the prelandfall hazard, there were actually only about six hours in which to safely evacuate flood-prone areas. To provide for the safety of all of the people, there could be no deviation in the evacuation schedule.

As the story suggests, to plan effectively for a disaster such as a hurricane, coordinators must develop a firm understanding of governmental emergency management plans. The government will place the safety and well-being of the citizenry before the interests of the business and, in so doing, may create a recovery environment in which business recovery plans will flourish or flounder. When there is a threat, governments will evacuate too often and too early. They will also be unsympathetic to the objectives of business planners if they are perceived as coming into conflict with civil plans aimed at preserving the lives of the population.

Evacuation is the first phase of the two-phase plan employed by most civil emergency management officials. The second phase is reentry. As noted previously, the Elena experience demonstrated that coordinators must consider where their recovery personnel reside when planning for facility reentry and damage assessment. If arrangements cannot be made to utilize only personnel who reside in the same area where business offices are located, coordinators may wish to pursue one of the following alternatives with civil defense professionals.

1. Determine whether an evacuation shelter exists or can be set up near the company facility for use by employees and their families. Not only will this reduce the distraction factor, but it will also reduce the likelihood that recovery will be delayed by prohibitions on travel in and out of the disaster area.

2. Discuss with emergency management officials the possibility of approving company ID cards as valid passes into disaster areas. In efforts to avoid looting, reentry into evacuated areas is often controlled by law enforcement officials who seek proof of *residence* (rather than employment) as the criterion for admission. As in the case of Hurricane Elena, company recovery personnel who cannot prove residence in the area of the business they want to access may be turned away, stalling damage assessment and disaster recovery. Preapproval of company ID with civil defense officials may expedite reentry into evacuated businesses once safety hazards have been cleared.

Coordinators from all types of businesses might find it useful to explore some of the generic issues, raised by the experience of Elena, with local government authorities. Depending on the business and its geographical location, there may be other issues that a coordinator may wish to explore in detail to bring business disaster recovery plans into agreement with civil emergency management plans. For example, local law enforcement and fire department officials may be consulted to determine the manner in which bomb threats or arson investigations will be handled, or to explore the roles that public safety officials will play in approving the reoccupation of salvaged facilities. The results of these and other investigations will aid in finalizing a plan which can coexist with other emergency management plans that comprise the recovery environment.

Professional Organizations

Information about the recovery management environment is available from a variety of sources besides publications and one-on-one interviews. Many professional organizations, such as those organized for risk managers, internal auditors, data processing and records management professionals, and other industry specific fields, occasionally offer special programs related to various dimensions of disaster recovery planning which the disaster recovery coordinator may wish to attend.

In addition to these educational forums, an increasing number of regional disaster recovery associations are available to coordinators. These organizations address the specific disaster recovery issues facing the business communities they serve. At meetings of these groups, disaster recovery planning is the central focus, rather than a peripheral issue. Members can compress a great deal of time-consuming research into several hours of concentrated discussion at a group meeting.

Through participation in the group, members can quickly develop an extensive network of contacts, including other users (and vendors) of disaster recovery plans, products and services. In addition, members are kept up-to-date with the latest advancements in disaster recovery techniques and technology, and can profit collectively from shared information on vendor or product performance, or from member discounts on expensive services.

The following disaster recovery groups in the U.S. and Canada were in existence at the time of publication. Telephone numbers and addresses are provided for further information.

- Association of Contingency Planners of California—ACP is a nonprofit, incorporated, mutual benefit association with the objective of becoming a national organization for contingency planners. Established chapters serve the business communities of Orange County and Los Angeles as well as Dallas, Miami, Denver, and Atlanta. Chapters are currently being formed in Phoenix, Boston and Baltimore. ACP produces a quarterly directory of vendor products and services for its members and holds monthly chapter meetings. ACP's address is P.O. Box 73-149, Long Beach, CA 90801-0073. Contact Diane C. Smith or David Williams for more information.

- Association of Contingency Planners of Ohio—This nonprofit organization, founded in 1986, is comprised of business professionals interested in contingency and business recovery planning. The organization's primary purpose is to provide an environment for the exchange of experience and information as well as the identification of common needs or problems shared by businesses in Ohio metropolitan communities. Monthly meetings consisting of a program in the area of recovery planning are followed by a brief business function. For more information, contact Terry Hunek, (216)252-7300, extension 2167, or Patrick Hughes, (216)650-7243.

- Contingency Planning and Security Information Exchange Group—CPSIEG is described as an organization for the exchange of information and promotion of education in the fields of disaster recovery and computer security. Established in 1985, the organization is sponsored by Weyerhaeuser Information Systems and serves the needs of its clients and other businesses in the area of Tacoma, Washington. Meetings of the organization are held quarterly and attendance is said to be in the range of 50 to 100 company representatives. For more information about the group, contact Gene Tallman, (206)924-7360, or write to CPSIEG, Weyerhaeuser Information Systems, Tacoma, WA 98477.

- Contingency Planning Association of the Carolinas—Information about this new group, its meeting schedule, and format are available from Bill Holt, *The Charlotte Observer*, P.O. Box 32188, Charlotte, NC 28232.

- Delaware Valley Disaster Recovery Information Exchange Group—One of the oldest organizations for disaster recovery planners, D.V.D.R.I.E.G. boasts over 500 members in the Delaware Valley. The address is: P.O. Box 8511, Cherry Hill, NJ 08002. Contact Jack Bannon at (609)486-6056 for more information.

- Disaster Avoidance and Recovery Information Group (DARING)—DARING incorporated as a not-for-profit organization within the State of Florida in 1985. Meetings of its Tampa Bay Chapter (there are also chapters in Orlando and Miami and more are anticipated) are held bimonthly and feature expert panels on a variety of disaster recovery-related topics. DARING also sponsors special seminars and has a speaker's bureau. The group attracts regular attendance in excess of 100 persons representing more than 50 member companies. For more information about DARING, contact the organization at P.O. Box 5214, Largo, FL 34294-5214.

- Disaster Recovery Information Exchange (DRIE)—DRIE formed in February 1986 in Toronto, Canada. For more information about the organization, contact DRIE through Graeme Jannaway, New York Life Insurance Company, 121 Bloor Street East, Suite 1600, Toronto, Ontario, Canada M4W 3N2, or call (416)620-3011 and ask to speak with DRIE President Mark Turnbull.

- Hartford Area Local Disaster Recovery Information Exchange Group—This group addresses the information needs of the Connecticut, Massachussets, and New York area. Its quarterly meetings feature expert speakers and vendor booths. For more information, contact Lewis P. Vasquez, (203)273-1187, or write to Mr. Vasquez in care of Aetna Life and Casualty, C14F, 151 Farmington Avenue, Hartford, CT 06156.

- New York Contingency Planning Forum—The New York Contingency Planning Forum is an exchange group of business people who are involved in some aspect of disaster recovery planning with their companies. Members are primarily from financial institutions in the

Wall Street area, but representatives also attend meetings from Connecticut, Massachussets, New Jersey, Pennsylvania, and New York state businesses. The group meets quarterly at member facilities. There are no dues or officers. A program committee meets 4 to 6 weeks before a scheduled meeting to arrange agenda and speakers.

For more information, contact Mark Haimowitz at (212)815-2064, or direct correspondence to his attention in care of Irving Trust Company, One Wall Street, New York, NY 10015.

- Three Rivers Contingency Planning Group—The Three Rivers Group is a recently-organized (June 1987) disaster recovery planning association serving the Pittsburgh area. Its membership numbers representatives from more than 50 businesses who meet bimonthly. Ed Appelt, the current chairman (and disaster recovery coordinator for Consolidation Coal Company), can be called at (412)831-4921. Correspondence may be directed to Mr. Appelt in care of Consolidation Coal Company, Consol Plaza, 1800 Washington Avenue, Pittsburgh, PA 15241.

Financing the Recovery

Another element of the recovery management environment with which the disaster recovery coordinator must become familiar is the financing of the recovery. While coordinators traditionally do not become involved in the planning for allocation of funds for evacuation, recovery, and relocation and reentry projects, they will have had, by the conclusion of the disaster recovery planning project, some influence over how much the recovery will cost and to whom disbursements will be made.

For example, by defining recovery strategies and identifying vendors of products and services to be used in plan implementation, the coordinator has determined the base cost of the recovery project. To this base cost will be added additional costs of transporting personnel to recovery sites; feeding and housing recovery teams; purchasing or leasing equipment until old hardware can be refurbished or replaced; salvage; administrative overhead; and supplies.

Some of these costs fluctuate and cannot be predicted. Some will be considerably more burdensome to the troubled company's treasury than others.   However, if an effective disaster recovery plan has been developed—one that will maintain vital company operations—the company should be able to pay its bills and ultimately recover full health and market share.

This assumes that some "stop-gaps" are in place to reduce the initial financial shock to the company of the disaster and to offset the base costs of recovery. For stop- gap, read insurance.

Business interruption insurance, especially policies designed to compensate for the loss of data processing operations, is a grossly misunderstood beast. Some business leaders still ask why they need a disaster recovery plan when they already have insurance. To others, insurance is considered a waste of money that cannot begin to compensate for a loss of the corporation's most critical, nonhuman asset—information.

Both views are erroneous.

The facts are: (1) Insurance should not be purchased until after a disaster recovery capability has been developed, and (2) insurance will cover the costs of restoring data if it is feasible to do so. According to representatives of the major EDP insurers, the following points need to be clearly understood by business leaders, information managers, and disaster recovery coordinators alike:

- **Types of EDP insurance.** There are basically four types of EDP insurance coverages available. One type covers damaged or destroyed hardware. The second type covers lost data and programs (or the cost of rebuilding data and rewriting programs from source documents, assuming that these are available). The third type of insurance is termed "extra expense" coverage, which includes costs above those for normal operation of the company data center. The fourth type is business interruption insurance to cover the loss of revenues to a company devolving from the loss of its data processing and network operations.[4]

- **Costs of insurance.** Insurance costs money. According to recent studies,[5] coverage for hardware and data loss (types one and two above) ranges between 20 and 30 cents per $100 insured in annual premiums. Thus, a medium-sized $5 million data center could be insured for approximately $10,000 to $15,000, assuming a $12,000 to $15,000 deductible. The cost of extra expense coverage is 40 to 60 cents per $100, and business interruption is double or triple that amount.

    These rates, of course, are available only to companies that have reduced their own exposures to disaster by installing disaster prevention capabilities (fire suppression systems, water detection systems, et al.) and by developing and testing a disaster recovery plan.

- **Considerations for buying insurance.** Fortunately, the pressures of the market have culled out the fly-by-night insurers from the EDP insurance industry. Only a few major companies still offer these lines. Thus, coordinators need not be too concerned about the reputation of the company that a broker recommends. The pricing of policies by most insurers providing the coverages listed above are fairly consistent. With two quotes, the coordinator can be fairly confident that the quoted price is sustained by the market.

  Thus, the major considerations in buying insurance are more internal to the company than external. One consideration that cannot be overlooked is the quality of the company's tested disaster recovery plan. If the plan can realistically provide for restoration of key company functions within 24 to 48 hours, and capabilities exist to prevent common causes of disasters, company risks are already substantially lower than those faced by businesses with no plan. There is no reason to buy insurance coverage for the restoration of data that is regularly duplicated and removed to off-site storage. Similarly, there is no reason to be redundant in insuring recoverable business functions. Items that should be insured include the following:

  1. Costs of replacing hardware. Many insurers will actually assist in obtaining hardware and having it delivered to the customer site in the event of a disaster. One insurer boasts of having replaced a major system within six days.[6]

  2. Known extra-expense items. The only way to know what extra expenses will be entailed in disaster recovery is to have a plan. With a plan, the dollar amount of a hot site disaster declaration fee is known. The cost for implementing a network rerouting plan is known. If preplanned, the costs of emergency off-site storage access, transporting media to the recovery facility, leasing user recovery space (over and above the lease rate for normal operations), and other plan components comprising the "base cost," can be predicted and adequate extra-expense coverages can be purchased.

  3. Interruption-sensitive functions. Business interruption insurance, while very expensive, may need to be purchased for those functions that the business cannot afford to be without even for the period of time it will take to implement the disaster recovery plan. For example, if a major securities brokerage firm loses network communications—its vital link to the markets—for any period of time, it may suffer extraordinary losses even in the brief period of time it takes to re-

store network communications according to the disaster recovery plan. Business interruption insurance would be a justifiable expense under these circumstances.

Beyond the point of insuring against losses in a way that complements the disaster recovery plan, planning for the financing of the recovery project is subject to the same pitfalls as planning for other aspects of disaster recovery. There are too many variations in too many scenarios to plan for every conceivable contingency.

REFERENCES

1. Wendy Goldman Rohm, "That's All That's Left!" *InfoSystems,* Vol. 34, no. 2 (February 1987).
2. Donna Raimondi, "Hot Sites: Disaster Plan Douses Flames," *Computerworld,* Vol. 20, no. 46 (17 November 1986).
3. William C. Symonds, et al., "How Companies are Learning to Prepare for the Worst," *Business Week,* 23 December 1985.
4. Maar Haack, EDP Underwriter, The St. Paul Insurance Companies, and Tom Cornwell, CHUBB Insurance Company, interviews with the author on December 5-6, 1987.
5. See David Stamps, "Disaster Recovery: Who's Worried?" *Datamation,* Vol. 33, no. 3 (1 February 1987).
6. Tom Cornwell, CHUBB Insurance Company, interview with author on December 5, 1987.

Chapter 9

Plan Maintenance and Testing

The plan is finished at last! Strategies for system, network and user recovery have been meticulously honed into straightforward, step-by-step procedures, tied together by a solid-but-flexible emergency decision-making flowchart. To the extent possible, there is now a document in place that will safeguard the company against the vicissitudes of nature and man.

Coordinators who reach this point in the disaster recovery planning project sense a special moment of exaltation, peering down from the summit of their accomplishment at the steep incline that they have just surmounted. Too many, however, end their efforts here.

The disaster recovery document for a large company with numerous critical functions can be voluminous and impressive looking. Perched atop a shelf in the office of the coordinator or information manager, it may be a source of pride, evoking awe from senior management and auditors alike. However, there on the shelf, gathering dust, the document is also useless.

Disaster recovery plans are living documents that must grow and change as the businesses they are to safeguard grow and change. Plans must be maintained and tested.

Plans must also exist not only on paper or diskette, but in the minds of those who will enact them. This presumes training and education.

These points are more than philosophical. With the increasing pressure of federal and state legislation, auditors are less inclined to pass untested plans without comment. They want to see proof that the plan will work and that the company's money has not been invested in anything less than the best capability their money can buy.

Disaster recovery plans should not be tested in use. That is, a disaster should not have to occur before erroneous conclusions and errant strategies are revealed. At that point, the plan's disaster is the company's as well. Plan components need to be tested in a context of rationality, not crisis, so that lessons learned are not learned at the expense of business survival.

Some of the elements of plan maintenance and some approaches to testing planned strategies and procedures are discussed in the following sections. Many experts, including those who owe their expertise to having recovered from smoke- and-rubble-type disasters, argue that testing is the most important element of disaster recovery planning.

Team Education

Before a disaster recovery plan can be implemented, whether in a test situation or in an actual crisis, those who will be called upon to implement the plan must understand their roles. Educating recovery teams requires a mix of classroom and hands-on instructional methods. Getting all team members to become committed to and conversant in the plan is often as great a challenge as developing the plan itself.

The coordinator needs to keep in mind that those who are receiving training in the plan are present for training because they have been told they must attend. Chances are that the majority of trainees do not share the coordinator's zeal for disaster recovery planning. Many may view the training as an unwelcome interference with their mainstream activities; others will see it as a vacation from other responsibilities. Being cognizant of this will help prevent misunderstandings on the part of the coordinator, and dissuade him or her from seeking the approval or applause of the class for a job well done.

The coordinator should focus as narrowly as possible on the specific sections of the plan that pertain to the team being trained. (Teams, by the way, should be trained separately; then, team leaders and alternates given special education in the bigger picture.) Teach trainees what they need to know, *not* how well the plan is organized.

There are a number of guidelines that coordinators need to keep in mind when presenting the plan in a training environment. Knowing what they are can aid in training even the most reluctant student.

1. Be brief and to the point. Especially when training technical teams, it is important to package the information in short, digestible amounts, appropriate to the skill level of the trainees. Unless asked, avoid lengthy digressions into the rationale behind the selection of a particular strategy.
2. Target the audience for level of presentation. Coordinators need not explain the differences between multidrop and point-to-point circuits to a network team. Where possible (i.e., where the coordinator clearly understands the concepts and jargon), use terms and language familiar to the trainee.
3. Use multimedia teaching methods. Coordinators should try to mix their methods for communicating information. Give handouts. Use overhead projectors, video, or slides; use flip charts—whatever is available and appropriate. Nothing is more dull than an hour of "talking head."

4. Make the presentation formal. Prepare an agenda. Rehearse. Designate start and stop times. Set objectives for the group and meet them.

5. Address all questions to the extent possible. If the coordinator cannot answer a question competently, he or she should make a note and follow up at a later time. Encourage constructive participation, and make notes of serious questions or concerns the trainees offer. They may be valuable considerations that will improve the plan.

6. Finish on time. If there is more material to cover, plan another session.

7. Indicate to the trainees that there is no test at the conclusion of the training, but that their performance in a forthcoming test of the plan may be evaluated by their managers.

8. Give the team members copies of the plan sections that pertain to them. Ask them to review the procedures and to submit any comments or corrections that they feel may be needed by a designated date. If the next test date is known, announce it so they are prepared.

Team leaders and their alternates require extra training to familiarize them with the big picture—how the activities of their teams will interrelate and combine to provide the business recovery capability. Here, some informality is suggested in order to create a sense of self-confidence and team unity. Team leaders are given some time-consuming and unrewarding tasks, such as maintaining their sections of the plan and ensuring that staff turnover does not leave a team position vacant. To offset this burden, coordinators should strive to develop a good personal rapport with team leaders.

Often the most difficult training problem exists at the senior management level. The emergency management team is typically comprised of senior managers. If at all possible, the coordinator should rely on his or her manager (usually an information manager or IS executive) to inform management of their role within the plan. If this is not the case, senior managers should nevertheless be given a high-level overview of the plan with emphasis on the emergency decision-making flowchart. Most decision-making flowcharts are fairly vague when it comes to the emergency management task path. Procedures for the emergency management team should consist of question lists management will need to address or guidelines for their consideration. Thus, this section of the plan requires little maintenance, and senior management is informed, rather than trained in their role.

Plan Maintenance

One of the least enjoyable aspects of the disaster recovery coordinator's job is maintenance of the plan. Changes to the functions that the plan seeks to protect (or in the systems and networks that facilitate the functions) come to the coordinator's attention in one of three ways. The first (and preferred way) is through the change management procedure. This procedure should be outlined in the plan to provide a means for regularly auditing plan procedures for their continued adequacy.

The second way in which changes reach the coordinator's attention is through tests. Tests are conducted for a variety of purposes, such as acclimatizing teams to their roles, checking new strategies, establishing restoration time frames, appeasing auditors, and so on. However, a test can also identify where a plan comes up short in the recovery of a given function.

The third way in which changing requirements affecting the plan are discovered is through negative audit reports. This is the least desirable method since it often casts aspersions on the effectiveness of the coordinator. With adequate testing, however, problems can be detected before an audit (or with an auditor present), demonstrating the efficiency of the testing strategy, if not the plan. (Auditors tend not to criticize test results inasmuch as testing is a sign of intent to correct. There is no such thing as a failure in testing. Tests are used to gain knowledge, not to disparage plans.)

Of course, there is one other way that problems in the plan can reveal themselves, but the last way one needs to discover plan inadequacies is in the implementation of the plan in an actual emergency.

Change Management

Change management procedures, combined with periodic testing, are the preferred approaches to plan maintenance. This section examines some of the considerations for developing change management procedures that will streamline the plan maintenance function.

To develop change management procedures, coordinators should look first to identifying which plan elements are likely to change over time. These elements probably include data, programs, documentation, supplies and forms, hardware, and personnel. Of these items, changes in the size and shape of company databases are probably the most expected and self-evident.

Changes in data have two ramifications for disaster recovery planning. First, the disaster recovery coordinator needs to be familiar with the procedures for purging old data and archiving data that needs to be preserved. The coordinator needs to ensure that backup and off-site storage procedures remain adequate to safeguard data against loss.

Also in the realm of data change management issues is the creation of specialized databases on PCs within the company. As new PCs are acquired, their uses need to be documented and provisions need to be made to secure and back up PC data. This task alone may pose as great a challenge as the entire disaster recovery planning process.

If, by great good fortune, PC acquisitions are controlled through a company IS department, or through an IS-directed information center, the coordinator only needs to develop an interface to the acquisition process to remain informed about where the computers are being installed. Controlled PC acquisition can yield other benefits as well. For example, users requesting PCs may be required to schedule time for disaster recovery and security awareness training in conjunction with microcomputer acquisitions.

However, it is more likely that PCs are not acquired through IS channels. As prices decline and user knowledge increases, the disaster recovery coordinator may find that PCs are acquired in the same manner as office supplies and that the number of company data centers increases from week to week. In this case, the coordinator may need to seek the assistance of senior management in order to be kept apprised of acquisitions. It is probably also a good idea to avoid being perceived as critical of the rationale behind the acquisition. If management cannot be convinced of the wisdom in placing control over the purchasing of computer technology in the hands of its IS professionals, the most one can do is to try to ensure that disaster recovery planning requirements are not viewed as a challenge to management prerogatives. With management support, the coordinator may be able to arrange with departmental managers to be informed of technology purchases.

The second ramification of data change is its impact on hardware. As databases grow, it may be necessary to acquire additional mass storage devices. The acquisition of these devices will have to be documented in the equipment inventory addendum to the plan. Also, if the company uses a hot site, the vendor will need to be notified of the additional hardware requirement and contractual changes may be required.

Program changes, enhancements, and modifications often reflect changing business functions. Some program changes do not affect the procedures for restoring the system in the event of a disaster. However, even these changes should be documented and copies of the documentation removed to off-site storage.

Major modifications or additions to the software inventory need to be documented and investigated for their impact on system recovery strategies. New software may carry with it new demands on processors, memory, and storage that have to be accommodated by the hot site to which the company subscribes.

Enhancements or additions to the software base may also reflect changing business functions and changing functional criticalities. Company business plans may offer insights into these changes, but more often the managers of end user departments can provide information about new directions for their operational areas. Thus, periodic questionnaires, accompanied by a copy of the original responses, should be circulated to end user managers with the request that managers update their information.

In the case of software changes and enhancements prompted by technical departments (IS, DP, etc.), recovery team leaders (who are generally employees of these departments) should be directed to update their sections of the plan at periodic intervals. Here, program changes may include changes to telecommunications switch programming as well as computer software.

Documentation changes may also entail a review of the disaster recovery plan's provisions for off-site storage. Coordinators, or their off-site storage team leaders, should regularly inventory documentation that is off-site to ensure that only the most current documentation is stored and outdated or obsolete documentation is destroyed. This includes the disaster recovery plan itself.

As business functions change, preprinted forms and other supplies are also likely to change. If stores of these materials are kept off-site or at a user recovery facility, they need to be inventoried periodically and outdated materials culled from useful supplies. The emergency supplier list (persons to be contacted to obtain replacement supplies and materials in the event of a disaster) also needs to be reviewed to ensure that changing supply requirements can be met by listed suppliers. This review should reveal whether a designated supplier has gone out of business. Where this is the case, any open purchase orders with the former supplier should be closed out and new suppliers should be identified.

Hardware changes require that plan inventories be updated and that hot sites be notified of these changes. Major system conversions may invalidate the existing hot site capability by creating backup requirements that the hot site vendor cannot meet. Thus, a major hardware change may necessitate evaluating new hot site vendors and negotiating a new contract.

Hardware change is a broad category that includes changes to communications as well as computer configurations. It is also important to review network configurations for line changes and additions, communications hardware changes and upgrades, and other network modifications that threaten to invalidate traffic rerouting plans or network backup strategies.

Handling personnel turnover is a critical dimension of disaster recovery change management. New personnel must be trained in the roles they will play in disaster recovery. Emergency contact directories also need to be updated to reflect new personnel and changed home and emergency telephone numbers. For the company as a whole, the maintenance of a general employee contact directory might best be delegated to the human resources or personnel department; while for teams, team leaders should be responsible for keeping contact lists up to date.

Testing the Plan

Plan testing is an important component of plan maintenance activity as tests are the crucibles in which the plan's validity is demonstrated. The central purpose of testing is to ensure that plans can be successfully applied to recover the business functions that they have been developed to safeguard. However, there are other purposes for testing the plan.

- Testing as an audit tool. Plan tests are often used to evaluate the efficiency of the plan and to reveal its shortcomings. Provided the criteria for evaluating test results are properly defined, tests can provide useful information about deficiencies in the plan so that they can be corrected.
- Testing as benchmarking. Plan tests may also reveal useful information about system performance at emergency service levels, network communication integrity over lines to the hot site, and time requirements for plan implementation. This data can be used to project the duration of downtime between invocation of the plan and restoration of critical systems and networks. This, in turn, may be used in the evaluation of business interruption insurance requirements.
- Testing as rehearsal. Tests are a valuable training experience for team members. They provide an opportunity for teams to become familiar with their roles in disaster recovery as well as how their activities relate to the activities of the other teams. Moreover, posttest debriefings of test participants can provide insights into implementation factors that the disaster recovery coordinator may not have considered.

Testing also provides a psychological benefit to participants. They become better prepared to function in a crisis due to the familiarity they acquire with procedures and tasks in a test situation. Furthermore, testing can help to build team unity by demonstrating the interdependence of team members upon each other.

Testing methodologies are numerous and the ones employed should be customized to the needs of a given business. Disaster recovery coordinators differ in their approaches to testing. Some prefer to test without prior notification of test participants in order to simulate the shock and crisis of an actual disaster. Others believe this approach has little merit, claiming that tests should be routine exercises that provide a basis for calm, rational implementation of plan procedures in an actual emergency. Some companies test sections of the plan separately (i.e., they perform a hot site test on one occasion and test various other plan components, one at a time, on other occasions). Other coordinators prefer a dry run of the total recovery plan.

The approach taken by a specific company will generally be determined by the tolerance of the company to interruption of normal work for testing. Few companies are willing to allow a coordinator to "pull the plug" on their computer systems in order to see how efficiently teams will react to a mock disaster. Not many more are willing to shut down normal operations for an evacuation drill. However, it may be argued that effective testing does not require these approaches. The following procedures are some of the basic requirements for effective testing of the disaster recovery plan.[1]

- Establish a scenario in advance. Before undertaking a test, a test strategy needs to be developed. The strategy, often set forth in a document, should identify the scope of the disaster scenario (total loss of facility, loss of CO services, fire in the user working area, flooding of the data center, etc.). The document should also indicate any assumptions that are being made, such as the anticipated duration of the outage, the availability (or unavailability) of key recovery personnel, or the opportunity to perform a last minute backup of critical data.

  In addition to these stage-setting directions, the coordinator may wish to provide details on specific production files that will be recovered, special security requirements, or other factors that will define the elements that are to be tested. In other words, although the disaster may encompass all systems, the coordinator may wish to test only the part of the system recovery plan that pertains to LAN software conversion and recovery or accounting system recovery. This will limit the actual procedures that are executed in the test.

- Set test objectives. Tests should be performed only after formal objectives have been set. Objectives should state clearly what the exercise is to test. For example, the test may seek to determine, under certain conditions, how quickly system and applications software can be brought up on hot site hardware. Or, the test may seek to determine how long data reconstruction will take if a disaster occurs at 3:00 P.M. on a working day and transactions entered since 9:00 A.M. have been lost. The test may also seek to measure the performance of a concentrator in conjunction with a set of user terminals thought to have low activity profiles.

Whatever the objectives, they should be clearly stated up-front to aid in the interpretation of test results at the conclusion of the exercise. Generally, the narrower the objectives, the more useful the information derived from the test will be.

- Define the rules. The rules in a test may be to perform the required function in strict adherence to planned procedures. Where deviation from the plan is required to accomplish the task, this reveals something about the adequacy of plan procedures, and participants may be required to make careful notes of what undocumented steps they must take to accomplish the objective.

    In rare cases, the rules for the test may be open-ended. Traditionally, this type of test rule is used to evaluate how well a team participant can improvise or develop procedures where none previously existed.

- Identify participants and observers. A list should be made of the team members and observers (often internal audit, IS executives, and others) who will participate in the test. Each should be made fully aware of his or her role *before* the test occurs (unless the test is a surprise). Observers should be told what to look for and what to do (i.e., take notes, ask questions). Team members should be told the rules and given any other directions that will help them to collect valuable information during the test.

- Document the test results. Depending on the objectives of the test, output may be printed in the form of system performance measurements, transaction logs, or other reports containing data sought from the test. This data will be analyzed, and both the original documents and the conclusions drawn from them retained with the plan. Test conclusions and source documentation are an important part of the documentation an EDP auditor will require when auditing the disaster recovery plan.

    In addition to machine data, test objectives may require written reports from test participants. Objective facts, such as elapsed time to perform a given task or prolonged delays in recovering systems, may be included in posttest documentation. In addition, subjective assessments of plan performance may be sought from participants. These subjective assessments may be balanced by obtaining more than a single viewpoint on a given subject. Conflicting views or interpretations necessitate a group discussion with the results summarized in a final test report. Written reports, like the machine output, should be kept with the plan document for review by auditors.

There is no rule of thumb for how often plans should be tested, but tests should be conducted as often as necessary. In stable, evolutionary data processing environments, system recovery plans should be tested quarterly or semiannually. However, in shops where system configurations and applications change often, more frequent testing may be required.

Managing the Results

Given the massive amounts of information that will often be generated by maintenance and testing, it is possible for the disaster recovery coordinator to lose sight of the purpose of the disaster recovery plan itself. Plans that need to be completely rewritten for each and every change that is made to company systems, networks, and user procedures are poorly written. By using a functional approach (organizing the plan into sections by recovery function) in plan construction, it should be possible to replace pages of the document when revisions are needed, rather than rewriting the entire document.

Still, changes may mandate substantive revisions to several sections of the plan. A change in the hardware configuration, for example, may require the updating of plan sections pertaining to system recovery, salvage, hardware inventory, and hot site configuration. However, the impact of other changes can be minimized if the plan is properly constructed from the start.

For example, highly variable elements of the plan—including team member names or supplier contact telephone numbers—should be kept in their own sections of the plan rather than being dispersed throughout the procedures. Procedures should refer the user to the section of the plan containing the name or number. In this way, a change in team personnel or a supplier can be readily incorporated into the plan.

For maintenance purposes, it may be valuable to have a copy of the plan stored on magnetic media as edits and changes can be made more readily using electronic means. If this approach is adopted, however, it is essential that both hard copy and magnetic media backups be made of the plan.

The idea of maintaining the plan by electronic means is not original. There are a number of vendors who market disaster recovery planning tools that are based on PCs and larger CPUs. PC-based tools, or "canned plans," can provide a valuable resource for in-house plan development. In fact, several consulting firms offer their basic plan on diskette to clients who cannot afford or do not wish to purchase the "full treatment."[2]

Canned plans range from boiler-plated, ASCII file documents that may be customized and maintained on a PC using any popular word-processing software package to "decision support systems" that "integrate" word processing-driven files with database, outline, and project management applications. Most planning tools offer basically the same feature—a generic plan. Each plan reflects its author's favored methodology for disaster recovery planning.

According to one plan author, the chief advantage of using a PC-based plan is that it eliminates the need to "reinvent the wheel."[3] For novice disaster recovery coordinators, a PC-based plan helps reduce the learning curve and the costs of the planning project. It can also reassure the coordinator that he or she has not overlooked something important.

While many PC-based planning tools have the drawbacks of being too generic to be of much practical use or requiring users to adopt someone else's planning methodology, the major advantage of these tools is their ease of maintenance. Some tools are word-processing driven or "secretary-friendly," in the words of one vendor.[4] Advocates of word processing-based plans argue that keeping the plan up-to-date is primarily a secretarial function. With a plan that can be maintained using any popular word processing package, there is no learning curve to overcome. Changes can be compiled by the disaster recovery coordinator and then referred to a secretary for input.

Word processing-based plans generally contain specific variables in the original software plan that the disaster recovery coordinator replaces with his or her own information using a Global Search-and-Replace function in the word processing software package. The use of Global Search-and-Replace, however, becomes problematic if the plan itself is not properly constructed. If variable information is dispersed and replicated throughout the plan, rather than being located in a single section, updating the variable using Global change can confuse coordinators.

One vendor told the story of a customer who replaced a certain item of hardware in accordance with a configuration change using Global Search-and-Replace, a process which does not generally reveal the context of the changed variable.[5] The net result was that the hot site configuration list was changed, but the hot site was never informed of the change. The coordinator failed to recognize the effect that variable replacement would have on the overall plan until a test revealed the error.

This factor, among others, has led to the development of database-driven planning tools. With database-driven plans, variable information is contained in an index, which is updated to reflect changes in the protected systems or recovery strategies. A series of reports are then printed which comprise the updated plan.

Detractors of the database approach argue that database management software is less familiar than word processing packages to the average disaster recovery coordinator. Thus, in addition to learning the principles and techniques of disaster recovery planning, the novice coordinator must also overcome a learning curve for new software.

Regardless of the relative merits of word-processing or database drivers, most canned plans share the following features that may or may not support their use:

- Most disaster recovery planning tools require the coordinator to adopt the methodology of the software author. Where company requirements dovetail with plan features, this factor may be a benefit. Where they do not, using such a tool can cause undue hardship for coordinators.

- Most disaster recovery planning tools focus only on the disaster recovery requirements of data processing. Most, but not all, ignore the recovery requirements of the company as a whole.

- Many disaster recovery planning tools set forth a systems recovery strategy that presumes the use of a hot site service. While this is certainly the current trend in the industry for systems recovery, companies that use service bureaus or other backup strategies may not benefit from the planning tool that has this strategy as its backbone.

Other factors being equal, the selection of which PC- based plan (if any) is right for a given company will be based upon the disaster recovery coordinator's personal preference for methodology and design. In the words of one observer, "Once you're comfortable with the basic methodology, the rest is a matter of taste. Plus, other factors such as company documentation standards, format, readability, and so forth may come into play."[6]

The point of this discussion is not to suggest that disaster recovery coordinators need or will profit from the use of a PC-based disaster recovery planning tool. Planning tools are not a replacement for sound planning practices. At best, they are an adjunct. However, an examination of the available software may result in a match with the coordinator's plan development and maintenance needs. At worst, obtaining demos of planning software may stimulate a few ideas about designing disaster recovery plans for ease of use and maintenance.

REFERENCES

1. Some of this information is derived from marketing literature provided by CHI/COR Information Management, Inc., EDP Security, Inc., and Total Assets Protection, Inc.

2. Much of the information in this discussion is extracted from Jon Toigo, "Your PC Can Help Avert Disastrous Consequences," *The Databus*, Vol. 4, no. 10 (November 1986), and Jon Toigo, "Alternatives For Disaster Recovery Plan Development," *Data Security Management* (New York: Auerbach Publishers, 1988).

3. Thomas Abruzzo, president, TAMP Computer Systems, interview with author, September 15, 1987.

4. Ibid.

5. Jill Chamberlain, vice president, CHI/COR Information Management, Inc., interview with author, September 17, 1987.

6. Ibid.

Chapter 10

Conclusion

This book was conceived as a practical guide for information managers. In reality, it is a compilation of all of the information that I wished I had known when, as a technical writer and documentalist for an MIS Division, I was handed the task of disaster recovery planning.

At that time, when asked how long I thought the project would take, I answered that the plan would be complete inside of two weeks. Two months and one hurricane later, I found myself still wrestling with the myriad details of a thousand what-if scenarios. Not one procedure had been written. Not one strategy had been developed. No testing had occurred. Yet, somehow, the document had grown to exceed the page count of the *New York Times* Sunday edition.

Assistance came in the form of an off-site storage marketing representative and a contingency planner-turned-consultant, who gave away more valuable advice than he should have, and who subsequently returned to the secure embrace of company employment. Through these persons, I was introduced to a network of concerned (and often overinvested) practitioners of the disaster recovery craft. One thing led to another and the nonprofit professional association, DARING, was born.

During the next two years, I became somewhat conversant in the rarified jargon of the disaster recovery industry. I learned to recognize both the charlatans and the earnest souls who populate this back-room world of disaster recovery. What I know, I learned from them.

The theoretical books and manuals I read on disaster recovery planning did not begin to capture the sheer pragmatism of their approach to disaster recovery planning. I promised to write one that would. To the extent that this objective has been met in the preceding pages, the credit goes to them.

Conclusions serve two purposes. One is structural as the book must have an ending.

The ending of this book is hopefully a beginning. Newcomers to the field of disaster recovery planning are now, I hope, a little better prepared to undertake the task that is before them. For accomplished coordinators, I hope the book will confirm that they are not alone and, just maybe, give them some added confidence that their self-made efforts are at least as valid as those of any high-priced consultant.

However, pragmatism dictates that this book must end with a sobering thought. It is this: No amount of planning can cover all the bases. When a disaster strikes, even the best plans may prove unequal to the challenge. In an actual disaster, creativity and improvisation and hard work will determine whether the business will recover.

What then is the value of disaster recovery planning? Just this: A company's chances of survival are better if it has a plan than if it doesn't. The enterprise of disaster recovery planning, involving as it does numerous company employees, forces the company as a whole to face a reality that most would prefer to ignore. This has the effect of sensitizing persons to the causes of disaster, and perhaps helping to avoid one.

In addition, employees who will serve as recovery team members are trained in the performance of these roles. While the realities of a disaster may render some of these procedures irrelevant, this does not alter one side-effect of training: Team members have been taught to reason in a crisis. This, and not the plan, is the foundation upon which business recovery will be built. Or as William Shakespeare expressed it in *Henry V*, "All things are ready, if our minds be so."

The second purpose of a conclusion is to serve as a repository for all the justifications of those quiet judgments that were rendered in the earlier chapters. It is where the author tries to comment on observations that he is sure will come in response to the book (although sometimes he only rationalizes his own complaints).

These are some of the issues that require closure.

1. "Short shrift was given to quantitative risk analysis techniques." This is probably true. However, as I am not an adherent of any of the major methodologies of quantitative risk analysis, and since there are already so many books on the subject, readers are directed to turn to their local libraries for more information on these methods.[1]

2. "Some system backup options that were brushed over in the book seem better suited to my company's needs than are the options that the author spent most of his time discussing." Again, this statement may be true. However, this book has sought to devote the greatest attention to those options that the apparent majority of companies with backup capabilities are using. Companies having tested disaster recovery capabilities, as stated in the Management Overview, comprise only a small percentage of all companies in North America.

   If coordinators who read this book determine that a mutual service arrangement with another company more closely meets their system backup requirements than a hot site, by all means enter into such an arrangement.

   Different companies clearly have differing needs. The caveats that have been offered are just that: things to consider before entering into such arrangements. If cautions are proved to be inapplicable in a given situation, coordinators should go with their best judgment.

3. "If I have only twenty employees, how can I have ten to twenty recovery teams?" or "I run my entire company on a minicomputer and a handful of local and long distance lines, so why do I need to use teams to perform tasks that a single individual could do blindfolded?" The size of a disaster recovery team should be guided by the following considerations.

    (a) Complexity of the task—If the task can be performed by a single person within an acceptable time frame, no team may be needed. If the task is somewhat complex, at least one other individual should be available to assist in the event of a problem. Very complex tasks may require several persons.

    (b) Extent of preplanning—If a task has been clearly defined, and no improvisation is required or expected, and the task can be performed by one person, designate a one-person team. If the strategy is not formalized, and the task is to be performed by "the seat of the pants," it may be necessary to allocate more than one person to the team assigned to perform the task.

    (c) Availability of trained backup—If the person responsible for performing the task cannot be reached in a recovery situation, is there another qualified individual to whom the task can be assigned? If the answer is no, then a team approach— with cross-training of team members—may be required.

4. "When you listed the skills that a disaster recovery coordinator would need to possess, you forgot to mention 'trainer'." Correct. However, this point should be clear in Chapter 9.

5. "You said that there is no such thing as a failed test. Considering the money, time, and effort spent in developing a plan, wouldn't the plan be a failure if the test proved the plan inadequate?" Personal embarrassment aside, coordinators need to view as beneficial any information that a test provides. If the plan fails in testing, the test is not a failure. It has succeeded in identifying areas of the plan that need to be reviewed and revised to make the plan better.

With those issues resolved, all that remains is to preview the appendices. Appendix A is the emergency decision-making flowchart that was presented in sections in Chapter 7. It is intended as a model, not as a guide. Coordinators should develop their own flowcharts or precedent charts based upon the tasks they have identified as necessary for the recovery of their own businesses.

Appendix B is a Glossary of terms and language used in this book. While every effort has been made to avoid jargon wherever possible or to explain its meaning in context, the glossary will provide a safeguard against lapses of attention to these objectives.

Appendix C is a directory of disaster recovery vendors, a *Who's Who* of disaster recovery planning. Neither the publisher nor the author endorses the products or services of the vendors listed in this appendix, nor is this list complete. It is a compilation of information available from a variety of sources at the time of publication. Readers are urged to evaluate a number of vendors before making any selection or purchase.

Appendix D is a sample user questionnaire that may be imitated for use in the collection of information for the purposes of criticality assessment.

One final issue needs to be addressed: "When should I start to develop a disaster recovery plan?" The question is typically followed by a lengthy list of all of the reasons why now is *not* a good time. Here is a brief summary of the rationalizations and how I respond to them.

- "We're just in the planning stages for bringing data processing in-house. We have no computers yet, except a few PCs. Most of our processing is done at a service bureau and they have a plan."—In this instance, the disaster recovery coordinator is afforded a rare opportunity. Not only can current manual operating procedures be documented fairly quickly, but the coordinator is in on the ground floor of a system development project and may be able to influence how that project develops in order to favor disaster recovery considerations.

  Second, the coordinator should test with the service bureau the service bureau's plan for disaster recovery. If the vendor has such a plan, but it has not included customers in the tests, I would have serious doubts about plan validity.

  Third, if facilities are being developed to house the company's new data processing capability, the coordinator should attempt to become involved in planning preventive capabilities to be installed in that facility.

  Finally, disaster recovery planning is not planning for the recovery of data processing alone. It is planning for business recovery. Thus, all components of the plan can be developed, leaving the systems recovery strategy for last.

- "We've been changing over to a new software package (or to new hardware) and I wonder if we shouldn't wait until the conversion is successful and complete before we take on disaster recovery planning."—Again, the coordinator has much more to protect than one system or application. Development of user and network recovery strategies should proceed, even if the systems recovery strategy is not yet able to be finalized.

  One other point: Conversions are not only destabilizing; they can also create disasters if not properly managed and controlled. Thus, a disaster recovery plan should be written before a conversion begins to handle the possibility of a disaster involving the conversion project.

- "We've had a shaky quarter, lots of expenses. I don't think that management will underwrite the costs of disaster recovery planning until maybe next quarter or next year."—Disaster recovery planning need not be a cost born solely by data processing. It is the protection of corporate assets from loss and may result in savings in the cost of business interruption insurance. The coordinator in this case may be surprised to find management receptive to the notion of disaster recovery planning, especially if audit remarks or legal mandates require that such a capability be put into place.

- "We're putting out daily fires. There's not much time for disaster recovery planning and no personnel are available for the job."—This comment suggests two things. One, the coordinator or IS manager is saying, "What we have right now is such a headache, I'm not sure that it's worth saving." If systems and networks provide critical functions for the company, they are worth something. Discerning that value and creating a plan that is commensurate to it is prerequisite to good management. If the manager doesn't agree, he or she is in the wrong job.

  The second comment, regarding the availability of personnel, is a valid one. Unless a full-time employee (or a consultant) is available or can be hired for the purpose of coordinating the disaster recovery planning project, it will probably not result in a workable plan. Assigning or hiring such a person should be a higher priority than hiring a new programmer or analyst, since an investment in disaster recovery protects an investment in new software.

The bottom line is that the time to begin developing a disaster recovery capability is *now*. Stop reading about it. The way to write the plan is to sit down and write it.

REFERENCES

1. For additional reading on risk analysis, see: Peter S. Browne, "Survey of Risk Assessment Methodologies," *Data Security Management* (New York: Auerbach Publishers, 1984); W. D. Rowe, *Anatomy of a Risk* (New York: John Wiley & Sons, 1977); U.S. Department of Commerce, National Bureau of Standards, "Guidelines of Automatic Data Processing Physical Security and Risk Management," FIPS PUB 31, Washington, DC, June 1984; and, U.S. Department of Commerce, National Bureau of Standards, "Guideline for Automatic Data Processing Risk Analysis," FIPS PUB 65, Washington, DC, June 1979.

Appendices

APPENDIX A: CHARTS

The foldout at the back of this book provides two charts that the disaster recovery coordinator may find useful. A-1 is a Master Emergency Decision Making Flowchart, combining all of the flowcharts found in Chapter 7. It can be imitated to create a master flowchart that will serve as the skeleton of the reader's disaster recovery plan.

On the second chart, A-2, is a Master Data Flow Diagram showing the combined disaster recovery planning activities described in the preceding chapters. It is hoped that the chart will be useful in orienting the reader to the complex and multifaceted processes that go into the making of a corporate disaster recovery capability.

APPENDIX B: GLOSSARY

Applications software: A set of programs that provides a specific function or set of functions.

Automatic rerouting: A method of reterminating wide area and local telecommunications traffic at alternate facilities in the event of a disaster. Automatic suggests that the rerouting of traffic may be accomplished rapidly by preplanning the alternate traffic patterns with a carrier service vendor.

Baud: A baud is a unit that measures the speed of data transmission. One baud equals 1 bit per second.

Circuit: A single communications facility or combination of facilities including satellite, microwave, fiber optics, or wire.

CO: A local carrier switch, provided by a commercial vendor of telecommunications services, which provides the interconnection of transmission devices.

Cold site: Cold site is a synonym for shell site. It is a facility that is prepared to receive computer hardware and which may be used on an on-going basis for emergency system operations if a primary facility is destroyed or rendered uninhabitable.

Concentrator: A programmable device which combines the functions of a multiplexor with a data storage buffer, message error checking capability, and device polling capability.

Encryption: A method of defeating attempts to eavesdrop on data communications by encoding the data according to a scheme known to both the originator and receiver of the transmission.

EPCOT Code: A set of codes, including a fire code, developed in conjunction with the construction of the EPCOT Center at Walt Disney World in Orlando, Florida. It is considered to be one of the most advanced codes in existence.

Firmware: Software that is stored in some fixed form, such as ROM (Read-Only-Memory).

Front-end communications controller: A programmable device that interfaces a communications network with a host computer. Some of the controller's functions may include polling, speed and code conversion, error detection, data buffering, and security authentications.

Gateway: A software- and/or hardware-supplied interface between communications networks.

Halon: An abbreviation for halogenated agent. It is a gas, which in relatively small concentrations of 3% to 5%, can effectively suppress fires. Available as an automatically-released system or in the form of hand-held extinguishers.

Hot site: A data processing facility that is equipped with hardware and communications capabilities that can be occupied by a subscriber in the event of a disaster.

ISO: An abbreviation for the International Standards Organization.

LAN: An abbreviation of Local Area Network. A method of connecting communications devices using privately-owned wire or fiber interconnecting numerous devices and a control program.

Micron: A unit of length equal to one one-millionth of a meter, or 39.3 microinches.

MODEM: An abbreviation for MOdulator-DEModulator. It is a device used to translate computer information into signals that can be sent along a telephone line, and then translate the signals back to computer data at the destination.

Multiplexor: A device that combines different data streams into a single stream for transmission at high speed. Multiplexed transmissions are commonly received by a multiplexor at the destination site where they are separated back into their component data streams.

Multidrop circuit: A configuration for connecting communications devices that allows the sharing of a communications facility. Like a "party-line," several devices share a single line. Generally, only one device can be active at a time.

NFPA: National Fire Protection Association.

OSI: An abbreviation of Open Systems Interconnection. It is a standard advanced by the ISO that segregates the process of network data communications into seven modular tasks: physical, data link, network, transport, session, presentation, and application.

Packet-switching: A data communications technique that allows messages to be divided or segmented into packets and routed dynamically through a network to a final destination point.

Packout: A stage of records salvage in which specific cleaning, packaging, labeling, and storage procedures are performed.

Particulate: A small particle of organic or mineral material that can collect in sensitive electronic equipment resulting in damage and possibly destruction.

Password: A character string (often a word) that must be entered by the user and validated by the system or network before the system or network may be accessed.

PBX: An acronym for private branch exchange. It is a leased or privately-owned programmable device that facilitates communications between a number of telecommunications or data devices within a company with the CO and wide area network.

Permissions: As the name suggests, permissions are read and/or write privileges assigned to users by the system administrator for programs and data sets. Permissions are often linked, via software, to device IDs or user passwords.

Point-to-point circuit: A method for connecting communications devices in which a dial-up or dedicated circuit provides the connection between two communicating devices.

Protocols: Typically, software-controlled rules that govern transmission between communicating devices.

Service bureau: A computer facility that provides processing services to subscribers on an on-going basis. In the context of disaster recovery, the vendor of a software package may be willing to make the software available on its own hardware for emergency use by a customer.

Shell site: A synonym for cold site. It is a facility that is prepared to receive computer hardware and which may be used on an on-going basis for emergency system operations should a primary facility be destroyed or rendered uninhabitable.

Software: A group of computer programs.

Trunk group: A group of circuits in a telecommunications network.

UPS: An acronym for uninterruptible power supply.

WAN: An acronym for wide area network.

APPENDIX C: PARTIAL DIRECTORY OF DISASTER RECOVERY VENDORS

This directory contains a partial listing of vendors of products and services that may be used in conjunction with disaster recovery planning activities. Inclusion or exclusion of vendors in this listing does not imply endorsement or detraction of a vendor's products or services.

The purpose of this list is provide disaster recovery coordinators with a starting point in their efforts to identify vendors and compare products on the basis of company objectives and requirements. Where possible, contact names have been provided.

Cold Sites, Shells

CompuSource
Cary, NC
Wayne Edge
(919)469-3325

Corporate Contingency
Services, Inc.
New Hudson, MI
Craig Fuller
(313)486-2110

Dataguard Recovery Services,
Inc.
Louisville, KY
Helen Below
(800)325-3977

Datashield
Greendale, WI
(414)421-7710

Data-Site
Greenville, WI
(401)949-1090

Digital Equipment
Corporation
(603)884-3042

Disaster Control, Inc.
Warminster, PA
Marie Mascio
(215)355-7800

Eloigne
Minneapolis, MN
J. Marquardt
(612)644-0882

Emergency Computer Center
Lenexa, KS
Mike Mahoney
(913)888-6200

Equicor Technologies
Bethlehem, PA
(215)861-2800

HSH Cold Site
Columbus, OH
(614)888-1050

Remote Computing
Palo Alto, CA
(213)386-6430

Iron Mountain
Boston, MA
(803)357-9034

Western Southern Life
Insurance Company
Cincinnati, OH
F. T. Schneider
(513)629-1717

Policy Management System
Columbia, SC
(803)748-2929

Computer-based Disaster Recovery Planning Tools

Advanced Information
Management
Woodbridge, VA
R. Phillips
(703)643-1002

Operations Services, Inc.
Tampa, FL
H. J. "Skip" Mathews
(813)888-8514

Systems Support, Inc.
St. Louis, MO
Richard Arnold
(314)846-1001

CHI/COR Information
Management, Inc.
Chicago, IL
K. F. Effgen
(312)454-9670

EDP Security, Inc.
Littleton, MA
John Negron
(617)486-8080

Tamp Computer Systems, Inc.
Merrick, NY
Tom Abruzzo
(516)623-2038

Consulting Services

CHI/COR Information
Management, Inc.
Chicago, IL
K. F. Effgen
(312)454-9670

Comdisco Disaster
Recovery Services
Rosemont, IL
J. E. Mannion
(312)698-3000

Corporate Contingency
Services
New Hudson, MI
Robert J. Dennis
(313)486-2090

Data Base Recovery Services, Inc.
Columbia, MD
(301)995-1433

Emergency Computer Corp.
Lenexa, KS
Mike Sheer
(913)888-6200

HOTSITE®
Niles, OH
Kevin Hephner
(216)652-9624

HDA, Inc.
Dublin, OH
Jon Raymond
(614)766-6881

Iron Mountain Group
Boston, MA
W. A. Dreyer
(617)357-9034

SUNGARD
Wayne, PA
Robert Bronner
(215)341-8749

Total Assets Protection
Arlington, TX
J. Stratton
(817)640-8800

Environmental Maintenance

CompuClean International
Miami, FL
Mark Sher
(305)666-9981

Randomex, Inc.
Signal Hill, CA
(213)595-8301

Facility Disaster Prevention

Ansul
Marinette, WI
(201)522-0130

Atlas Fire Equipment
(609)456-3299

Automatic Sprinkler
(216)526-9900

Borrell Fire Systems, Inc.
Tampa, FL
Tom Butler
(813)223-2121

Chemetron Fire Systems
(312)534-1000

Digital Pathways
(415)493-5544

Fenwal Incorporated
Ashland, MA
(617)881-2000

Fike Metal Products
(816)229-3405

Fire Suppression Systems
Association
P.O. Box 28279
Baltimore, MD 21234

Great Lakes Chemical
(317)463-2511

Keystone Fire Protection
(215)426-3600

National Fire Protection
Association
Batterymarch Park
Quincy, MA 02269

Power Solutions
Technology
(215)245-4242

Pyrotronics
(201)267-1300

Raychem Corporation
(TraceTek®)
Menlo Park, CA
Laurie C. Conner
(415)361-6693

TAPP of Delaware
(302)429-9348

Fireproof Vaults and Cabinets

Diebold
(216)489-4000

Meilink
(800)537-3266

Mosler Safe
(201)575-4666

Oxford Pendaflex
(516)741-3200

Schwab Safe
(317)447-9470

Hot Sites (IBM)

Alternative Marketing
Systems
Bensalem, PA
(215)244-1777

Bessemer Information
Services
Monroeville, PA
(412)829-3336

Bradford National Computer
Teaneck, NJ
(201)883-1020

Comdisco Disaster
Recovery Services, Inc.
Rosemont, IL
J. E. Mannion
(312)698-3000

CompuSource
Cary, NC
Wayne Edge
(919)469-3325

Computer Recovery Facility
Mississauga, Ontario, Canada
M. B. Moore
(416)821-2800

Continental Computer
Assurance Corp.
Newtown, PA
Robert Fritsky
(215)968-6000

Corporate Contingency
Services
New Hudson, MI
Scott Sarasin
(313)486-2110

Equicor Technologies
Bethlehem, PA
(215)861-2800

Eloigne Corp.
St. Paul, MN
J. Marquardt
(612)644-0882

HOTSITE®
Niles, OH
Kevin Hephner
(216)652-9624

Neshaminy Valley
St. Trevose, PA
(215)322-2285

Policy Management
Systems
Columbia, SC
(803)748-2929

Software Research
Needham Heights, MA
(617)449-5310

SUNGARD
Wayne, PA
Robert Bronner
(215)341-8749

Weyerhaeuser Recovery
Services
Tacoma, WA
Gus Bader
(206)924-4200

Hot Sites (Non IBM)

Arbat Systems
(DEC)
Hoboken, NJ
(201)963-4440

Cadre
(Burroughs)
Avon, CT
(203)674-1285

Computer Alternatives (NCR)
Ridgewood, NJ
(201)652-0400

CRA
(Honeywell)
Phoenix, AZ
(602)944-1548

Dataguard Recovery Services,
Inc.
(Honeywell)
Louisville, KY
Helen Below
(800)325-3977

Disaster Control, Inc.
(Burroughs)
Warminster, PA
J. Saint George
(215)355-7800

Hale Systems, Inc.
Palo Alto, CA
T. J. O'Neil
(415)494-6111

Information Network
(DEC, IBM)
Dallas, TX
(214)630-1240

Phoenix Services
(Prime)
Lexington, MA
(617)863-5040

Remote Computing
(Burroughs)
Palo Alto, CA
(213)386-6430

Wang Information Services, Inc.
(Wang)
Burlington, MA
Frank Mundo
(617)270-8519

Weyerhaeuser Recovery Ser-
vices
(DEC, Honeywell,
Hewlett-Packard)
Tacoma, WA
Gus Bader

Off-Site Storage (Regional or Archival)

Acme Visable Records
(804)823-4351

Advanced Information
Management
Woodbridge, VA
R. Phillips
(703)643-1002

Archives
(901)386-5560

Association of Commercial
Records Centers
9715 James Avenue South
Minneapolis, MN 55431

AT&T American Transtech
Maitland, FL
Al Carozza
(800)447-0012

Berkins Records Management
(213)466-9271

BIMS
Tampa, FL
Thomas Brasser
(813)626-0470

Data Base Company, Inc.
(301)995-6433

Dataguard
(617)875-4300

Dataguard
(201)592-7868

Data Networking Services
(314)343-2858

Data Protection Inc.
Orlando, FL
Pam Freeman
(305)851-8557

Datasafe
(404)256-5840

Data Safe, Inc.
(201)989-1000

Data Security
(206)581-4200

Data Security
(416)293-1161

DataVault Corp.
Needham Heights, MA
B. Stoddard
(617)444-8908

Digital Equipment
Corporation
(603)884-3042

Digital Equipment
of Canada Limited
(416)624-3466

Fireproof Records
Center
Columbus, OH
(614)299-2121

First National Safe Deposit
Corporation
(215)576-1300

Florida Data Bank, Inc.
Winter Haven, FL
Joseph Bogdahn
(813)965-3691

Fort Knox Safe
Depository
(404)292-0700

Iron Mountain Group
(617)357-9034

Off-Site Storage
(617)454-8033

Perpetual Storage, Inc.
Salt Lake City, UT
J. L. Nowa
(801)942-1950

Peirce Business Archives
(215)586-1545

Security Computer Data
Limited
(604)873-4581

The Holding Company
(215)527-8010

The Vault, Inc.
Reno, NV
D. L. Andrews
(702)785-8408

The Vault, Limited
(302)652-2202

Vital Records, Inc.
Raritan, NJ
P. Catalano
(201)526-7557

Wright Line
(215)852-4300

Power Conditioners and UPS

Abacus Controls
(201)526-6010

Elgar
(619)565-1155

Adley CES, Inc.
(609)667-6681

Emergency Power Engineering
(714)557-1636

Amtek Systems
(214)238-5300

Emerson Electric
(714)545-5581

Atlas Energy Systems
(213)575-0755

Exide Electronics
(919)872-3020

Best Energy Systems
(608)565-7200

General Electric
(615)824-7260

Clary
(213)287-6111

Georator
(703)368-2101

Computer Power
(201)735-8000

Gould
(619)291-4211

Computer Power Products
(213)323-4181

International Power Machines
(214)288-7501

Computer Power Systems
(201)515-6566

ITT Power Systems
(419)468-8100

Cuesta Systems
(805)541-4160

Kalglo Electronics
(215)837-0700

Cyberex
(216)946-1783

K/W Control Systems
(914)355-6741

Deltec
(619)291-4211

LEA
(213)944-0916

Liebert
(614)888-0264

Ratelco
(206)624-7770

Litton Industrial Products
(414)481-6000

RKS Industries
(408)438-5760

Lortec Power Systems
(216)327-5050

Shape Magnetronics
(312)620-8394

Micron Industrial
(312)345-0788

Sola Electric
(312)439-2800

Nova Electrical Manufacturing
(201)661-3434

Solidstate Controls
(614)846-7500

Pilgrim Electric
(516)420-8989

Teledyne Inet
(213)325-5040

Power Conversion Products
(815)459-9100

TII Industries
(516)789-5000

Powermark
(619)565-8363

Topaz Electronics
(619)279-0831

Power Solutions Technology
(215)245-4242

UPSystems
(213)634-0621

Power Systems & Controls
(804)355-2803

Welco Industries
(513)891-6600

Salvage and Restoration

American Freeze Dry
Atlantic City, NJ
John Magill
(609)546-0777

CompuClean International
Miami, FL
Mark Sher
(305)666-9981

Blackman Mooring Steamatic
Catastrophe, Inc.
Fort Worth, TX
W. Blackman
(817)926-8251

Document Reprocessing
California
Eric Lundquist
(415)362-1290

Randomex, Inc.
Signal Hill, CA
(213)595-8301

Security-access Systems

Amcard Systems
(617)562-7111

Analytics
(703)893-2124

Butler National
(913)888-8585

Cardkey Systems
(213)998-2777

Datakey
(612)890-6850

Emidata
(301)363-1600

Fingermatrix
(914)428-5441

Honeywell
(612)332-5200

Identatronics
(312)437-2654

Mastiff Systems
(404)448-4100

Medeco Security
Locks
(703)387-0481

Rusco Electronics
(213)240-2540

Schlage Electronics
(408)727-5170

Sensormatic Electronics
(305)427-9700

Sielox Systems
(408)374-3049

Simplex Security Systems
(203)693-8391

Stellar Systems
(408)946-6460

Sutton Designs
(607)277-4301

Sycon
(408)374-3049

Synergistics
(617)655-1340

Systematics
(213)799-6696

TEC
(602)792-2230

TelTech
(212)921-0250

Other Backup and Recovery Services

Premier Network Services, Inc.   VIPS, Inc.
Dallas, TX   Hunt Valley, MD
(Network Recovery)   (Check Processing Backup)
Leo Roebel   Sherri Nowicki
(214)733-6870   (301)667-8477

APPENDIX D: SAMPLE USER QUESTIONNAIRE

The following five-page questionnaire has been successfully used to gather preliminary information regarding departmental disaster recovery requirements. Note that the wording of the questionnaire can be changed to correspond to the reading level and technical level of the user community.

As a follow-up to this questionnaire, the coordinator may wish to interview respondents to achieve a more comprehensive and detailed understanding of their responses. Respondents should be interviewed separately, rather than in a group. The coordinator should facilitate communications and not dominate the discussion as the point is to learn all that is possible from the respondent in a brief period of time.

If discussions reveal the need for more information, the respondent should be given a written list of follow-up questions and a target date for returning the answers to the coordinator.

Responses to the questionnaire are the foundation upon which the disaster plan is based. They provide a picture of which systems are critical, how they are used, and what minimum level of service could be provided without undermining the function that the system is to provide. Also, responses will provide data of use in cost-justifying the plan.

In some companies, departmental personnel who respond to the questionnaire become disaster recovery representatives for their department. They may take part in development of the plan or serve as recovery team leaders or members.

Finally, data from the disaster recovery questionnaire will be considered during the development of strategies for system, communications, and user backup strategies. The disaster recovery coordinator provides an interface between user departments and technical specialists in the company by translating user objectives into technical requirements.

D I S A S T E R   R E C O V E R Y
Q U E S T I O N N A I R E

DEPARTMENT _____

MANAGER/SUPERVISOR NAME: _____

EXTENSION: _____   DATE COMPLETED ____/____/____

S E C T I O N   I :   W O R K   A C T I V I T I E S

INSTRUCTIONS: Identify in short, complete statements what jobs/tasks are perfomed by your department using computer systems (including PCs). Task 0 is provided as an example. Attach additional pages of tasks as needed.

TASK 0   Enter manual Receipts and Disbursement ledger data into Accounting System.

TASK 1. _____

_____

_____

TASK 2. _____

_____

_____

TASK 3. _____

_____

_____

TASK 4. _____

_____

_____

TASK 5. _____

_____

_____

SECTION II: IDENTIFY INPUTS AND OUTPUTS FOR TASKS

INSTRUCTIONS: For each numbered task above, list on a separate page all forms, documents, reports, and other sources of information used to complete a task. Then, list what is created by the task: reports, updated computer files, printed checks, etc.

EXAMPLE: Task 0, Input Receipts and Disbursements Ledger data into Accounting System, has the following Inputs and Outputs.

INPUTS	OUTPUTS
(Information and materials required to complete the task.)	(Results or products of task completion.)
1. Completed R&D Ledgers from Production Offices (via FAX machine, U.S. mail and internal mail.)	1. Updated electronic R&D Ledger files.
2. Access to Accounting System terminal and system time.	2. Daily Ledger Activity Report.
	3. Monthly Ledger Balance Report.

SECTION III: TASK FREQUENCY

INSTRUCTIONS: Indicate how many times in an average workday, work week, or work month you perform each task intemized in Section I. Attach additional pages as needed.

TASK	FREQUENCY	COMMENTS
0	3 Times per Day	Average input: 10 ledgers per session (30/day)
1		
2		
3		

SECTION IV: SYSTEMS USE

INSTRUCTIONS: Please answer the following questions.

1. Identify how many and what types of computer terminals are installed in your department (i.e., 23 IBM, 3 Data General, 10 AT&T):_____

2. Do users share terminals? If yes, how many users share a single terminal?_____

3. How many PCs are installed in your department?_____

4. What software is used with the PCs?_____

   _____

   _____

5. How often is PC data being backed up currently? (i.e., once per day, per week, per month)_____

   _____

6. Where are PC software and data stored when not in use?_____

   _____

7. Are backups of PC data stored in locked desks or cabinets, in fireproof safes, or are they removed off-site to employee homes or to a commercial storage facility?_____

   _____

8. Please list all peripheral equipment installed in your department including printers, modems, tape drives, external disk drivers, etc._____

   _____

   _____

SECTION V: SYSTEM CRITICALITY

INSTRUCTIONS: On a separate sheet of paper, please answer the
                following questions. Refer to tasks itemized
                above.

1. By task, please identify the costs that would accrue to your
   department if the system (or PC) used to perform each task
   were unavailable for use for a period of 24 hours. Express costs
   as dollar amounts, and identify what factors were used in your
   calculation. Repeat the above for a 48-hour outage.

2. By task, please identify how you would cope (would carry out
   task activities) if the system (or PC) used in performing the
   task were to become unavailable for a prolonged period of
   time. For example, could you convert to a manual method of
   performing the task? If you could NOT perform a task without
   access to the system (or PC) normally used in task fulfillment,
   please indicate this. Also, if a manual method of task performance could only be used for a brief period of time, please so
   state.

SECTION VI: COMMUNICATIONS

INSTRUCTIONS: Please complete the following questions as they
                pertain to previously identified tasks.

1. Do any of the tasks listed above require the use of telephones,
   FAX machines, or data communications terminals (used for
   electronic mail functions)? If yes, please specify which tasks
   utilize which communications devices._____

   _____

   _____

2. How many telecommunications devices (including
   telephones, FAX machines, data communications terminals)
   are installed in your department?_____

3. By task, identify how a telecommunications outage of 24 hours
   would effect task completion. If possible, estimate the costs
   in dollars to your department of a telecommunications outage
   of 24 hours. Explain the rationale you used to calculate costs.

SECTION VII: EMERGENCY OPERATIONS

INSTRUCTIONS: Please answer the following questions, referencing the tasks and coping methods you identified in Section V.

1. By task, identify the minimum number of personnel you would need to sustain work performance at an acceptable level in the event of an outage. Explain your answer.

2. By task, identify the minimum number of computer and telecommunications resources you would need to sustain the acceptable level of work performance in an emergency. (Give numbers of terminals, PCs, telephones, FAX machines, and data communications terminals.)

SECTION VIII: GENERAL CONSIDERATIONS

INSTRUCTIONS: The following questions are intended to gauge the importance of various capabilities that tend to be taken for granted until an emergency occurs. Please answer the questions as completely as possible.

1. By task, how important would a photocopying machine be to task performance in an emergency? Indicate whether the photocopying machine would be necessary for the task, nice to have, or not at all necessary.

2. By task, how important would U.S. mail be to task performance in an emergency? Apply the same criteria as above.

3. By task, how important would it be to redirect incoming long-distance telephone traffic to the relocation site? If you rely heavily on incoming long-distance calls for task performance, the answer is "very important." If incoming long-distance calls do not play a role in task completion, the answer is "not important" do not play a role in task completion, the answer is"not important."

4. Does your department maintain a home and emergency telephone directory of its staff? Is a copy of the directory kept off-site, at a commercial storage facility, or supervisor's home?

5. What are the normal working hours of your department? Are there shifts or weekend hours?

Thank you for your assistance in completing this questionnaire.
Please forward your answers and the questionnaire document to:

Jon Toigo
Disaster Recovery Coordinator
ABC Company

You will be contacted in 1 to 2 weeks to schedule a follow-up interview.

Index

TEAR OUT THIS PAGE TO ORDER THESE OTHER HIGH-QUALITY YOURDON PRESS COMPUTING SERIES TITLES

Quantity	Title/Author	ISBN	Price	Total $
_____	Building Controls Into Structured Systems; Brill	013-086059-X	$35.00	_____
_____	C Notes: Guide to C Programming; Zahn	013-109778-4	$21.95	_____
_____	Classics in Software Engineering; Yourdon	013-135179-6	$39.00	_____
_____	Concise Notes on Software Engineering; DeMarco	013-167073-3	$21.00	_____
_____	Controlling Software Projects; DeMarco	013-171711-1	$39.00	_____
_____	Creating Effective Software; King	013-189242-8	$33.00	_____
_____	Crunch Mode; Boddie	013-194960-8	$29.00	_____
_____	Current Practices in Software Development; King	013-195678-7	$34.00	_____
_____	Data Factory; Roeske	013-196759-2	$23.00	_____
_____	Developing Structured Systems; Dickinson	013-205147-8	$34.00	_____
_____	Design of On-Line Computer Systems; Yourdon	013-201301-0	$48.00	_____
_____	Essential Systems Analysis; McMenamin/Palmer	013-287905-0	$35.00	_____
_____	Expert System Technology; Keller	013-295577-6	$28.95	_____
_____	Concepts of Information Modeling; Flavin	013-335589-6	$27.00	_____
_____	Game Plan for System Development; Frantzen/McEvoy	013-346156-4	$30.00	_____
_____	Intuition to Implementation; MacDonald	013-502196-0	$24.00	_____
_____	Managing Structured Techniques; Yourdon	013-551037-6	$33.00	_____
_____	Managing the System Life Cycle 2/e; Yourdon	013-551045-7	$35.00	_____
_____	People & Project Management; Thomsett	013-655747-3	$23.00	_____
_____	Politics of Projects; Block	013-685553-9	$24.00	_____
_____	Practice of Structured Analysis; Keller	013-693987-2	$28.00	_____
_____	Program It Right; Benton/Weekes	013-729005-5	$23.00	_____
_____	Software Design: Methods & Techniques; Peters	013-821828-5	$33.00	_____
_____	Structured Analysis; Weinberg	013-854414-X	$44.00	_____
_____	Structured Analysis & System Specifications; DeMarco	013-854380-1	$44.00	_____
_____	Structured Approach to Building Programs: BASIC; Wells	013-854076-4	$23.00	_____
_____	Structured Approach to Building Programs: COBOL; Wells	013-854084-5	$23.00	_____
_____	Structured Approach to Building Programs: Pascal; Wells	013-851536-0	$23.00	_____
_____	Structured Design; Yourdon/Constantine	013-854471-9	$49.00	_____
_____	Structured Development Real-Time Systems, Combined; Ward/Mellor	013-854654-1	$75.00	_____
_____	Structured Development Real-Time Systems, Vol. 1; Ward/Mellor	013-854787-4	$33.00	_____
_____	Structured Development Real-Time Systems, Vol. II; Ward/Mellor	013-854795-5	$33.00	_____
_____	Structured Development Real-Time Systems, Vol. III; Ward/Mellor	013-854803-X	$33.00	_____
_____	Structured Systems Development; Orr	013-855149-9	$33.00	_____
_____	Structured Walkthroughs 3/e; Yourdon	013-855248-7	$24.00	_____
_____	System Development Without Pain; Ward	013-881392-2	$33.00	_____
_____	Teams in Information System Development; Semprivivo	013-896721-0	$29.00	_____
_____	Techniques of EDP Project Management; Brill	013-900358-4	$33.00	_____
_____	Techniques of Program Structure & Design; Yourdon	013-901702-X	$44.00	_____
_____	Up and Running; Hanson	013-937558-9	$32.00	_____
_____	Using the Structured Techniques; Weaver	013-940263-2	$27.00	_____
_____	Writing of the Revolution; Yourdon	013-970708-5	$38.00	_____
_____	Practical Guide to Structured Systems 2/e; Page-Jones	013-690769-5	$35.00	_____

Total $	_____
Discount (if appropriate)	_____
New Total $	_____

AND TAKE ADVANTAGE OF THESE SPECIAL OFFERS!

a.) When ordering 3 or 4 copies (of the same or different titles), take 10% off the total list price (excluding sales tax, where applicable).

b.) When ordering 5 to 20 copies (of the same or different titles), take 15% off the total list price (excluding sales tax, where applicable).

c.) To receive a greater discount when ordering 20 or more copies, call or write:

Special Sales Department
College Marketing
Prentice Hall
Englewood Cliffs, NJ 07632
201-592-2498

SAVE!

If payment accompanies order, plus your state's sales tax where applicable, Prentice Hall pays postage and handling charges. Same return privilege refund guaranteed. Please do not mail in cash.

☐ **PAYMENT ENCLOSED**—shipping and handling to be paid by publisher (please include your state's tax where applicable).

☐ **SEND BOOKS ON 15-DAY TRIAL BASIS** & bill me (with small charge for shipping and handling).

Name _____

Address _____

City _____ State _____ Zip _____

I prefer to charge my ☐ Visa   ☐ MasterCard

Card Number _____ Expiration Date_____

Signature _____

All prices listed are subject to change without notice.

Mail your order to: Prentice Hall, Book Distribution Center, Route 59 at
Brook Hill Drive, West Nyack, NY 10995

Dept. 1   D-OFYP-FW(1)